2022 Edi

Freight Dispatcher Training Guide

Freight Dispatcher Training Guide © 2022

Created on 04/2020 ID:V1.1.2022

Legal Disclaimer

This document and any files transmitted with it are confidential and are intended solely for the use of the individual or entity to which they are addressed. This document contains material that is proprietary and confidential. Any use, dissemination, forwarding, printing or copying of this document by and/or to unauthorized parties is strictly prohibited. Any redistribution or reproduction of part or all of the contents in any form is prohibited other than the following.

1. You may print or download to a local hard disk extracts for your personal and non-commercial use only.

You may not, except with our express written permission, distribute or commercially exploit the content. Nor may you transmit it or store it in any other website or other form of electronic retrieval system.

The materials in this document are provided "As-Is," without warranty or condition of any kind whatsoever. FreightBrokersCourse.com does not warrant the materials' quality, accuracy, timeliness, completeness, merchantability or fitness for use or purpose. To the maximum extent provided by law, FreightBrokersCourse, it agents and officers shall not be liable for any damages whatsoever (including compensatory, special, direct, incidental, indirect, consequential, punitive or any other damages) arising out of the use or the inability to use the materials provided in this document.

Table of Contents

Introduction

What are the responsibilities of truck dispatcher?

The trucking industry relies on many working parts to complete a delivery safely and on time. The role of a truck dispatcher is an important one within the trucking industry. In general, a dispatcher schedules drivers to pick up and deliver loads to customers or vendors. But their responsibilities are much broader than that since there are many steps in this process to ensure deliveries arrive safely and on time. They act as the go-between customers and drivers keeping records, monitoring logs, and handling equipment availability. The Chronicle states, "dispatchers are the backbone of the trucking industry, helping truck drivers concentrate on routes and roadways and securely deliver their cargoes."

What are the responsibilities of a truck dispatcher?

Balance responsibilities

Each day presents a new array of challenges, and the dispatcher is responsible for resolving them quickly and efficiently. This action isn't just beneficial for their drivers but it also protects the company from missed opportunities or delays. Acute attention to detail and the ability to work under highly stressful situations is essential when your primary goal is to get the best results possible. Accommodating the client and ensuring driver safety requires a balancing act. A dispatcher has to feel comfortable with managing multiple tasks and know how to prioritize when a decision needs to be made quickly.

Be one step ahead

Especially these days keeping the driver's health and safety in mind while meeting the requirements of the customer is a tough job. Every state has different rules in relation to health and safety. The primary goal of every truck driver is to get their delivery to the destination on time. The long hours require a different focus, and the dispatcher helps by utilizing technology to manage loads, assist with fuel efficiency, and check for potential weather issues. Avoiding setbacks requires foresight and staying on your toes.

Provide value to the drivers

To achieve success, dispatchers have to rely heavily on the truck drivers to not only transport product from point A to point B but to communicate any issues they might encounter along the way. Developing a working relationship with the driver helps a dispatcher identify issues before they become challenges that halt the progress of the delivery. Some challenges are uncontrollable, for example, the weather, other times it's understanding how your driver operates. For a truck driver, the hours are long, and they are often away from home for several days at a time. Taking stock of how fresh the drivers feel and their ability to complete the task, will allow the product to move efficiently.

Plan for weather delays

Weather accounts for a great majority of delays for shipments and the U.S. Department of Transportation provided the following statistics highlighting potential challenges for truckers and the dispatch:

Each year trucking companies lose an estimated 32.6 billion vehicle-hours due to weather-related congestion in 281 of the nation's metropolitan areas.

Nearly 12% of total estimated truck delay is due to weather in the 20 cities with the greatest volume of truck traffic.

The estimated cost of weather-related delay to trucking companies ranges from $2.2 billion to $3.5 billion dollars annually.

Maintain a relationship with the costumers

The responsibility of the dispatcher doesn't start and stop with the truck driver; it also involves keeping the client happy. When you are in the business of helping other businesses, you need to find solutions to their ever-changing problems such as time-frame, budget, and capacity. Direct communication with the customers develops trust that is essential when you need to navigate quick changes. To get the most out of the drivers you work with, treat them as partners and you both will see the fruits of a successful partnership.

Optimize

Often times less is more, a dispatcher works to save the driver time and customer money. Each day the dispatcher manages the progress of current loads and locates opportunities to consolidate deliveries. Sending two drivers to the same location costs a lot of time and wastes money. Identifying opportunities to reduce travel time helps the customer with cost, the driver to deliver in a timely fashion, and the dispatcher with time management. There are a few ways dispatchers work to build the perfect load:

- Consolidate by allocating items to a container to maximize the available space.

- Optimize cost by reducing unnecessary expenditures before a delivery hits the road.

- Find ways to collaborate with outside sources to complete operations.

- Comply with loading and unloading regulations.

Be Nimble

Transporting goods is a twenty-four-hour service, which means problems can happen around the clock. Drivers encounter obstacles daily, and the dispatcher has to work to find quick solutions. These problems could be a breakdown, sickness, or a customer changing their mind on load size or timeframe. Regardless, the dispatcher needs to look at the bigger picture while making decisions to prevent costly delays. This could be reassigning different loads when a driver is unavailable to complete the task or keeping the customer informed of the delivery status through constant communication.

Freight Dispatcher vs. Broker

What is the Difference?

When it comes to finding freight in the trucking industry, motor carriers have several options. Load boards, freight brokers, and dispatchers dominate the industry. If you do not have time to search through the load boards yourself then you are probably thinking of using a freight broker or a dispatcher. Both work as intermediaries between shippers and the trucking company, but which one is best for your business?

What is a Freight Broker?

Freight brokering is when a broker agent works with both shipping companies and carriers and serve as the middle man. Many freight brokers pick up their profit by negotiating rates with shippers and negotiating a different rate with owner-operators. The difference between the two rates is the freight broker's commission. As a result, freight brokers are motivated to encourage shippers to pay high rates while offering carriers a rate that helps them make a profit. If you do not have good negotiation skills, knowledge of pay rates in certain lanes, and know your operating cost when dealing with a freight broker, it is easy to accept loads that can sink your business. It is important to be very selective when choosing a broker (some are more motivated by profit than others). If the freight broker also offers quick pay, they take another percentage from the carrier's agreed-upon rate.

Example

X Shipper has an open load and reach out to Y Broker to find them a carrier. X Shipper and Y Broker agree on a rate $2,000. Y Broker then reaches out to ABC Trucking about the open load. Y Broker is not required to disclose the originally negotiated amount to ABC Trucking. As a result, ABC Trucking agrees haul the load for $1,600. Y Broker keeps the $400 difference as commission.

ABC Trucking also uses Y Broker's Quick Pay option, which takes 2% out of the $1,600. The end result is ABC Trucking receives $1,568 for a load originally negotiated for $2,000. Y Broker makes $432.

What is a Truck Dispatcher?

Dispatchers represent the carrier when negotiating freight. They take a percentage off the carrier's negotiated rate, so they are motivated to find carriers high paying freight. The higher the rate they can find for the carrier, the more money they make. Good dispatchers will keep portfolios with their carrier's lane preferences, desired freight rates, and equipment specifications. Using this information, the Dispatcher then contacts the shippers or freight broker on the carrier's behalf to negotiate loads that meet the carrier's requirements. Only after a load is agreed upon does the dispatcher charge the carrier a fee for the service. Also note, if the carrier uses factoring, many dispatchers will create and submit invoices to the factor on the carrier's behalf. However, all dispatchers are not created equal, as some will charge additional fees or make you book a monthly minimum. As always, be sure to ask those questions before hiring a dispatcher or signing a contract.

Example

Let's continue with the example above. X Shipper agreed on a rate of $2,000 with Y Broker. However, this time instead of using Y Broker directly, ABC Trucking is using Z Dispatcher to find freight. Z Dispatcher knows ABC Trucking needs to make at least $1,600 on the load to stay in business, and also has knowledge of what each load should pay. Z Dispatcher contacts Y Broker about the open load. Y Broker offers the load at $1,600, but Z Dispatcher declines the offer. The two negotiate until Y Broker agrees to a $1,800 rate. Z Dispatcher contacts ABC Trucking about the load and ABC Trucking agrees to haul it. Z Dispatcher charges ABC Trucking a 5% fee. When everything is done, ABC Trucking pockets $1,710, Z freight Dispatcher makes $90, and Y Broker receives $200.

ABC Trucking also uses Y Broker's Quick Pay option, which takes 2% out of the $1,600. The end result is ABC Trucking receives $1,568 for a load originally negotiated for $2,000. Y Broker makes $432.

Freight brokers tend to have close relationships with shippers, so they are convenient to use. However, they make more money by offering carriers lower rates. Their goal is to find the fine balance between offering carriers' lower rates while also enticing carriers to continue taking loads directly from them. Some brokers are better to work with than others.

Dispatchers work closely with carriers to find them the best freight rates. However, most dispatchers work with freight brokers or load boards to find freight; if you find one that works directly with a shipper, that's great! Remember, dispatchers do not make money unless you do, so a dispatcher's goal is to negotiate the highest paying freight possible.

How to Become a Work from Home Dispatcher

The role of a work from home dispatcher is just as important in the $700-billion-dollar Logistics and Trucking industry as their office-based dispatch counterparts.

Dispatchers find freight for trucking companies to transport. While the job may look similar to customer support jobs, dispatchers actually have more tasks to fulfill.

They are in constant communication and negotiation between the driver, broker, trucking company, shipper, receiver, and other parties involved in freight logistics.

A Day in the Life of a Home-Based Dispatcher

A work from home dispatcher may be miles away (or across the world), but he/she can manage a group of truck drivers via phone.

Dispatchers are experts in spreadsheets, real-time maps, and Skype (or other messaging platforms).

As a truck dispatcher, your day would likely involve tasks such as:

- Finding loads/freight and negotiate rates with brokers: This is the main job of truck dispatchers. They find freights to keep trucking companies busy and make sure the rates are agreeable to all parties. Dispatchers may also be responsible for checking credit-worthiness of suppliers.

- Arranging package pickups and deliveries: If you already have customers and would no longer need to find packages every day, your job would likely revolve around arranging pick-up, deliveries and other handling concerns.

- Picking out the best routes for drivers: Because you are the one scheduling all the logistics of a delivery, you'll also determine the best routes for truck drivers to reach their destinations safely and on time.

- Managing daily schedule of drivers: Sometimes, cancellations occur. Bad weather conditions make it impossible to reach destinations. Or other instances wherein scheduled delivers may have to be rescheduled. During these instances, the job of a dispatcher is to update drivers throughout the day to save gas and other resources.

- Conducting team meetings: As a work from home dispatcher, you may be far from your team, but you're going to serve as the leader to all drivers.

- Logging records: At the end of the day, what you're doing is part of a larger trucking and logistics business. Ensuring the drivers log their schedules, incidents, route changes, and other details of the trip is just as important.

- Generating invoices: You've negotiated on fees between all parties involved, so it's only fitting that you handle the invoicing as well.

- Keeping up-to-date with weather conditions: As I explained earlier, you need to be on top of things that could affect the schedule of deliveries.

Generally speaking, a trucking dispatcher must decide on the most efficient and most cost-effective loads for all the trucks on the team.

How Much do Dispatchers Get Paid?

Trucking dispatchers are non-emergency.

The emergency dispatchers take care of distress calls and work with emergency services like ambulance, fire department or police. The rates of emergency dispatchers are higher (about $18 an hour), while trucking dispatchers who are employed with a company earn around $15/hour.

A freelancer dispatcher is paid with commissions (either prepaid or by the number of load/freight/job closed within a week). On average, a dispatcher could handle around 3 to 5 trucks at a time with each truck bringing you in an average income of $1000/month, so that's around $3000 to $5000 monthly. This is the main reason why many prefer independent truck dispatcher jobs than being tied to just one company.

How to Start a Dispatching Home Business

The trucking and logistics industry has many players.

As a dispatcher, you play only one of the several important roles.

As such, when you decide to launch a dispatching home business, you should know the ins and outs of this role already. You also need the following:

- Dispatcher training – Experience is important but the training you are taking will help you hit the ground running and hopefully get you a leg up on the competition!
- A small office – Ideally, your office should have a computer, internet, printer, fax machine, and a landline. Ideally, the office should be in a quiet environment, so you could answer and make calls without any issues.
- Dispatching software – This can be a life-saver when organizing invoices, names, schedules, shipping information and so on. It also keeps records of past transactions, help in keeping tabs on payments made.
- Employer Identification Number (EIN) – All businesses in the U.S. require an EIN from the IRS.
- Get paperwork – Write contracts, so all transactions you do are documented. Pick a business structure (LLC, sole proprietorship, etc.) that you think is most suitable for your business.
- Create a marketing plan – Are you taking this business to the next level? Craft a marketing plan that will outline how you're going to promote your dispatching services.

Truck dispatching is definitely more complicated than call center jobs, or other ways to make money off your phone.

In fact, dispatching is a high-paced position, you must be able to work under pressure gracefully. This is probably the most important characteristic of dispatchers because burn out in this field is very real.

Being a work from home dispatcher doesn't make the job any easier. There's a lot that is required of a dispatcher. First, your communication and negotiation skills must be top-notch, since your goal is to always find the middle ground with other players of the trucking/logistics industry.

Second, you should be highly organized, expert in spreadsheets, good with numbers, and have leadership skills.

Requirements For All Dispatchers

Your first step when thinking about getting into any business especially transportation is to check your local business registration/license issues and insurance coverage needs

As a dispatch service you need to have an agreement for services with a carrier that would have to grant you, via Power of Attorney, the permission to negotiate, and do business on their behalf. The arrangement can vary but your business needs to ideally be listed as a certificate holder on the carrier's insurance policy, or you need to be directly employed by the carrier and forego having your own dispatch business. Without the Power of Attorney, you cannot legally represent a carrier to a broker or shipper and should you try, there is always the chance your actions to do so could be considered fraud since the MC#/DOT# are issued by the FMSCA directly to the carrier strictly for the use of the carrier and without express written agreement you have no right to use any carriers' registrant numbers of profile. This is the situation that unfortunately gives Dispatching a bad name.

Another issue that arises with new dispatch companies is that they believe they do not have to have insurance. This is again where the agreement is important, that will show whether you are covered under the carrier agreement or they agree not to hold you responsible. In reality neither exempts you from being liable in the event of certain circumstances. Your personal liability insurance also may not cover you. Again, this is research that should be done with your state before starting your Dispatch company!

Records, Rules, & Accounting

A dispatcher shall keep a record of each transaction. For purposes of this section, dispatchers may keep master database lists of consignors and the address and registration number of the carrier, rather than repeating this information for each transaction. The record shall show:

- The name and address of the consignor;
- The name, address, and registration number of the originating motor carrier;
- The bill of lading or freight bill number;
- The amount of compensation received by the dispatcher for the dispatching service performed and the name of the payer;
- A description of any non–dispatcher service performed in connection with each shipment or other activity, the amount of compensation received for the service, and the name of the payer; and
- The amount of any freight charges collected by the dispatcher and the date of payment to the carrier.

Dispatchers shall keep the records required by this section for a period of three years. Each party to a transaction has the right to review the record of the transaction required to be kept by these rules.

Misrepresentation

When working as a dispatcher, you may not do business, including advertise, in any name other than the name stated on your registration or operating authority.

- A dispatcher shall not perform or offer to perform any brokerage service
- A dispatcher shall not, indirectly or directly, represent its operations to be that of a carrier.

Accounting Requirements, in Compliance with Regulation, 49 CFR §371.13

If you operate other businesses in addition to your dispatching service, especially other transportation businesses such as motor carriers, then you must maintain your financial accounts so that revenues and expenses from your dispatching service are separate from those of the other businesses. If your dispatching service and the other businesses share common expenses, then your records must show which expenses belong to the dispatching service.

Doing Business Only with Motor Carriers Having Valid USDOT Numbers and Operating Authority, 49 CFR §371.105

As a dispatcher, you may do business **only with a motor carrier that has a valid USDOT number and valid** household goods motor carrier authority. You may not arrange transportation with motor carriers having only property motor carrier authority or household goods authority that is under suspension or has been revoked. You are encouraged to regularly verify the authority status of motor carriers that you do business with. You can check the status of a motor carrier's operating authority by going to the FMCSA Licensing and Insurance Web site at http://li-public.fmcsa.dot.gov. When you arrive at that Web site, click "Continue" at the bottom. On the next webpage, click "Choose Menu Option" in the upper right corner. When the drop-down menu appears, click "Carrier Search." On the next webpage, enter the motor carrier's USDOT or MC number and click "Search." You will see the results of your search, provided that the motor carrier is registered with FMCSA. If the carrier you are searching for appears, then choose either "HTML" or "PDF" to get a status report. http://safer.fmcsa.dot.gov/CompanySnapshot.aspx

Starting your Truck Dispatch Service

Things to Know before you Start

First thing to start up the business professionally is to decide the form of business and giving it a name. Incorporation is not mandatory but recommended. Other forms that can be well considered are the sole proprietorship, partnership, Sub Chapter S Corporation and the Limited Liability Company (LLC). Incorporation can be easily processed without hiring an attorney. You can search for the Articles of Incorporation over the Internet. They are not more than two pages in length.

The Federal Identification Number (FEIN) is needed for incorporation or partnership businesses. You need to apply to get the FEIN. However, for Sole proprietors Social Security Number is sufficient for completing the paper works.

Forms of business you can consider for your dispatching service business:

1. Incorporation
2. Proprietorship
3. Partnership
4. Sub Chapter S Corporation
5. Limited Liability Company
6. UCR Registration (Page 9)
7. SCAC Code Registration (Page 74)

Regarding the selection of the business name, it can be your own name or any other name you would like your business to be called as. The name has to be unique and the dispatching service needs to enquire that the name is available and not being used by someone already. The terminology used is doing-business-as name or the fictitious name. A country or state level search can be done to confirm its availability.

If the business you are planning is a partnership business then it is highly recommended to work out the partnership agreement. The partnership will form an outline for the scope of functions and expectations of each of the partner. The business set-up requirements for a dispatching service are very basic and inexpensive. A toll-free number is highly desirable but not essential. We recommend using Twilio and http://www.nethram.com/main-page/ chrome plugin for all your voice and sms needs. They offer great features like click to call, voicemail drops and an autodialer to help you reach out to more prospects more quickly.

Creating an office is quite simple as a freight dispatcher. Being a freight dispatcher is the perfect business that can be operated within the confines of your home. When you decide to increase the size of your dispatching service by adding freight agents, a true office will definitely be needed at that time. Whether you're telecommuting to your new office or working at home, running your freight, setting up your office requires some diligent thought and planning. Consideration needs to be made with thought to functionality, lighting, and ergonomics. Another important thing to remember that if you tend to take a home office deduction on your federal income tax return there are other issues you will to be aware of. Startup requirements include:

1. A personal computer.
2. High-speed Internet connection: cable or DSL.
3. A telephone with twilio and nethram
4. A reliable online fax service
5. Filing cabinet
6. Load Board membership (FindFreightLoads.com)
7. Microsoft Office (Word & Excel Mainly)
8. Email system (Gmail or Yahoo)
9. Website – (Included with Dispatch Plus course)

Common Equipment Types

Dry Van – Box Trailer

Freight trailers (also called dry vans or simply "boxes") are designed to carry virtually any kind of boxed, crated, or palletized freight.

Configurations

Standard lengths: 28', 32', 36', 40', 42', 43', 45', 48', and 53'

Standard widths: 96"–102"

Maximum weight loaded: 46,000 lbs.

Standard heights: 12.5'-13.5' overall Shorter trailers are typically used for local deliveries or in tandem with "truck trains."

Standard axle/wheel configuration: 2-axle/8-wheel.

Features and Options

- Roll-up doors, rear swing doors, one or two side doors, and roller beds.

- When used for moving produce, "produce vents" are added and insulated with roofs of wood, tin, or fiberglass.

Reefer (Refrigerated Trailer)

Reefers are insulated and refrigerated trailers designed to transport perishable items. Commodities transported include vegetables, fruits, milk, juices, meats, and poultry.

Configurations

Standard lengths: 28', 32', 36', 40', 48', and 53'

Refrigeration Unit

Equipment Type	Average Legal Weight	Average Legal Dimensions
FLATBED — 40' to 50'	40,000 - 80,000	Length : 40' - 53' Width : 8'6" Height : 9'
EXTENDIBLE [STRETCH] BED FLAT — 40' to 50'	40,000 - 44,000	Length : 40' - 75' Width : 8'6" Height : 9'
STEPDECK [DROPDECK] — 11' — 37'	40,000 - 44,000	Length : 35' - 37' Width : 8'6" Height : 10'
EXTENDIBLE [STEPDECK] — 11' — 37' to 60'	37,000 - 40,000 40,000 - 44,000	Length : 37' - 60' Width : 8'6" Height : 10'
DOUBLE EXTENDIBLE DROP — 10' — 26' to 50' — 5'	35,000 - 40,000	Length : 24' - 30' Width : 8'6" Height : 11'8"
DOUBLE DROPDECK — 10' — 30' — 5'	35,000 - 40,000	Length : 26' - 50' Width : 8'6" Height : 11'8"
DOUBLE DROP/LOWBOY [R.G.M] — 10' — 24' TO 30' — 5'	36,000 - 42,000	Length : 24' - 30' Width : 8'6" Height : 12"

- Standard widths: 96"–102"

Standard heights: 12.5'–13.5' overall. Shorter trailers are typically used for local deliveries or in tandem with "truck trains."

- Standard axle/wheel configuration: 2-axle/8-wheel. For heavier loads: 3-axle/12-wheel or 4-axle/1-wheel configurations are also available.

Features and Options

- Rear swing doors or roll-up doors.

- One or two side doors.

- Moveable bulkheads, lift gates, and temperature recording and monitoring systems.

- Single- or multi-temperature models.

Flatbeds and Single Drop Decks (Step Decks)

- Platform (flatbed) trailers are designed to transport oversize cargo that normally would not fit into standard freight trailers.

- Platform trailers are used especially for the transport of goods that must be loaded from the side or top of the trailer.

- Standard cargo for platform trailers includes: ocean freight containers, machinery, construction equipment, lumber, plywood, steel, pipe, and rebar.

Variations

- Standard lengths: 26', 40', 42', 45', and 48'

- Extended Lengths: 60', 65', and 70'

Double Drops and RGNs (Removable Goose Necks)

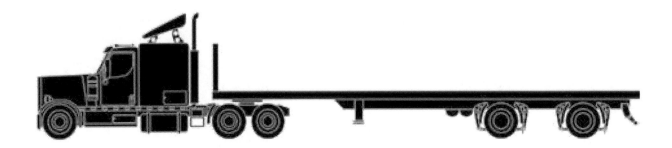

- These specialty trailers are designed to transport oversize cargo that normally would not fit onto standard freight trailers.

- Specialty trailers are used especially for the transport of goods that must be loaded from the top of the trailer.

- Standard cargo for specialty trailers includes: heavy equipment, machinery, farm equipment, windmills, transformers, etc.

Variations

- Standard lengths: 48' and 53'

- Extended lengths: 60', 65', and 70'

- Weight allotted for hauling is determined by the axles included on trailer and configuration

Containers (Skeletal Carrier / Drayage)

- Container carriers are designed to transport standard international cargo containers of 20'–45' length.

- Some models are able to transport non-standard and oversize containers.

Configurations

- Models are designed to transport a single specific size container (20', 40', 45', etc.).

- Models can also be designed in adjustable ("zoom") configurations to work with a range of standard and non-standard containers of different sizes.

- Axle/wheel configuration standard: 2-axle/8-wheel. For heavy loads: 3-axle/12-wheel configurations are also available.

- Brackets are especially designed to hold the container carrier.

Tankers (Food Grade / Chemicals / Petroleum)

- Tanker trailers are designed for carrying a wide range of goods in the form of fluids.

- Standard cargo carried includes: refined gasoline, heating oil, natural gas, acids, industrial chemicals, caustic soda, clay and mud, cooking oils, corn syrup, orange juice, milk, and other foodstuffs.

- Some tanker trailers need special design considerations depending on type of fluid cargo being carried. For example, carriers designed to transport caustic soda and acids require some special aspects, such as exterior paint and equipment that can withstand the effects of corrosive goods.

Variations

- Standard lengths: 40', 42', 43', 45', 48', and 53'

- Axle/wheel standard: 2-axle/8-wheel. For heavy loads: 3-axle/12-wheel or 4-axle/16-wheel configurations are also available.

Features and Options

- Multiple compartments (1-7)

- Vacuum pumps

- Measurement equipment

- Insulated tanks

- Pressure tanks

- Ladders

- Walkways

- Hose carriers

- Belly cabinets

Dry Bulk Trailer - Hopper

Dry trailers are mainly used in the transportation of dry commodities such as grain, shelled corn, hulled rice, beans, gravel, limestone (loose and pulverized), and sand. It is a safe transportation method and very useful for long distances.

Variations

- Standard lengths: 26' to 42'

- Standard widths: 96"-102"

- Hopper configurations: single, double, and triple.

- Open and closed end configurations.

- Steel and aluminum models.

- There are available as singles, doubles, and three-trailer "truck trains."

Notes

- Dry bulk trailers use rolled tarpaulin tops rather than rigid tops.

- Typical dry bulk trailers usually use hoppers to unload or empty conveyor systems.

- International trailer manufacturers produce a variety of models that are designed for different freight configurations.

<u>Logistics Van & Deep Drop Furniture</u>

Deep drop vans are designed especially for transporting large, bulky, and relatively light cargo (weight to volume).

- Deep drop vans are mainly used in the transportation of specific kinds of goods such as furniture, household appliances, and electronics.

Variations

- Standard lengths: 45', 48', and 53' overall

- Standard heights: 13' 6" overall

- Standard widths: 96"–102" overall

- Rear door(s): Standard swing doors.

- Side doors: 1 or 2 side swing doors.

Options & Features

- The lower rear surface is used to facilitate loading.

- Air ride suspension is provided to protect the fragile cargo.

- Compartments have belly cabinets and ramps.

<u>Auto Transport Tractor Trailer</u>

These trailers are used to transport auto transport cars, sports cars, or small trucks. It mostly facilitates the movement of these goods from the manufacturing plants to distributors, or from most common ports (Ro-Ro ships) to distributors of the interior.

Auto variations:

Auto transporters are produced in two general configurations:

- Trailers capable of transporting up to nine vehicles pulled by tractor unit standard.

- Truck tractor is up to three vehicles while the trailer transports up to six cars.

There are also private covered car trailers that are specially used in the transportation of high-value cars.

Notes

- Different trailer manufacturers from all over the world produce a wide range of models that have been designed for different shipping configurations.

- There is a large market for private party auto transporters in the transfer of families and the transfer of specialized and high-value vehicles locally and internationally as well.

- Dimensions, weight, and capacity are the data that varies according to the requirements of cargo, manufacturers, national model, state, as well as the requirements of the provincial road.

General Guidelines

Maximum Overall Dimensions (Un-Permitted) Width: 96 inches
Width: (Designated Highways): 102 inches
Height: 13 feet, 6 inches
GVW: (Gross Vehicle Weight): 80,000 lbs.
Length of Semitrailer: 53 feet
Length of Semitrailer: (Non-Designated Highway): 50 feet
Length of Combination Tractor Trailer: (With or Without Load): No Limitation Units
Permitted in Train: Two (2) Semitrailers, or Truck and Semitrailer

The Semitrailers that are longer than 50 feet shall have a wheelbase of 37 feet to 41 feet. This is measured from the kingpin coupling to the center of the axles or to the center of the tandem axle assembly in case it is equipped with (2) axles.

Semitrailers longer than 50 feet are limited to 3 axles and shall operate only on designated highways.

The measurement of Semitrailers and Trailers shall be done from the front vertical plane of the foremost transverse load-supporting structure to the rearmost transverse load supporting structure. Safety and energy conservation devices are not supposed to be included in the length measurement, but not limited to, impact-absorbing bumpers, rear view mirrors, turn signal lamps, marker lamps, steps and handholds for entry and egress, flexible fender extensions, mud flaps or splash and suppressant devices, load-induced tire bulge, refrigeration or heating units, or air compressors. However, any device that is not designed or intended to be used in the cargo-carrying process shall be excluded from the length determination.

Projection Beyond Front of Vehicles: 3 feet

Overhang beyond rear of vehicles: Any amount is permissible as long as it doesn't exceed the legal length. However, if this overhang is 4 feet or more, then a 12-inch red square flag in the daytime and a red light or lantern at night shall be displayed on the extreme rear.

The Weight Distribution Analysis Process

Position of Trailer Tandems

Performing a weight distribution analysis can prevent building trucks that are overloaded in normal use and hence cause problems for users and the equipment installer. Overloads can shorten the life of a vehicle and its components. Overloads can also prevent compliance with weight laws and federal safety standards.

Sliding your trailer tandems toward the front or back of the vehicle will primarily change the weight distribution between the tractor's drive axles and the trailer tandems. Sliding the tandems can also affect the weight on the steering axle, but to a rather small degree. For the purpose of focusing exclusively on positioning the trailer tandems, we're going to ignore the minor changes to the weight of the steer axle. It's rarely a factor when deciding where to place your trailer tandems. By sliding the trailer tandems forward, you will put more weight on the trailer tandems and take weight off the tractor's drive axles. Conversely, by sliding the trailer tandems toward the rear of the trailer, you will take weight off the trailer tandems and put more weight onto the tractor's drive axles. The #1 most important concept is redistributing weight across axles. Sliding the trailer tandems forward adds weight to the tandems, sliding them back removes weight from the tandems.

Amount of Weight Moved Per Hole – The What & Why of Weight Distribution

Weight distribution is the amount of the total vehicle weight imposed on the ground at an axle, a group of axles, or an individual wheel. The weight on a truck must be distributed on the axles to comply with the chassis manufacturer's axle ratings and weight laws.

Having the correct wheelbase on the chassis and placing bodies and loads in the proper place will ensure that axles are loaded correctly. Performing a weight distribution analysis identifies the proper axle loadings before building a truck.

Axle capacities are limited either by the axle capacity or legal weight limits, whichever is lower. Both trucks in Image A have a front axle rated at 12,000 lbs., limiting the weight on those axles. The rear axle on the single-drive truck is limited by the axle capacity or legal weight restrictions to 20,000 lbs. The two rear axles on the tandem-drive truck are limited either by axle capacities or legal weight restrictions to 17,000 lbs. for each axle, or a total of 34,000 lbs. for the pair of axles.

The trailer tandems lock into place with a set of locking pins that slide into holes drilled into the tandem slider rail. You can see the holes in the slider rail in the picture to the left (click to enlarge).

The distance between the locking pinholes on the trailer will be the main factor affecting how much weight is moved per hole. This distance varies between the different trailer manufacturers, and the larger the distance between the holes, the more weight will be shifted with each hole. The two main hole spacings you'll find are 4 inches and 6 inches. You can estimate that you will move 250 pounds per hole for 4-inch spacing, and 400 pounds per hole for 6-inch spacing. This will help you estimate how many holes you'll have to slide the trailer tandems to move the proper amount of weight necessary in order to get the axle weights legal. Again, we're assuming the weight won't change on the steer axles for these examples, but in reality, it might change a little bit. Most of the time the change in weight of the steer axle will have little or no effect on where you'll put the trailer tandems. The weight on the steering axle is significantly altered by the amount of fuel you have and the position of your 5th wheel.

Calculate the weight distribution of a vehicle using the following steps:

1. Determine the weight and center of gravity location for all of the components and items to be considered.

2. Multiply the center of gravity distance times the weight to get the moment for each component and item.

3. Add all of the moments and divide by the wheelbase to get the weight on the rear axle.

4. Subtract the rear axle weight from the total weight to get the front axle weight.

AB – Distance from the center of the front axle to the back of cab.

AF - (After Frame) Distance from the center of the back axle to the rear end of the chassis frame.

BA - Distance from bumper to axle.

BL - (Body Length) Overall length of the body.

CA - (Cab to Axle) Distance from back of the cab to center of the rear axle.

CB - (Cab to Body) Distance between back of cab to front of body.

WB - (Wheelbase) Distance from center of the front axle to center of rear axle.

Example 1:

Steer: 11,590

Drives: 34,700

Trailer: 32,100

Gross: 78,390

You scale your truck at a truck stop and receive your scale ticket. The slider rail hole spacing is 6 inches which will move 400 pounds of weight per hole, and let's assume the steer axle weight won't change. What would you have to do in order to get your truck legal?

 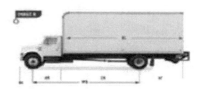

Steer	11,590	Steer remains unchanged for this example
Drives	33,900	Drives: 34,700 – 800 (2 holes x 400 pounds each)
Trailer	32,900	Trailer: 32,100 – 800 (2 holes x 400 pounds each)
Gross	78,390	Remains the same

Example 2:

Steer:	11,320
Drives:	31,300
Trailer:	35,050
Gross:	77,670

You scale your truck at a truck stop and receive your scale ticket. The slider rail hole spacing is 4 inches which will move 250 pounds of weight per hole, and let's assume the steer axle weight won't change. What would you have to do in order to get your truck legal?

In this example, the trailer tandems are overweight by 1,050 pounds (35,050 – 34,000 pounds maximum). Assuming each hole in the tandem slider rail moves 250 pounds, you would have to slide your trailer tandems toward the rear of the truck a minimum of five holes to transfer enough weight from your trailer tandems to your drive axles in order to get your axle weights legal. The end result would be approximately:

Steer	11,320	Steer remains unchanged for this example

Drives	32,550	Drives: 31,300 + 1,250 (5 holes x 250 pounds each)
Trailer	33,800	Trailer: 35,050 – 1,250 (5 holes x 250 pounds each)
Gross	77,670	Remains the same

<u>Types of Pallets</u>

TRAILER CAPACITIES

1. Maximum weight is 46,500 lbs. per trailer (48' or 53').

2. 22-24 single-stacked standard (48x40") pallets in a 48' trailer.

3. 26-28 single-stacked standard (48x40") pallets in a 53' trailer.

4. Every two single-stacked standard pallets take up 4 linear feet of truck space.

MEASUREMENT CALCULATIONS

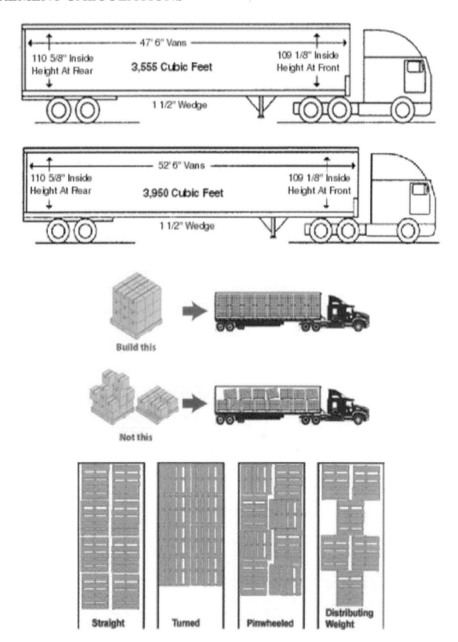

1. Compute Cubic Feet = L x W x H x # of Pieces/1728

2. Compute Dimensional Weight = L x W x H x # of Pieces/DIM Factor

3. Convert Kilograms to Pounds = # of Kilograms x 2.2046

Pallets and Configurations

Shipping & Logistics managers all need to know the basics of loading trailers of different types and sizes. Whether you have a 48-foot trailer or a 53-foot trailer will make a difference. If you have **40×48** skids, you have the choice of running them straight into the trailer, **pin-wheeling**, or turning them all **sideways.**

The following scenarios would apply:

48 foot trailer:	53 foot trailer:
24 skids loaded straight into the trailer	26 skids loaded straight into the trailer
26 skids pin-wheeled	28 skids pin-wheeled
28 skids turned sideways	30 skids turned sideways

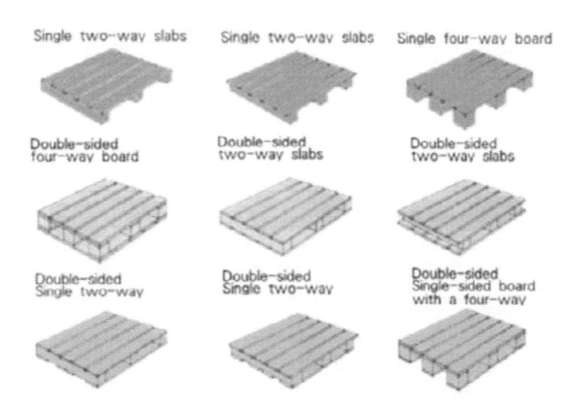

Finding and Soliciting Shippers

Developing Shipper Relationships

Searching for shippers is one of the initial stages of the dispatching business. However, before you begin any marketing operations, you'll need to have at least a good website as a place to start off your marketing campaign. Your broker's course includes free website templates. Even if you are operating a small dispatching business, a professional website will be helpful in giving your clients and shippers the impression that you are an established freight dispatching company. When you market your services to shippers, they will want to see your website and more than likely, your website will be one of the key factors affecting their decision of doing business with you or not. Your website will be the main source that describes all your services, testimonials, and contact information.

Within your broker's course, you will be provided a shipper and carrier database of over 250,000 profiles in Excel format. By using this list of data, you will be able to market your business by sending out emails to potential clients, mailing brochures to their business address, and making phone calls to set up appointments. Pay attention to plan a marketing strategy rather than just making indecisive searches or phone calls. Define your target area, set goals, and work from there. It is good to start with e-mail marketing as you will reach a lot of clients with little effort, but making calls and setting up appointments is where most of your leads will start to convert into reality.

The Approach

One of the best approaches is to target a specific market segment. By developing certain markets, you will be referred to other customers within that market. In addition, it is much easier to find other carriers through this method as well. Try targeting your business based on the following search criteria:

• The shipper's location and the freight's destination.

• Type of cargo (agricultural, perishable, oversized, bulk commodities, etc.)

• Load size, specific industries, or some other special shipping segment

Upon choosing a particular demographic, you must consider what type of cargo will be best suited and comfortable for your brokering business. You may choose to broker general commodity freight, which is more stable and less volatile, or you may focus your expertise in areas such as heavy haul, temperature controlled hazardous material (HAZMAT) loads or oversized loads.

Once you find a shipper, you will need to approach the right person—the one in charge. Generally the "Traffic Manager" is the person that you'll need to contact. Thankfully, the "go-to people" in this industry are not that evasive, and there are very few loops to jump through to get to the right person.

Key Contacts:

• Transportation Manager

• Sales Agents & Brokers

• Logistics Department

• Traffic Manager

As mentioned previously, your first goal is to look for shippers who need shipping services. As a service industry, you have no physical store that the customer can visit, nor do you have a product that the customer can hold or examine. Therefore, your website acts as a "virtual" storefront for you.

Your marketing campaign should include:

1. Telephone calls

2. Brochure distribution

3. Promotional emails with cover letters

Also, you need to pay attention to marketing over the internet through social networks like Facebook, Twitter, Craigslist ads, and transportation blogs.

Shipper Requirements: The shippers are always concerned about constraining their shipment to their limited budgets. However, the budget varies according to fluctuations in the supply and demand of any load type. Shippers want carriers to transport their cargo with safety, efficiency, and within their estimated costs. They do not usually have industry knowledge or the time to find reliable carriers themselves. Therefore, your clients (shippers) are constantly looking to find reliable and honest freight dispatchers to build strong business relationships with.

There are two types of brokers: Truck Brokers (**the motor carrier with Authority and a Broker's License**) and Property Brokers (Only having a broker's License, **CANNOT** move freight). A property broker has NO LIABILITY, and only makes a commission for facilitating the move of the load, while the truck broker HAS LIABILITY and may hire other carriers / owner-operators to move the freight, thus creating liability. This difference arises due to having an "Authority" versus having a "License." A carrier has "Authority," which means it has the shipper's permission to take ownership of the cargo to deliver the load by interstate or intrastate transportation. When taking over the cargo, the carrier must show proof of cargo and liability insurance, as upon the receipt of the cargo for transportation they indirectly become responsible for it. A broker obtains a "License" and can only arrange the transportation of the shipper's cargo with carriers (owner-operators with Authority). A broker's license is NOT a "mode" of transportation and a property broker cannot take ownership of the bill of lading. Property brokers are in a fiduciary (trust) relationship with the motor carrier actually hauling the brokered freight. The broker collects the money from the shipper, then pays the motor carrier their rate, less his own commission.

In case a carrier (broker) loads their excess onto another motor carrier (sub-hauler), there is no broker's license required. However, both parties need to share 100% liability for the cargo. So many truck brokers think that they are not responsible for freight that they subcontract from one motor carrier to another.

Carrier Requirements:

Carriers are certainly looking for the best price that they can get for shipping the cargo. The motor carriers and shippers also have to face cost constraints. The carrier company takes care of many different costs such as truck maintenance, employee salaries, fuel costs, etc. If they learn how to manage such costs efficiently, they can achieve good profit.

To facilitate a smooth process, a freight broker is required to make a win-win situation for all. This can be achieved by excellent negotiation skills to devise a transaction in which all parties (broker, carrier, and shipper) are satisfied.

Broker Requirements:

The broker looks for shippers who need their cargo shipped, and then they look for reliable carriers who are able to cover the loads. It's the freight broker's responsibility to do perfect load and carrier matching while keeping the shipper's costs as low as possible or at least within their budget.

When starting a new brokerage business, a broker may need to do a lot of research on the phone and the Internet to gather a useful database of carriers and shippers. This course will give you a database of 350,000 shippers and carriers to help you overcome this step.

The broker's **key role** is to achieve reliable relationships between the shippers and carriers, and provide the shipper with a list of different options that can meet their needs of delivering their cargo. This is an art that greatly determines broker performance and drives recurring business. The next important step to success in the business is to do a credit check in order to be on the safe side of deals with new shippers. Try to avoid problems before they occur. Don't let your guard down even if a shipper has good credit— it may take 45, 60, or even 90 days to receive a check from them, so you either need to have GREAT cash flow management, or factor your invoices with freight factoring companies that will pay faster (less their processing fees).

With new carriers, you'll need to do a similar credit/background check. The broker needs to pre-qualify carriers, which means they should have all their operational and insurance documents ready. A carrier should not have too many traffic citations or Highway Patrol Inspections. Also, there are some web services that can help check the carrier's authority status, such as SAFER (https://safer.fmcsa.dot.gov/CompanySnapshot.aspx).

Use the carrier's USDOT# to search the SAFER web service. Cargo insurance is not required to be obtained by freight brokers, as they use the cargo insurance of the carrier. But the "Contingent" cargo insurance should be purchased as a plan B insurance in case the carrier's insurance does not pay or only partially pays the insurance claim. This is always a great backup to protect both you and the shipper, and many new brokers who ignore this are often driven into financial troubles, so never think that you can skip insurance coverage.

In order to start your business relationship with the shipper, you'll need to first get **"set-up"** with the shipper. The "set-up" process involves faxing the shipper an information packet, including all important documents such as their motor carrier number, proof of surety bond, insurance certificate in case the contingent cargo coverage is purchased, W-9 form, and any other crucial information that you as the broker may want to include or that the shipper may have specified. As soon as the shipper accepts and verifies your information, you are good to officially start working together. This information packet **IS NOT** like the marketing packet that you will send out to potential clients. This "set-up" packet is specifically meant to provide more information about your brokerage to the shipper who intends and agrees to start a business with you.

Some professional freight brokers often send a "broker-shipper" agreement, but this is rarely done by new brokers as they still do not have enough experience to justify such agreements. This agreement assures the shipper that their loads will be covered by the broker. This course includes a sample of a broker-shipper agreement contract. If you are a creditable broker, you will make demands in your contract that you can fulfill.

The shipper might ask you (the broker) to give your quote to deliver one or more loads, before deciding to start the business relationship with you. In the previous chapter, we reviewed how to do rate calculation; this will be helpful in preparing your rate sheet well in advance so it is ready to be sent out in your "Set-Up" package in case the shipper requests to include your rate sheet.

What Do You Say?

When you contact your customer, whether via phone or e-mail, you must speak in terms that they understand so you do not appear uneducated in the industry. Shippers desire to deal with reputable and established companies that can handle the movement of their freight with the smallest number of problems. The only thing they may need to be convinced about is consistency and reliability for the shipment of their various products.

It is preferred that you have a good working knowledge of the transportation vernacular prior to contacting a shipper for the first time. Human resource experts say that we only have **15 seconds** to make a first impression. Do not worry if you have never had any previous experience in **direct sales,** as most of the work in freight brokerage is completed via telephone or email. It would be beneficial to spend a little time on the phone or in practice sessions by role-playing with a partner prior to setting up a perspective sales meeting with a client personally. This is also called the "Elevator Pitch." You have the time to go from one floor to another in an elevator to get your pitch in. Can you do it?

Prospecting For Customers

Find Your Customer Base

In order to be a successful freight dispatcher, you will need to have a good database of customers. Shippers are always looking for the safest, most efficient and cost-effective methods to transport their products. The information mentioned below will provide you a general knowledge base and grant you the required skills to manage and find appropriate freight and customers.

Gather the Information

There are several useful methods to find your customer database. It can be as easy as a phone call. Products manufactured in the United States have to be shipped to the retail or wholesale distributor.

Targeted markets:

• Distributors

• Warehouses

• Cold Storage Facilities

• Growers & Packers

• Membership Associations

• Trucking Companies

• Manufacturers

• Wholesalers

Databases

The information databases are provided by third-party resources. However, before paying your money, you must be aware of what kind of information is included in the database you are purchasing and whether it is useful and up-to-date for your needs. You may try one of the following resources:

• Contact DB (Website Link - http://www.contactdb.com)

• Data Axle USA (Website Link - https://www.dataaxleusa.com)

• Dunn and Bradstreet (Website Link - https://www.dnb.com/business-directory.html)

How to Search?

You can access a wide range of sales and contact information by performing searches of various membership databases. You can perform the search process for membership directories, and get the membership directories and their buyer's guide for free and easily via various trade organizations.

Using Truck Load Boards

Load boards are websites that are widely used by freight brokers to post the shipper loads available with them, in order to find available ready trucks to cover them.

On the other hand, the load boards are used by carrier companies to post the availability of their trucks.

So simply put, the carrier companies are searching for brokers and loads matching their post request.

Load boards operate differently. Some may allow the broker to post load information and perform searches for trucks as well, while other load boards automatically notify carriers that match the broker's posting, achieving a quick response.

Nowadays load boards provide many customized services, but the primary one of interest to freight brokers is posting loads and searching for available trucks to cover those loads.

Government Contracts

There is another option to acquiring good paying freight, and that is government freight.

Government freight doesn't have to be just from the federal government, but also state and local governments. They, too, have goods and products that need to be moved, and not just in times of natural disaster.

Trucking services are also desperately needed for disaster relief.

What Types of Trucks Can Haul Government Loads?

Dump trucks, agriculture haul, refrigerated trucks, auto haulers, flatbed and traditional cargo trucks are all eligible to haul government loads. The government accepts all types of hauling, especially when it comes to bringing relief after a natural disaster.

DOT maintains a Subcontracting Directory to search for opportunities, but the Small Business Administration (SBA) also offers a service, a Subcontracting Network website, Sub-Net, where prime contractors may post subcontracting opportunities for smaller businesses looking for opportunity. The database lists opportunities by state. Here are some good search queries (https://tinyurl.com/y3sz3ocg) (https://tinyurl.com/y3sz3ocg)

Another resource is the GSA, which provides government agencies with cost-effective transportation services, including the military. The majority of opportunities were listed on FedBizOpps.gov they were moved to here now though: (https://tinyurl.com/y543sdxj). The site currently lists tens of thousands active opportunities – not all in freight movement.

Lastly, this is another great place to look for freight loads. FPDS.gov (https://tinyurl.com/yxbnqshv)

Any carrier that hauls government freight may also have to meet requirements under the Service Contract Act (SCA). (https://tinyurl.com/y6o7p3y)

Qualifying Prospects
Sales Strategy

You need to gain and maintain very strong negotiation skills so you can market your freight dispatching business successfully. Most people aren't good at negotiating; many are intimidated by the person on the other end of the line. If you are not comfortable with negotiations, then keep in mind that negotiation skills are highly involved in the daily procedures of your business. You can enhance your negotiation skills by coming up with a few ideas and mental exercises to overcome your fears, which can make you a successful negotiator.

Before quoting freight rates, it is very important that you remember your service value. You should know and understand your product and its value, which you introduce to your customers. Every new customer you work with will point out your weaknesses and strengths, and listening to that feedback and making improvements will surely give you an edge over your competitors. It is necessary to be open-minded and accept their criticism in order to develop yourself. If you do that, you will gain new customers and grow your business.

Study your competition:

It is essential to know which rates are being quoted on lanes and how your competitors are meeting them. You should understand other's pricing and strategies in order to improve your predictive abilities. You should study and research your competitors. Customers are always looking for a better deal, so they are going to hang around for the best possible price. If you understand your competitors and develop your business accordingly, you can end up getting the lead during negotiations.

Understand Your Sales Strategy

Firstly, you should define your strategy before beginning negotiations. Have a list of possible alternative plans that you may propose as further opportunities to your client in case your first suggestion isn't accepted. Your strategy should be flexible enough to work efficiently with all of your provided opportunities when negotiating a rate. If you succeed in developing such a strategy for marketing your service, then you will definitely acquire the forefront in negotiations with your clients.

Rates Quoting

Define spot quote

A spot quote is a group of rates for a month. It is calculated based on the current market and it is done without a contract. So the spot quote is a rate quote for an individual line haul. Before you start talking to carriers who run this line, you must gather all information that they are going to ask you about.

Information and Actions Needed for Quote

- Origin & Destination

- Truckload / LTL

- Dimensions

- Commodity

- Weight / Trapping Required?

- Pallet Exchange Required?

- Date of Pickup & Delivery

- Contact information of five (5) carriers to get their quote on the Line Haul.

- Post the load and request rates from carriers that call you for the details

- Get an average price for the load and then contact your shipper with the rate.

Dedicated Lanes

When you quote dedicated lanes for shippers, you will need to do some research. Dedicated means moving constant loads weekly from the same origin to destination. Carriers usually love this type of freight, so they will give you a better rate than the normal spot quote line haul rate. Because of the demand, this type of freight is very competitive and your quotes will be compared and considered against many others.

It is essential to offer your shipper a quote that actually can transport the freight, especially if you are a non-asset-based freight broker. Most brokers will provide low quotes to shippers so that they can get the freight in hopes of brokering it out to carriers. In such a scenario, many of these freight brokers will not be able to move the freight since their quotes are not accurate. This is one of the main reasons why shippers refuse to deal with many freight brokers. You must set yourself as apart from the rest. Here are a few ways to do that.

Rates of Market prices:

Sometimes shippers will need carriers to move their freight due to a truck falling out or another vendor's inability to provide the service. In such a case, the shipper will have to pay the going rate for a truck to move the freight, making it possible to have a relationship with a lot of carriers. You can make huge commissions on these loads, as the shipper will most generally pay whatever is necessary to transport the load.

Do not gouge your shippers!

Rates Calculation

Freight charges vary according to a number of variables, but the two main factors are the weight of the load and the distance it must travel. The type of truck also affects the rates, regardless of the driver's needs to make one or more stops to pick up the freight or to deliver it. However, rates for additional stops are usually negotiable.

You'll need to get an idea of the current "going rates" for the types of shipments that you can handle before you begin shopping for rates for specific shipments. This can be achieved by requesting copies of tariffs from several carriers and studying them. There are different methods to calculate these rates, as mentioned below. Using load boards and calling for rates on posted loads is another way of getting information on current market rates. The National Motor Freight Traffic Association (NMFTA) classes products according to four characteristics: weight, handling, storability, and liability. There are 18 freight classes beginning from class 50 (the least expensive) to class 500 (most expensive). For more information on NMFTA classes, visit: http://www.nmfta.org/Pages/welcome.aspx

1. **Flat Rate:** The broker can set up a flat rate for a shipper's load that might need to be hauled from one state to another. For example, if the loads are to be shipped from Miami FL to Houston TX, then the broker can decide upon a flat rate of $2,200.

2. **Rate per Mile:** Rates can be determined based on mile. For example, suppose the rate per mile is $1.5 and the carrier covers 2,500 miles then the total cost to cover the loads will be $3,750.

3. **Rate per Unit:** The shipper may prefer to pay the broker per unit price. For example, the payment for a carton of juice cans to be delivered may be set at $1.75.

4. **Rate per Hundred Weights:** The shipper can also choose the payment option of pay per hundred weights. Say $6.25 is the price per hundred weights and the total weight of the loads to be shipped is 32,000 lbs. Then the total amount the shipper will pay is $2,000.

The broker should find if there is any extra cost involved in the shipment such as extra picks, unloading fees, etc. The broker should have good negotiation skills to ask the shipper for some add-ons (e.g., fuel surcharge) above the regular rate. With increasing fuel prices, more and more truckers want the fuel surcharge payment to be added in the deal.

The broker should have good knowledge about all loading techniques and regulations. He should be aware of the loading terminology like Full Truck Load (FTL) and Less than Truck Load (LTL). He should keep himself well informed to avoid any future problem related to loads transporting.

Commissions that you earn on each load form your main source of income. There are two methods to receive your payment: You can bill the shipper the amount you're going to pay the carrier plus the amount of your commission, or the carrier can bill the shipper directly and then pay you a commission from its revenue. The most common and efficient way to handle billing and commissions is to have the carrier bill you, and then you bill your customers.

Freight rates are based on many factors, including

1. The distance that the shipment will cover

2. The shipment's weight

3. The density of the shipping goods

4. The commodity's susceptibility to damage

5. The value of the commodity

6. The commodity's load ability and handling characteristics

All of the above factors affect the classification of a commodity. The NMFC, or National Motor Freight Classification tariff, contains all product classifications. There are eighteen possible classes ranging from 50 to 500. Higher the class, higher the rate for every hundred pounds you will ship. Most less-than-truck-load (LTL) rates are stated as a rate per hundred pounds, or per hundredweight. The rate per hundred pounds decreases as the total shipment weight increases. For example: a shipment weighing 100 pounds may cost $41.00 per hundred-weight, while a heavier shipment, say 500 pounds, of the same commodity (moving to the same destination) may only cost $35.00 per hundredweight. But doing the math, we see that the total charges for the 500-pound shipment are higher (5x$35 is greater than 1x$41). For very light shipments, most LTL carriers state a minimum charge.

Carrier expenses such as fuel mileage, driver wages, IFTA (International Fuel Tax Agreement) fuel taxes, as well as the road tolls play a critical role in the line haul rates you submit to your customers, simply because carrier's rates are based on mileage. Regardless of the line haul rate, which is broken into mileage, there are additional costs that necd to be calculated. For example, if that very same $1,500 load has two extra stops, you should add another $50 to $100 per stop to the gross line haul rate.

Carriers tend to use two major formulas to determine shipping rates:

1. The linear foot rule

2. The cube rule

The standard carrier linear foot rule states that shipments occupying 10 linear feet or more of trailer space are charged for 1,000lb per foot. Usually, this rule applies when there are at least five pallets single-stacked or 10 pallets double-stacked. For example, say a 10-pallet order of stackable freight occupies 10 linear feet. If those pallets were not stackable, they would occupy 20 linear feet. In the former scenario, a shipper would be charged for 10,000lb; in the latter, they would be charged for

20,000lb. Here's a simple rule of thumb to remember: for stackable pallets, take the number of pallets on the floor of the trailer and multiply by two—that's how many linear feet you should be charged for. For non-stackable pallets, multiply the total number of pallets by two to get the linear foot count. Review your invoices to see if this rule is being applied.

How To Calculate Linear Foot from number of Pallets

Example

Units: 16, Width: 42, Length: 48, Height: 42, Stackable: 1, Weight: 5000, Not

Turnable: Turn pallets resulting in width of 48. Number Across: 2

Base Linear Feet: $(42 / 12) = 3.5$

Linear Feet after accounting for 2-wide in Trailer = $(3.5 / 2) = 1.75$ Linear Feet after Stacking: $(1.75 / 1) = 1.75$ Linear Feet for all Units: $(1.75 * 16) = 28$

Here is a great link to calculate linear ft.: http://www.wpg.org/Member/LinearFootCalc3.asp

To reiterate, linear feet = square feet / width.

What is meant by fuel surcharge?

A fuel surcharge aims to compensate carriers and balance spiraling fuel expenses. In case the fuel cost has risen to $750 per gallon, then it's not feasible for a carrier to haul a load at the rate of $150 per mile. We try to resolve this issue by getting the clients to pay a fuel surcharge, which is then handed over to the trucking company.

How is fuel surcharge calculated? The average of most trucks is approximately 5 mpg. The base fuel cost should range from $1.10 to $1.20 irrespective of the existing cost of fuel. For instance, here we will assume the base price to be $1.20. You now have to divide the fuel expenses for more than $1.20 for every gallon by 5 (which is the average mpg for majority of the trucks).

If the existing fuel rate is $2.50 per gallon then you will have to deduct the base price (in this case $1.20). The amount which remains ($1.30) will now be divided by the average MPG (5 as decided in the example). Thus you get $0.26 cents, which is your fuel surcharge.

Regional/National Fuel Prices

The fuel surcharge depends on the national average retail price of diesel fuel in the specific region from where the load begins. You can get the details about the average retail price from the Federal Government's Energy Information Administration which is updated every week on Wednesdays.

You can also call: (202)586-6966 or visit http://www.eia.gov/petroleum/gasdiesel/ to find out more details.

Often freight brokers decide on a floating fuel surcharge with their clients. This surcharge is modified every month. It is better to ensure that you update your customers about the changes in the fuel surcharge which will be applicable for the following month. In case you do levy a fuel surcharge, then sincerely ensure that it reaches the carrier. Never be overcome by greed as it could spell doom for your business.

Fuel Surcharge Rate Confirmation

The fuel surcharge must be included separately on the rate confirmation sheet and you must never levy any commission for this amount. It is better to have a detailed rate confirmation with all the overheads like the line-haul rate, the paid miles, the tarp pay, additional stops, and fuel surcharge. Itemizing the confirmation sheet will give you better clarity in revenue sharing. You do not have to pen down the fuel surcharge on any other shipping documents like the Bill of Lading. But it is essential to include it on the load rate confirmation agreement as well as the invoice that you send to the client.

Freight Rate Variables

The freight rates differ from day to day. Besides, they are not uniform throughout the nation. The freight rates depend on the supply and demand at a particular location, and as long as there's no sudden hike in the fuel rates, the rates you finalize should be stable for around a month. After you have finalized a line haul rate, it is easier to keep the base rate stable and negotiate with the rate variables like the truck fuel surcharge.

The motor carrier will have to order the proper permits for all the states through which the load is going to be hauled. But you too should find out if the load requires any additional permits. The customer too should be fully updated of the same.

A load must have individual state permits in case:

- Its width exceeds 8 feet.

- Its length exceeds 53 feet and it is hanging over the back of the trailer.

- In case the GVW or Gross Vehicle Weight of the truck exceeds 80,000 pounds after being loaded.

Because of the extra expense for the carrier, it is better that you get a good deal for such loads.

Extending Credit to Shippers

The credibility of information, efficiency of communication, and control play a vital role in managing credit in your small business. Before you can even begin to think about granting any kind of credit terms, it is essential that you research and get the correct information you need to obtain reasonable assurance that you will get paid on time and in full. Transparent communications, an excellent flow of information, and complete and clear documentation will contribute in building positive business relationships with your customers and clients. Most importantly, having a strong contact relationship with the accounts payable and following up will be a key aspect in your collections and cash flow.

Freight Brokerage & Credit

It is a normal procedure to perform buying and selling operations on credit. Establishing and maintaining a clear credit policy and following the proper credit practices and procedures should be an integral part of your small business operation. Marketing and sales, production and delivery, and customer service are essential aspects of your business, and your credit and collections practices complete the operating cycle.

Three key concepts involved in credit are:

- Communication

- Control

- Information

To sell on credit is agreeing to deliver the products ordered by your customers, or to perform their requested services based on a promise to pay at a determined future date. Therefore, you will need to make an informed decision about extending credit, before committing your time and resources.

Clear communication with the customer will avoid any misunderstandings that may happen later. Once you have decided to extend credit to a customer, the terms should be documented so that they can be clear to both parties. It is also important that all your employees who work in sales and marketing, production and distribution, or accounting operate from the same base in terms of credit.

Your credit policy will only be effective if it is carried out in practice, and in order to have a proper control you'll need to perform constant follow-up. Guidelines should be consistently applied in the sales and billing phase, and enforced through follow-up in the collections stage.

Common Credit Practices

When establishing a credit policy, you should consider the factors that are the standard practices in your line of business. It is common for many businesses to have customers with 30-day payment terms. In spite of the fact that you are not obligated to accept terms imposed by your customers, it is extremely important to recognize these standard or common practices. Most businesses operate on a standard pay cycle, issuing payments once a week, for example, based on an accounts payable system that looks up invoices and calls up for payment those that are due. In many cases, when the invoices are entered into the system, the due date will be assumed to be, or will default to, 30 days.

The 30-day payment period is an example. It can vary according to the business's nature, type of industry, general economic conditions, and the individual company's financial policies and practices. You will need to provide your small business cash flow permits, by making it easier for your customers to pay you. It may be beneficial to accept the standard terms of your customers as your company is new established.

However, you may be in a business that normally involves payment on cash terms; which means, you receive payment for your sales essentially by cash, check, credit or debit card, or electronic transfers of funds. Your credit policy would involve the exceptions, when you would extend credit to a particular customer based on a certain set of circumstances. Though even in the case of an exception, the same principles would apply in deciding whether to grant credit to that customer.

Considerations regarding the potential customer

Some of the following questions may form part of a credit evaluation of a particular company:

- How long has the company been in operation?

- Are you familiar with the company?

- Is the company generally recognized in your market, industry, or community?

- Does the company have a physical address?

- Do you know the manager?

- Has the company undergone a change of management or a restructuring?

- Who are the owners?

- Has the company undergone a change of ownership?

- What is the company's PAYDEX score?

- Is the company in bankruptcy or has it declared bankruptcy in the past?

Dunn - Bradstreet PAYDEX:

The most important thing to know as a business is your Paydex score. A company's Paydex score is the business equivalent of your personal FICO score or personal credit score. Knowing what this number is and having the secrets to increasing your Paydex score can mean acquiring the financing necessary to start or grow your business. On the flip side, not managing your Paydex score will cost your business.

The exact definition from Dunn & Bradstreet or D&B is: The D&B PAYDEX® Score is D&B's unique dollar-weighted numerical indicator of how a firm paid its bills over the past year, based on trade experiences reported to D&B by various vendors. The D&B PAYDEX Score ranges from 1 to 100, with higher scores indicating better payment performance.

Understanding Payment Patterns

100 (Anticipated) – Payment detail may state: payments are received prior to date of invoice

90 (Discount) – Payment detail may state: payments are received within trade discount period

80 (Prompt) – Payment detail may state: payments are received within terms granted

70 – 15 Days Beyond Terms

60 – 22 Days Beyond Terms

50 – 30 Days Beyond Terms

40 – 60 Days Beyond Terms

30 – 90 Days Beyond Terms

20 – 120 Days Beyond

UN – Unavailable

The payment details section may include the following comments on your payment patterns:

- Antic – payments are received prior to date of invoice (Anticipated).

- Disc – payments are received within trade discount period (Discount).

- Ppt – payments are received within terms granted (Prompt).

- Slow – payments are beyond vendor's terms. For example, "Slow 30" means payments are 30 days past due.

- Ppt-Slow – some invoices are paid within terms, others are paid beyond terms.

- (#) – indicates that no manner of payment was provided; the number merely reflects the line where it appears in the listing. For example, (004) means it is the fourth experience listed.

Closing Deals

All small business owners either hate or completely ignore the cornerstone of the business: the sales process. The main idea of closing a sale is even less appealing. Sales and marketing are the foundational functions that keep every business alive and growing, and enable every successful business owner to make good deals. Selling is much more about educating and informing, than pushing and listening. A truly good salesperson, regardless of what they are selling, is a master at determining their customer's needs and finding answers for them. The quicker a business owner realizes the importance of selling and closing, the sooner he makes a positive business decision to educate himself on techniques and principles associated with selling and closing, the faster his business will grow.

The last and most critical step in the sales process is closing: asking your prospective customer for their business. Closing is a critical step, but unfortunately many people close without thinking. They make the age-old mistake of assuming that their prospect will just automatically give them their business. Of course, this does occur occasionally. But it's difficult to pay your bills every month if you rely on what may occur occasionally. Closing the sale is as important as crossing the finish line at the end of a race. Many business owners do not like going into "close" mode, as they fear being rejected. You should not be afraid to close and ask for the business, whenever possible. That is the purpose for having the business in the first place. With practice, you will know when your potential customer's interest is high; make sure you take advantage of the timing by asking for their business. Never, ever be afraid to close. Even if your attempt at closing is unsuccessful, you must tell your potential customer that you are able to offer them your service/product, as you will have an instant indicator in order to know where they are in the sales process.

Frequently, customers will show interest in asking about details related to your service. This is an indication that their interest is high, so this is the time that a nudge puts them over the buying edge. If they committed after your initial close, there is some type of objection standing in your way. You must determine that objection or concern, then address it and go for the close again.

Trial Close:

In order to close your prospective customer, you should estimate their level of interest by using a "trial close." A trial close is a very simple question that gets the customer to think about the possibility of using your services. Lots of car sales representatives may use a trial close with an interested buyer by, for example, asking them about the color that they prefer. If the buyer answers with a color, then the sales representative has determined that the buyer's interest is high, simply because the customer has already imagined owning that car in a particular color. Therefore, using trial close technique is very helpful in determining your prospective client's level of interest. In fact, a trial close builds interest in your customer by getting them to think of you as a service provider who has what they need.

Assumptive Close:

Assumptive close is considered as one of the most effective closing techniques. Simply, it is a statement that implies that you will do business with your prospect. The assumptive close has the same aim as the trial close: to gets the prospective customer to consider you as a service provider. It should also be used throughout the sales process to determine and build interest. Nevertheless, unlike the trial close, the assumptive close is normally posed as a statement. The close should be a very conscious part of the sales process and when you enter into a closing opportunity, confirm that you:

- Successfully create enough interest in your service.

- Familiarize yourself with closing options.

- Have clear pricing objectives.

- Have mental and emotional clarity about closing.

- Have prepared a way to accept payment.

- Have an agreement or contract ready if it is necessary.

Alternative Choice Close:

"Alternative choice close" is an extremely strong and very powerful closing technique, which gives your prospective client several options on any particular aspect of your service. The alternative choice close is formed as a question that prompts your prospective client to consider how to do business with you. This can be done throughout the sales process.

You should limit your choices to two possibilities when using the alternative choice close. After the potential customer answers the question by selecting one of the possibilities, have them commit to specifics immediately after that. A free analysis or a free offer form is highly recommended to be added to your website. It will help to initiate the sales process by letting you cultivate a contact with the potential client to determine their needs and be educating them on how you can become a solution to their needs. Closing and selling is not a way of manipulating your prospective clients, but an opportunity for you to show them that your service can serve their needs. It is vital that you are successful at closing and selling and persuading your client that there is a great need for your service. Your job is to be proactive by making others aware that they need your service. As a salesperson, you know that there is always some resistance to change among those considering using your services. Selling and closing are the tools by which you can overcome that resistance.

Additional Closing Tips:
- Ask for the order.

- Ask for the order again.

- Ask for commitment using the alternative choice close.

- Create a sense of urgency with temporary discounts and promotions.

- Keep your energy and enthusiasm high, don't lose steam at the end.

- Don't oversell. Ask for the order and quietly wait for a response.

- Move into closing seamlessly and without hesitation.

- Visualize yourself successfully getting the business.

- Ask for the order again.

Remember, you should not be hesitant or fearful in promoting your services proactively. As a business owner, we know that most people need our services. Take it as a conscious mission to improve your sales and closing processes and then use as many of the techniques as possible, in order to essentially grow your business.

Additional Closing Techniques:

If it's a low-ticket retail purchase, most people won't say "Okay, I'll buy it!" out of their own initiative, especially if it's a purchase that will require financial commitment. In order to be successful at closing a sale, you'll have to convince them by using these ten sales closing techniques. The idea behind closing a sale is encourage the buyer to ask the right questions that will make the buyer want the product. This is not to say that sales closing techniques should be clever, manipulative, or deceptive. Rather, closing a sale should come as a natural conclusion of the selling process. Here is what many consider as the top ten sales closing techniques that will make the customer say the magic words, "I'll take it!"

Affordable Close:

Price is the key element of any buying operation. In fact, it is the first objection most people have about buying a product, especially a major one like a car or house. But did you know that "I can't afford to buy it" is more an excuse than an actual objection? You'll need to restructure the payment scheme according to your client's budget in order to change his prospective mind. This is called the Affordable Close technique. To do that, you have to find out their budget and how much they can spare, and present a payment scheme that can fit the buyer's capacity to pay. Supplement this by showing the price of not buying (e.g. the current car's cost of continued ownership).

You can also make the product more affordable by stripping it down to the bare minimum and selling the other options, accessories, or add-ons as separate products. Alternately, you can present a different product that fits their budget. Your very last option is to bring the price down to something the buyer is prepared to pay.

Opportunity Cost Close:

The "opportunity cost" is the cost of not doing something—there is a cost for everything in the world of business. We can understand that the cost is not equal to the price. The price refers to what the buyers pay, but cost may refer to the problems you may face by not buying the product, such as "hassle" and "dissatisfaction," which are not valued by money.

No Hassle Close:

The no-hassle close is a way to win over the prospective buyer by making the purchase process very simple and avoiding giving the buyer any trouble or hassle. For example, you can fill all forms and papers on the buyer's behalf.

Best Time Close:

If your client says that he does not have the time now, then try to persuade him that it is the best time for that, as once the client goes away, he will not be back again. So you should try to close the deal now.

You can do that by showing him the advantages of your product and how it will be suitable in this time.

Minor Points Close:

This means you persuade the buyer to close the deal by closing the minor points; that is, asking him about small details like the color, delivery time, fitting options, etc. This may make it easier for the buyer to decide and help you to close the sale as well. In the same time, you should know the factors that may help him to take the decision.

1-2-3 Close:

There are three main items in this technique: cost, quality, and time. There are two ways for doing this; they may be used together to make a single point, or may be separated in order to gain greater coverage. We all know that every customer wants free, perfect, and delivery on-time products.

Adjournment Close:

We know that the relationship between the seller and client is very important as it will be a long-term relationship. So it is not recommended to push him to take a decision before he is ready. So you can use an Adjournment Close to let your client take his time before deciding what he really needs. The Adjournment Close is better and easier to manage when the salesperson is in a face-to-face meeting rather than waiting on a call phone. So you tell him that you will put his deal on the table and give him time to think.

Use this when:

1. You are seeking a long-term relationship, and if the client makes the wrong deal that may affect the relationship.

2. You do not need to make the sale today, for perhaps you've made your quota, and this sale would be just fine for next month.

3. You are confident that the client likes your products and he will come back.

4. You know that they are not going to decide now.

5. Given more time, it is very likely that they will buy more, if they are at the edge of a budgetary period and their current funds are low.

Balance-Sheet Close:

This works through building trust by seemingly taking a balanced and fair approach. It can save customers from wasting their time and it helps them to know their positive and negative sides, so their lists will be different.

Squeeze Close:

Give the customer three different offers. First, offer them something that is well beyond their target budget number, but not so far beyond that they would not consider it. Ideally, it should be something they look at wistfully but just cannot justify the purchase. Then, as another option, offer them a good deal that is within their price bracket. It may not have all the bells and whistles they want, but it is clearly a very good value for the price they want to pay. Lastly, offer a severely stripped-down deal in which very little of what they want is included. More than likely they should, and probably will, go for the middle option.

Bracket Close:

The Bracket Close works by contrasting the preferred option both upwards and downwards. Rejecting a higher option lets the other person feel good about not spending too much. By comparison, the option they choose seems quite obvious and they may even feel that you have saved them some money. Rejecting the lower option makes the customer feel they are not a cheap who can't afford something of value such as the service you provide.

Charmer:

Deal with your customers gently and express your admiration for their personality. Boost their self-confidence and make them feel that they have the necessary expertise to determine what they want to buy. You have to entice the customers and massage their ego to become more concerned about themselves. Link your customers to the product and let them feel that the product meets their personal needs. Praise their earlier decisions and express your confidence that they can take new successful ones.

Carrier "Set Up" Package

When starting a business with a new carrier, you will need to get them **"Set Up"** in your carrier database. For this, you will need to collect the following information from the motor carrier.

FMCSA Contract Authority

The **"Authority"** or **"MC"** number of the motor carrier is required to be placed on file for your protection. You can check the accuracy of information provided by the motor carrier here:

- http://www.safersys.org/CompanySnapshot.aspx

Insurance

You will also need a copy of the motor carrier's **"Liability & Cargo"** insurance. You can verify the accuracy and minimum requirements here:

- http://li-public.fmcsa.dot.gov/LIVIEW/pkg_carrquery.prc_carrlist

IRS W-9 Form

You will also need a copy of the carrier's IRS W-9 Form. You can download a blank one here:

- http://www.irs.gov/pub/irs-pdf/fw9.pdf

Broker Carrier Agreement

This agreement will regulate the provided services by the carrier for your freight brokerage. It will also list the exclusionary rules of how the carrier should operate and also help prevent back solicitation of your customers.

Company Profile

You'll need to have a **"Company Profile"** to obtain a better idea of the capabilities that the motor carrier possesses. The carrier's company profile should include the following information:

- Payment Information

- Factoring Company

- Type of Equipment

- Dispatch Contacts

- Operating Areas

- Emergency Contact Information

- Endorsements

- Insurance Contacts

Daily Routine

Being a freight dispatcher will involve a huge amount of phone time and computer screen time daily. You have to communicate with potential shippers efficiently to discover their needs. You will be very busy finding carriers or just providing lane quotes for the shipper to use at a later date. These communications are very important to build your database of contacts and get your name out there to the shippers. The first two to four hours of your day are the most critical. You can maximize your time by receiving calls and booking loads for the shipments you posted the previous day, rather than spending that time performing freight inquiries. Therefore, it is preferred to implement inquiries in the afternoon when things begin to slow down. Customer freight inquiries should be looked at as another form of time management that can make you money.

- The initial load details that will be collected by each broker will generally be: commodity or cargo type, pick-up and delivery locations, type of carrier required, anticipated rate for the load, and any special instructions to the carrier regarding the load.

- As soon as you collect this information, you will begin entering these notes into your contact manager indicating when and where this shipper's loads move, and also the frequency of shipping. Remember to start as early as possible preferably by 6:00 AM. These offices start work early as the shippers are usually preparing to arrange their freight early in the morning.

- After establishing your relationship with a shipper, getting loads wouldn't be a problem. The shipper will tell you on what lanes carriers are needed. You have to note everything about the load since this information will be relayed in detail to the carriers that are interested in moving the freight.

- The shipper will either give you a rate that they want to pay for the load or they will ask you to submit a quote for the lane. Once you have the numbers nailed down, you now know what to offer the carrier to haul the freight. On average, freight brokers make about 10% of the load amount. Try to average 15%-20% of the load. It might take a bit longer to find a carrier, but it will work out better at the end of the day.

- In case you do not have a carrier already in mind for the freight, then you should start posting on load boards such as Internet Truckstop, Get Loaded, or The DAT. These are not the only load boards on the Internet, but are the load boards that receive the most traffic and most prospective carriers.

- Once the load has been posted, then you can move on to find more freight or you may start calling your database for interest in the load. While calling the database, you will also start to receive calls from prospective carriers who saw the postings on the load boards. Once you have reached an agreement with a carrier to accept the line haul, immediately call the shipper to inform them that the load is **"Covered"** and that you have a truck.

- If you have reached a deal with the shipper, then you'll obtain from them the rate confirmation and load sheet for you to sign and return immediately. It might take a while to receive the rate confirmation; this is common as most shippers are extremely busy moving several loads.

- Now it is the time to clear your carrier through the FMCSA to make sure they have no prior history of accidents and that they have the proper insurance. Once this has been done, you will then fax your **"Set Up"** package to the carrier for him to sign and return.

- Once the carrier has completed your initial **"Set Up"** package, you will then prepare the rate confirmation sheet and loading order and fax that to them. They will also sign and fax that back to your office for your records.

- Now that you have received the signed rate confirmation from the carrier dispatcher, you have to call the truck driver and verify the entire load details and dispatch them to the location to pick up the load.

- The carrier should contact you daily with a status of the whereabouts of their truck. This is called a **"Call Check."** It is standard operating procedure to impose fines to the carrier for failure to comply with your **"Call Check"** policy. This policy should be noted on the rate confirmation sheet.

- As soon as the load has been delivered, contact the shipper to let them know the status. It is standard operating procedure to require the carrier to fax a copy of the signed bill of lading when the load has been accepted; then you are aware of any problems with the load or can verify delivery to the recipient.

- If there have been any problems with the load, you should contact all parties immediately, that is, Shipper, Carrier, and Recipient, and resolve them amicably. This is your responsibility as a broker.

Though this may all seem to be a complicated and very mundane procedure, you must follow these steps strictly to ensure smooth deliveries and returning customers. Keep in mind that all situations that may arise concerning any given load can be resolved with the exception of force majeure incidents, or **"Acts of God."**

Dispatching

Always be calm and speak professionally. Never get into a verbal altercation with a driver while he is dispatched on your load; it is pointless to risk getting into a situation that could potentially turn bad.

Dispatching means the process of assigning motor carriers to your loads. Once you and your client have discussed the line-haul rate, you will have to start searching for a motor carrier willing to haul the load. There are many ways to find motor carriers. You will have to complete some formalities like signing the set-up contract, preparing the rate sheet, and scrutinizing the safety ratings of the motor carrier before you can start the dispatch process. It is important to complete all the formalities to prevent any legal or financial issues at a later stage.

If you are brokering a load, you will be following the roles and responsibilities of a contractor. While availing the services of the motor carrier, you need to have an arrangement or "set-up" with the carrier. "Set-up" means the contract agreement which has been chalked out between you and the motor carrier. In case you aren't aware of the process of creating a contract, then you should seek assistance from a lawyer who will draft a proper contract with the help of a sample contract form.

There are numerous forms and agreements which have to be filled before you can begin to dispatch. Such forms and agreements are used during various stages of the dispatch process. However, it is important to know the purpose of these forms and agreements.

Majority of the companies include a lot of legal terms in their set-up contracts to protect their prospecting endeavor. It is also necessary for the brokers to have a "back end solution clause," which is informally called a "non-complete" agreement, with their set-up contract to avoid the possibility of the carrier hauling directly from the clients. Thus as a freight dispatcher, you are sure that the efforts of procuring a client have not gone waste. In case the motor carrier ends up directly dealing with your customer, it will be mandatory for them to share a certain percentage of the revenue they have earned from that customer. Thus, this is the best solution to safeguard your business.

Motor Carrier Snapshot/Safety Rating

In case you do not have any setup agreement with a carrier and intend to dispatch for the first time, then it is better to find out more about the Motor Carrier Snapshot or Safety Rating. By doing so, you can find out a lot about the motor carrier. Some vital information you will get is the number of units on file with the FMCSA, the drivers they have employed, and their safety snapshot. You will also get to know their "Out of Service" ratio.

A motor carrier can be termed "Out of Service" by the USDOT in case it does not adhere to the regulations which have been laid down by the FMCSA. But this is not always accurate. For instance, in case a carrier has just one truck and yet was given a 100% Out of Service rating, it may mean that the truck was being handled by the owner himself and had once been declared "Out of Service" due to a small or major issue.

This could have happened unintentionally due to ignorance about the law. Besides, if the carrier has two trucks, out of which one got an "Out of Service" label then it amounts to 50%, which indeed cuts a sorry picture. However, if the same carrier had 100 trucks out of which one was labeled "Out of Service" then the rating would be a mere 1%.

Hence, focus on looking for a carrier that has a low Out of Service percentage. However, this will not make sense unless you find out about the total number of units they possess.

After you dispatch the carrier, do not assume that everything is moving smoothly. You should keep in contact with the truck driver directly or the agent and dispatch personnel responsible for that carrier. Typically, you would ask the carrier to contact you:

- When the truck is loaded

- Each morning or once daily while under the load

- Immediately after the load is delivered to the final destination

Have you ever heard the term GAP? It stands for Grab A Pen! Each time the carrier contacts you for a check call, Grab a Pen! Make a note of the following:

- Who you spoke with

- Motor Carrier Snapshot/Safety Rating

- Broker/Shipper Agreement

- The date and time (always use your local time zone)

- The driver's location (or nearest town if you're entering these notes into software)

- The estimated time of arrival at the final destination

Your customer is depending on you to know where their freight is and whether or not it's going to be on time for delivery. And if there is a change in plans, such as a mechanical failure or bad weather conditions, your customer may also need to notify their customer. If the motor carrier does not contact you, you should contact them each day while they are dispatched under your load. When contacting customers and carriers, consider the time zone in which they are located.

Dispatch Cancellations

Cancellation occurs when the carrier has already signed a rate confirmation agreement and agreed to transport your freight, then for whatever reason, chooses not to haul it. In case the carrier fails to pick up a load after agreeing to do so, you will have to find an alternative truck to service your customer.

Motor carriers use backhaul loads to get back into their home or to an area where they have direct shipper contacts. Obviously, motor carriers can secure better paying freight from their own customers. For this reason, carriers opt to pre-plan their trucks in a direction that will put them closer to their direct customer base.

Carrier Fines & Carrier Communication

Brokers will impose a system of fines on carriers to ensure the successful transportation of the cargo and consistent communication throughout the load. It is simply not enough to ask the carrier to do his job and move the load with no problems. A freight brokerage is not a daycare center, so we may not put the carrier in **"Time Out"** if he fails to hold up his part of the contract moving the load.

A freight brokerage will use carrier fines to help avoid a multitude of problems. Below is a list of infractions in which a carrier will be fined. Also included are suggested amounts to charge for each infraction.

- **Daily Call Check** ($100.00 Per Instance) -It is important to impose fines on carriers who do not maintain communication with your brokerage. These fines are to be clearly listed on your rate confirmation sheet to the carrier. If these are not listed on your rate confirmation sheet, you have no legal recourse to impose the fine toward the carrier.

- **Late Delivery** (25% Of The Load) -This is generally only enforced if a shipper has placed time constraints on the arrival of the load. The above amount is on the high end of the spectrum. Fines could range from $100 -$1,500 per load.

- **Failure to Fax BOLs** within specified time ($100.00) -A number of shippers want the BOLs faxed to them within 4-6 hours of the load being delivered.

- **Dispatching of Drivers** (10% of the load) -Fine is enforced if the carrier requires the broker to dispatch his driver. This is the carrier's responsibility. Do not create additional work for yourself.

- **Truck No Show Fee** - ($250.00) -You should bill the carrier's company this fine if the truck does not show up to take the load. This is a rarity.

- **Failure To Load Complete Order** -Occasionally, trucks will not load a complete order as prescribed by a shipper. It is recommended that you place specific quantities needed to be loaded on the rate confirmation sheet. If these are not on the rate confirmation sheet, the truck can literally leave half your order behind. This fine will vary depending on the load. This is on an as-needed basis.

Freight's Types

LTL - Less than Truckload

LTL freight refers to Less Than Truckload, which usually weighs between 151 and 20,000 lb. (68 and 9,072 kg). The main task of Less Than Truckload carriers is collecting freight from shippers and consolidating that freight into enclosed trailers to the delivering place, where this freight will be further sorted for additional distances. Drivers usually make deliveries first, and then they make pickups after the trailer has been emptied. Generally, most pickups are made in the afternoon and most deliveries are made in the morning.

How does the LTL model work?

Pickup/delivery drivers as a rule have particular routes that they travel every day or several times a week, as this gives the driver a good chance to develop a rapport with their customers. Once the driver has filled their trailer or completed their assigned route, the driver returns to their destination for unloading. The trailer is unloaded and the individual shipments are then weighed and inspected to verify their conformity to the description contained in the accompanying paperwork.

All LTL freight is subject to inspection for this purpose, though not all freight is inspected. Freight that is shipped LTL (less than truckload) has an increased risk of damage or loss as the freight may be handled multiple times while passing through freight terminals and being consolidated with other shipments on its way to the ultimate destination. Next, the freight is loaded onto an outbound trailer, which will later forward the freight to a breakbulk, a connection, or to the delivering terminal. An LTL shipment may be handled only in the transit, or it may be handled many times before final delivery is accomplished.

The times for LTL freight are more than that for FTL, as they are not related only to the distance between shipper and sender. But LTL transit depends on the making network of terminals and break bulks, which are operated by the nominated carrier and belong to agents and interline partners. For instance, if a shipment is delivered by the same freight terminal, or if the freight must be sorted only in transportation, the freight will be delivered the next day after pickup. If the freight must be sorted and routed many times or if there are more than line haul that are required for transportation to the delivering place, then the time of transportation will be longer. So if the delivery is going to remote areas, the transit time will be increased.

There are several advantages for the LTL carrier. The most important one is that a shipment may be transported for a fraction of the cost. The second advantage is that accessorial services are usually available from LTL carriers, but not offered by FTL carriers. These optional services include lift gate service at pickup or delivery, residential (also known as "non-commercial") service at pickup or delivery, inside delivery, notification prior to delivery, freeze protection, and others. These services are usually charged at predetermined fees that are based on the weight.

What's the difference between an LTL Common Carrier and a Volume Consolidator?

Common carriers usually handle small LTL (1-5 pallets) less than 4,500 lbs. Common carriers use the NMFC classification 50-500 to charge for freight. Usually, there is a maximum linear feet measure before it has to change to a volume spot rate quote... Rule of thumb: if your freight is over 10 feet in length, double check your LTL rates and possibly get a volume rate quote. If your freight is light and the linear feet you take up is more than 10 feet, you may be violating their low-density minimum charge rule.

Consolidators do exactly what the root word is, they consolidate freight. They charge based on the linear feet you take up in the trailer. So if you have 10 non-stackable pallets with dimensions of 48 x 48 x 96, you will be taking up 20 linear feet. You will be charged for 20 linear feet, not for classification. Some things to keep in mind: you are only entitled to 1,000 lbs. per linear feet. So if your 10 non-stackable pallets weight 18klbs but only take up 20 linear feet, your price would be the same. But if your 10 non-stackable pallets weigh 21,500lbs, you are entitled to pay for 22 linear feet because of the 1,000lbs per linear foot.

NMFC Classifications: http://www.nmfta.org/pages/nmfc

Carrier Integration of FTL & LTL

Shippers that have large volume of LTL freight may choose a Full Truckload Carrier to move the freight directly to a break-bulk facility of an LTL carrier. For instance, if a North Carolina shipper has a large quantity of shipments for Western US States such as CA, NV, OR, WA, and ID, then the shipper can realize significant cost savings by having an FTL carrier, known as a line haul carrier, transport the freight to a break-bulk facility nearest the center of such shipments in terms of the carrier's network. In this case, the shipper may choose to send the freight to a break-bulk in CA. The use of an FTL carrier to transport this freight will save your money because the freight will travel fewer miles in the LTL carrier's network, and a further benefit will be realized because the freight will not be unloaded and reloaded as many times. This reduces the incidence of loss and damage in transit.

Double Load vs. LTL Load

As long as each piece of freight is within the standard legal dimensions, the weight of a shipment is the primary concern. Distinguishing a double load from an LTL load begins first with origin, destination, and timeline similarities. Does the load pick up or deliver to points close to the other load? Are loading times flexible enough to make room for the other loads' delivery times? If so, the next things to examine are weight and load dimension. The main factor in determining whether a double load can be booked is the carrier's ability to handle the job, with respect to trailer, size, type, etc. If you maintain a good carrier equipment list, the chances you'll have to swiftly recognize when a double load is possible will greatly increase.

(LTL) Carriers

Access America Transport

http://www.accessamericatransport.com

2515 East 43rd St., Suite B Chattanooga, TN 37407 **Phone:** (866) 272.2057 **Fax:** (423) 648.7782

Click Ship N Go

http://www.clickshipngo.com

PO Box #102 Medford, New Jersey, 08055 **Phone:** (877)859-6217

Global Forwarding Enterprises LLC

http://globalforwarding.com

Manalapan, NJ 07726 **Phone:** (877)287-0804

Freight Classes

Freight Identification and Classification Standards

The National Motor Freight Classification (NMFC) is a standard that offers a comparison of commodities moving in interstate and foreign commerce. In concept, it is near to the groupings or systems that serve many other industries. Commodities are grouped into one of 18 classes—from class 50 to the highest class 500—based on an evaluation of four transportation characteristics: density, storability, handling, and liability. Together, these characteristics establish a commodity's "transportability."

The four transportation characteristics were prescribed by the Interstate Commerce Commission (ICC) in 1983 and then mandated by its successor agency, the Surface Transportation Board (STB). Although the ICC no longer exists and the STB no longer regulates the classification process, by analyzing commodities on the basis of these characteristics and only on the basis of these characteristics, the NMFC provides both carriers and shippers with a standard by which to begin negotiations and greatly simplifies the comparative evaluation of many thousands of products moving in today's competitive marketplace.

Packaging, Rules, and Bills of Lading Standards

The NMFC minimum packaging requirements ensure that goods are adequately protected in the motor carrier environment and can be handled and stowed in a manner that is reasonably safe and practical. Those specs contain various rules that govern and otherwise relate to the classification and/or packaging of commodities as well as procedures for the filing and disposition of claims. It also contains the **Uniform Straight Bill of Lading** and the **North American Uniform through Bill of Lading**, including their terms and conditions.

Resources

National Motor Freight Traffic Association, Inc.

http://www.nmfta.org

Truckload (TL)

Truckload shipping is the movement of large amounts of cargo, generally the amount necessary to fill an entire semi-trailer or intermodal container. A truckload carrier is a trucking company that generally contracts an entire trailer-load to a single customer. But a less than truckload (LTL) company generally mixes freight from several customers in each trailer. One advantage full truckload carriers have over LTL carriers is that the freight is never handled end route, as an LTL shipment will typically be transported on several different trailers.

Normally full truckload carriers deliver a semi-trailer to a shipper that will fill the trailer with freight for one destination. After the trailer is loaded, the driver will return to the shipper to collect the required paperwork **(i.e., bill of lading, invoice, and customs paperwork)** and depart with the trailer containing freight. In most cases, the driver then proceeds directly to the consignee and delivers the freight themselves. Sometimes, a driver will transfer the trailer to another driver who will carry the freight the rest of the way. Full Truckload (FTL) transit times are normally constrained by the driver's availability according to Hours of Service regulations and distance.

Since truckload carriers are asked to ship a large variety of items, a truckload carrier will often specialize in moving a particular kind of freight. Some carriers will primarily transport food and perishable items, and others may specialize in moving hazardous and poisonous materials. Carriers will only transport specific freight because different equipment and insurance is needed for the different loads. There are also federal laws that state which types of freight can be shipped together in the same trailer.

General Freight

Shipments that are larger than about 7,000 kg (15,432 lbs.) are generally classified as "Truckload" (TL) in the United States of America, since it is more efficient and economical for a large shipment to have exclusive use of one large trailer rather than share space on a smaller LTL trailer. The total weight of a loaded truck (tractor and trailer, 5-axle rig) cannot exceed 36,000 kg (79,366 lb.) in the U.S. In ordinary circumstances, long-haul equipment will weigh about 15,000 kg (33,069 lb.), leaving about 20,000 kg (44,092 lb.) of freight capacity. Similarly a load is limited to the space available in the trailer; normally 48 ft. (14.63 m) or 53 ft. (16.15 m) long and 2.6 m (102.4 in) wide and 2.7 m (8 ft. 10.3 in) high (13 ft. 6 in/4.11 m high overall). Express, parcel, and LTL shipments are always intermingled with other shipments on a single piece of equipment and are typically reloaded across multiple pieces of equipment during their transport. TL shipments usually travel as the only shipment on a trailer and usually deliver on exactly the same trailer as they are picked up on.

Truckload (TL) carriers generally charge a rate per kilometer or mile that depends on the distance, geographic location of the delivery, goods being shipped, the type of required equipment, and the time of required service. TL shipments usually receive a variety of surcharges very similar to those described for LTL shipments above. In the TL market, there are thousands more small carriers than in the LTL market; so the use of transportation intermediaries or "brokers" is extremely common.

Facilitating pickups or deliveries at the carrier's terminal is another cost-saving method. In this way, shippers avoid any accessorial fees that might normally be charged for lift gate, residential pickup/delivery, inside pickup/delivery, or notifications/appointments. Carriers or intermediaries can provide shippers with the address and phone number for the closest shipping terminal to the origin and/or destination.

Shipping experts increase their service and costs by similar rates from many carriers, brokers, and online marketplaces. When the shippers get rates from different providers, they may find quite a wide range in the pricing offered. If a shipper uses a broker, freight forwarder, or other transportation intermediary, it is common for the shipper to receive a copy of the carrier's Federal Operating Authority. Freight brokers and intermediaries should be licensed by the Federal Highway Administration. Experienced shippers avoid unlicensed brokers and forwarders, because if brokers are working outside the law by not having a Federal Operating License, the shipper may face problems. Also, shippers normally ask for a copy of the broker's insurance certificate and any specific insurance that applies to the shipment.

Truckload Carriers

Schneider National, Inc.

http://www.schneider.com

3101 South Packerland Drive Green Bay, Wisconsin 54306-2545 **Toll-Free Phone:** (800)558-6767

New England Motor Freight

http://www.nemf.com

1-71 North Avenue East Elizabeth NJ 07201 **Phone:** (908)965-0100 **Fax:** (908)965-0795

GT Logistics

http://www.gtlogisticsllc.com

3 Crafton Square, Pittsburgh, PA 15205 **Phone:** (888)588-5850 **Fax:** (412)920-1899

Evans Distribution Systems

http://www.evansdist.com

18765 Seaway Drive Melvindale, MI 48122 **Phone :**(313)388-3200 **Fax:** (313)388-0136

Resources & Links

Fairgrounds Transportation

http://www.arlwest.com

6833 Indiana Ave. #202 Riverside, CA 92507 **Phone:** (951)786-9372 **Fax :**(951)786-9399

There are several types of freight that move daily on America's interstates. It is the job of a freight broker to decide which type of freight will be the most profitable and easily placed by your brokerage.

Produce Freight

America's appetite for food and delicacies keeps reefers running continuously from all parts of the country. Produce warehouses, wholesalers, and supermarkets need to replenish their inventories daily with fresh vegetables to keep up with the demand of the American consumer. Produce is the easiest type of freight to get. Your customer will be the grower, packer, produce cooler, produce broker, or the consignee himself.

Produce loads are generally very competitive for pricing depending on the type of produce. Shippers will require minimizing the carrier load or paying on weight. Shippers will do this so they can be assured that the carrier loads are the maximum amount of product by law. Outlined below is how most shippers will require the carrier to load for specific types of products around the country.

- **Rates** -Overall rates for the transportation of products are most generally low throughout the country. Unless you have access to a core group of carriers, these types of loads will require a lot of work.

- **Claims** -To keep claims to minimum, use carriers with a great deal of experience in hauling produce. These carriers will have newer equipment that is maintained accordingly, temperature thermometers, and good insurance.

- **Detention** -Inexperienced carriers will frequently attempt to bill you for detention because of the long periods of wait time to load for produce. This is because of product unavailability, number of carriers loading, or seasonal delays.

- **Carrier Fines** -Produce shippers and receivers are notorious for implementing fines for delays in delivery. These fines are incurred because the receiver has to purchase their product at terminal markets in their area. Shippers will then impose fines for the price differences to the carrier due to the delay.

Great Link for Shippers
- http://www.producemarketguide.com/

Consigner Procedures:

When produce or refrigerated freight is prepared for shipping, it is most generally fresh from the field. When your carrier arrives for their scheduled pickup, the product may or may not be ready due to product availability. They will be waiting onsite until the product arrives at the shipping location.

Produce must be cooled down prior to loading.

When the shipment is loaded on trucks, spoilage or damage may occur during transit. This will occur because the outer layers of produce that is palletized, whether bagged, boxed, or loose, will cool down to the temperature of the trailer. However, they will also serve as an insulation barrier against the product that is underneath the top layers. Encourage your carrier to exercise due diligence as produce shippers file the most insurance claims on freight because the profit margins on their products are so slim and freight charges are usually very high during peak seasons and in peak areas.

Consignee Procedures

When produce or refrigerated freight is delivered, most generally consignees have a set of guidelines that they should follow before receipt of the freight. If these guidelines are not followed the load could be rejected and a claim situation could arise. Here is a scenario of a consignee's receiving procedures.

- The condition of the trailer will be examined. If there are any insects or rodent infestation, the load will be rejected. If the floor of the trailer is dirty, the load will be rejected.

- Pulp temperatures of product are taken and recorded from each pallet removed from the trailer. (Industry standard is tail, middle, and nose of the trailer.) These recorded temperatures are then compared to tolerant temperatures for the product.

- Product quality is examined on each pallet.

Links & Resources

- Produce Marketing Association – http://www.pma.com

Refrigerated Loads

When you are transporting refrigerated loads, there are several variables you need to be aware of prior to the loading of cargo and during the lifecycle of the load. The list below contains items you need to be aware of about what your carrier will go through while transporting your freight and also what will happen if a problem occurs once delivered. Refrigerated loads, also known as reefer loads, require increased rates because it costs the carrier more money to run a refrigeration unit on their trailer to keep the goods from spoiling. You should try to negotiate an additional 20 to 40 cents per mile above of your standard rate to help them cover the fuel and maintenance costs for that reefer unit.

- Your carrier must arrive **clean and dry** to load your cargo.

- You carrier must arrive at the consignee **pre-cooled** to the determined temperature for the load.

- When your cargo is loaded your carrier will need to make sure that the cargo is not loaded above the danger line in the trailer. If this happens, the cool air will not circulate properly and your load could be damaged.

- When your cargo is loaded, your carrier will need to make sure the air chute in the trailer is not blocked as the air will not circulate and the load will run at inconsistent temperatures.

- Most shippers will require the load to run at consistent temperatures during transport.

- When your load delivers, whether it is produce or other food-grade products, the consignee will check the freight before he accepts it to make sure the load was transported correctly. If there has been evidence of a problem such as thawing, discoloration, or wilting of your products, the consignee will likely reject the load. The carrier at this point does have the option of contacting the U.S.D.A. and requesting an on-site inspection of the cargo. This is at the carrier's expense. The cost of this inspection will generally range from $200 -$250. If the U.S.D.A. determines that load has not been compromised or that the evidence of spoilage is not the fault of the carrier then the consigner cannot reject the freight.

- If the freight has evidence of spoilage and the load is rejected, the consignee will have to notate this on the **"Bill of Lading."**

- Once this happens, your shipper will then want to possibly move the freight to another location in the area if they can find a buyer for the product depending upon the condition of the goods. In both cases, you and the carrier are now in charge and you re-negotiate the new freight rate for the load to the new location or back to the original consigner of the product.

- If the carrier has been found at fault, generally the load will be rejected by the consignee. The carrier will then be responsible for disposing the freight. A claim will be filed by the shipper to the carrier's insurance company and they will instruct the carrier on how to get rid of the contents of the trailer.

Time-sensitive loads, also known as expedited loads, are handled by team drivers. You should secure rates comparable to that of a reefer load. If it is both refrigerated and time-sensitive, set your per-mile rate accordingly. If you plan to coordinate dry van or refrigerated freight, there are two terms you should familiarize yourself with: DRIVER UNLOAD and DRIVER ASSIST.

A Driver Unload is when the driver is required to unload the trailer and, when necessary, break it down for storage. A Driver Assist is when the driver is required to assist in the loading or unloading of the freight. For both of these, the carrier must be compensated.

Some carriers allow their truck drivers to act as the lumper or driver assistant by participating in a Driver Unload or Driver Assist loads to earn extra money. Some will not. Some carriers are owner-operators who own and operate their own trucks and simply refuse to unload their own trailers. In such cases, the owner-operator becomes responsible for hiring and compensating the lumper or driver assistant.

What are Lumper Charges?

A freight lumper is basically a dockworker or a driver assistant whose work involves loading and unloading trucks. Often, they are hired independently by shippers as well as receivers for loading or unloading their trucks. In fact, companies are more comfortable outsourcing these activities to lumpers. Typically, lumpers deal with delivering the products from inbound carriers, which would have to be unloaded by the drivers.

Truck drivers have a very busy and hectic schedule and they seldom get any free time. So if they hire a lumper for the unloading process, then they can take some rest while the trailer is unloaded. They can also get ready for their next assignment. The drivers who are required to segregate the load, split it, or modify it to make it fit in the warehouse of the consigner often leave this task to the lumpers.

Due to insurance liability, the drivers aren't allowed to use forklifts and similar motorized equipment for unloading their trailers.

For dry vans and frozen or refrigerated freight, the consignee provides the driver with a pallet jacket for manually unloading the trailer. In a Driver Unload, the driver has to personally unload the trailer, and if needed segregate it before storage.

When it comes to Driver Assist, the driver will have to help in the process of loading and unloading. In both the cases, the carrier is compensated.

Often carriers let their truck drivers work as lumpers or driver assistants to make some quick money. However, some restrict their drivers in being a part of the loading and unloading process. At times carriers are operated by the owners who do not agree to unload the trailer themselves and so they have to hire and compensate a lumper or a driver assistant to complete the task.

Requirements for Freight Delivery

Make it a point to ask the customer whether the load is a Driver Unload or a Driver Assist, and pass the information to your carrier. However, if you fail to do so, then the driver will assume that he can take a rest at the destination. Besides, the driver will not be prepared to unload the trailer and segregate the containers which contain the boxes. This is an unpleasant situation and is sure to tarnish your reputation since truck drivers tend to take communication flaws to heart. They prefer to be well prepared and hence you should do the needful and find out the proper details before updating the driver or carrier.

Dry vans and refrigerated shipments often hire lumpers or driver assistants. Hence if your freight includes this, then you should find out whether the customers need a lumper service or not.

Lumper service rates are not static and depend on the type of work they are required to do. Besides, the amount depends on how much they are expected to load and unload. You do not have any say in the negotiation. The remuneration is decided by the carrier or the driver on reaching the destination.

But after you have decided to opt for a Driver Unload or a Driver Assist option, then you should add around $50-$100 for the shipment so that you can cover the cost involved in hiring a lumper service for the unloading process.

Lumper fees are additionally calculated and added to the line-haul rate similar to stop off fees, fuel surcharge, etc. This amount should be included independently in the rate confirmation agreement.

Flatbed & Step Deck (Open Top)

Steel & Machinery

Industrial freight is one of the largest facets of the transportation industry. This freight will typically consist of a variety of types of steel products and/or machinery. The loads could move as little as 65 miles and up to 3,000 miles depending upon your customer. This type of freight is typically very easy to move as there are rarely any claims involved with it and the rate of damages is very rare. Such freight is usually loaded on trailers such as flatbeds, step decks, double drops, etc. If it requires an open trailer such as a flatbed, or step-deck trailer, you will need to determine if the load must be kept dry or under a tarp.

Oversize loads are nearly always transported on an open trailer such as a flatbed, step deck, double drop, lowboy, RGN, or multi-axle trailers. These carriers will have to carry the tools of the trade to haul these loads, which is called "**Dunnage.**" Several different types of "**Dunnage**" are shown below.

Dunnage

Boards	V-Boards
Nylon Straps	Drop Tarps
Chain Protectors	Pallets
Padded Chains	Coil Racks
Canvas Straps	Side Kits

Lumber & Agriculture

The agriculture industry offers a great deal of cargo for freight brokerages in order to be available to carriers. This type of freight is generally seasonal and also regional. You will find these loads will most typically have a line haul of 500 miles or less. This type of freight is transported by a number of different trailers. Please see the table below for the specific commodity and trailer type needed.

Machinery

The majority of machinery such as lathes, press brakes, augers, etc., is transported on flatbeds and step decks across America. These loads can be full truckloads or partials. This is the type of freight to work consistently for profit and stability.

Remember: When you are moving this type of freight, always get dimensions and details in this order from your shipper. The truck will require them to give you an accurate quote.

Length x Width x Height

Taping Required – Yes/No

Gross Commodity Weight

Driver Assistance Required – Yes/No

Overweight & Over Dimensional Freight

Oversized Loads: Oversized loads, also called "Over Dimensional" or "OD," are shipments exceeding the standard legal length, width, or height limits for commercial vehicles. Shipping over-dimensional and overweight freight represents special challenges. Oversized shipments require specific knowledge of government regulations and the necessary trucks and trailers to accommodate the freight that you are moving. Over dimensional freight requires permits and special routing through cities and is frequently escorted by pilot cars, so the trucks can only travel certain hours of the day for safety reasons.

Gather the Information

When considering movement of an "**Over Dimensional Load or Oversized Load**" you will need to get very specific information for the carrier to give you an accurate quote. If a truck does not have an adequate number of axles to carry and stop the additional weight of an overweight load, you will need to search for a truck and trailer capable of doing so. In order to do that, you'll need to familiarize yourself with the types of trailers commonly used to transport oversized and overweight shipments. The general information required is typically put in this table:

Required Load Information	
Origin & Destination	Equipment Required
Length -Width –Height	Trip Insurance
Make & Model Of Machinery	Escorts
Exact Weight	Rigging Charges
Specifications & Drawings Permits	

It is the motor carrier's responsibility to obtain their own permits. In addition to federal laws, each state has different regulations regarding over dimensional loads. State transportation permit fees vary. **A permit for your freight is typically required if your vehicle dimensions or weight exceed the following:**

Dimensions	
Width	8 feet, 6 inches
Height	13 feet, 6 inches
Length -(Single vehicle and load)	40 feet
Length -(Combination of 2 vehicles)	65 feet
Length -(Truck/tractor and semi-trailer)	75/65 feet
Axles	**Weight**
Any wheels supporting one end of an axle	11,000 Lbs.
Truck tractor steering axle	13,000 Lbs.
Single axle	20,000 Lbs.
Tandem axles	34,000 Lbs.
Maximum gross vehicle weights on all axles	80,000 Lbs.

Overweight & Over Dimensional Loads

Escort Vehicles

Escort vehicles are used for transporting over dimensional or overweight loads. This is an additional cost or **"accessorial charge"** that will generally be included above the original transportation charge. Commercial vehicle escorts are used to assist truck drivers in all areas of maneuverability. They communicate with the driver via CB or other two-way radio. Truck escort services are also used for over length shipments to assist in securing traffic lanes during difficult turns and other maneuvers.

These could include but not be limited to:

1. Pilot Cars / Chase Cars –

This is an escort vehicle that displays signage on its front and rear bumper of an impending oversize /

overweight load that is approaching or passing. These are required as part of the permitting process in individual states and cities. These vehicles are generally one (1) mile in the front of the load, and on occasion, by jurisdiction a chase car may also be required in the rear of the load.

2. Pole Cars –

This is an escort vehicle that has a pole affixed to the front of the bumper in order to measure height of a load. This is required on loads generally over **14'3"** tall, but can be also required for less depending on the specific Department of Transportation laws where the load is traveling through. The use of this vehicle will ensure that the load will be able to travel under bridges and overpasses safely without obstruction.

3. State Police Escorts –

The assistance of State Police is often required on **"super loads"** as part of the permit process when the load has exceeded **"maximum"** dimensions or weights by state.

Frost Laws

Frost laws are seasonal restrictions on road traffic weight limits and speeds.

In climates of freezing temperatures, frost-triggered damage to roads leads many states to enact laws. The state of Michigan, for example, during the months of March, April, and May reduces legal axle weights of vehicles by up to 35%. Some areas also require heavy vehicles to travel a maximum of 35 miles per hour, regardless of the posted limit. Frost laws have a significant impact on excavation and construction industries.

Route Surveys

A route survey is conducted by either mapping out the route to be traveled for an overweight or over-dimensional load. There are **two** types of surveys that can be found. The type of survey needed depends on the type of load moved and the laws of each state. This is an additional cost or **"accessorial charge"** that will generally be extra charges that will be added to the original charges.

- **Digital Survey** -This type is performed by a topographer and it includes "**mapping**" of the route.

- **Physical Route Survey** -This is only valid when the surveyor verifies that the noted route will allow safe travel and sufficient clearance for the noted dimensions of the load. These surveys are usually performed by State Licensed Escort Vehicles.

- Physical Route Survey

This type of survey ensures the safe travel and sufficient clearance for the noted dimensions of the load. That is usually performed by State Licensed Escort Vehicles.

General Conditions:
1. **1'0"** on each side of vehicle/load

2. **1'0"** under load clearance

3. **6"** under trailer/semi-trailer clearance

4. **6"** clearance under overhead obstacles. Axle weights and gross vehicle weight must not exceed highway and/or structural weight postings for routes shown. All roads and highways must be shown for route continuity.

Utility Assistance

"Super Loads" may need utility assistance, which requires the carrier to seek the assistance of local power and gas companies to temporarily divert services while the load is being transported through certain areas or jurisdictions. This is also an additional cost or **"accessorial charge"** that will generally be included over and above the original transportation charge.

Bonds

Municipalities, state governments, and the federal government require surety bonds so that they can cover the cost of possible damage to highways. These can be attained from any insurance company or surety bond company.

Links & Resources

Specialized Carriers & Rigging Association –

The Specialized Carriers & Rigging Association (SC&RA) has over 1,200 members in over 40 countries. The goal of the SC&RA is to help improve the safety and quality of its members and end users of crane rental, heavy lifting equipment, and services.

- http://www.scranet.org

Check List & Heavy Haul Action Plan

Any new freight dispatcher or agent must be cautious prior to moving any over dimensional shipment. You should only let your most experienced agents undertake these loads as you could easily lose more than what you would gain in profit. You must possess a basic knowledge of heavy equipment transport. These loads are transported by specialized carriers with the equipment needed. For over height loads, the escort will measure the distance from the ground to the highest point on the load.

Steps

1. Calculate the length, width, height, and overall weight of the commodity you will transport. Know the specific location of pick-up and delivery, and have the details of directions to these locations.

2. Determine the equipment necessary for the load.

3. Make the **"Riggers"** the responsibility of the shipper or carrier as they specialize in this. You are

a freight broker, not a carrier or rigging company.

4. Find the carrier that is necessary for the load. Check his references and insurance if you have not hired him before. When you check the rate confirmation and load details, make sure this is an **"all in"** rate for the load. If this does not happen, you could be in for a ton of **"accessorial charges"** when the invoice comes for the transport of the freight.

5. Communicate with the trucking company to determine how long it takes to acquire heavy equipment hauling permits, if your load is overweight or oversize. A permit is required for every state through which the load travels. The transporting must take place during daylight hours with exception to a few cities to limit you to nighttime transport because of traffic congestion. You are also set within a restricted number of days because of your permits.

6. Plan the pick-up and delivery dates accordingly, and allow additional time for limited driving time for oversize and overweight loads.

Road Weight and Size limitations: By State

TRUCK SIZE AND WEIGHT, ROUTE DESIGNATIONS -- LENGTH , WIDTH AND WEIGHT LIMITATIONS

State	Maximum Cont. Length (Ft. & In.)	20' Std. Steel	40' Std. Alum	40' HC, Alum	45' HC, Alum	40' Std. Steel	40' HC, Steel	Std Rfr, Alum	HC Rfr, Alum	Open top, Alum	Open top, Steel	Flat Rack Steel	Flat Plat, Steel	40' Rear	20' (with slider) Rear	Maximum Weight Legal Gross Weight	Legal Gross Weight W / Permit	Permit Cost	Comments
Alabama	53-6	38,200			43,500	43,900	43,600	42,400	40,800	43,900	43,200	38,800	44,200	Reference Bridge Law Formula		80,000	100,000	$15	
Alaska	48-0				43,500	43,900	43,600	42,400	40,800	43,900	43,200	38,800	44,200	Reference Bridge Law Formula		80,000	Variable		per dot and bridge
Arizona	57-6	38,200			43,500	43,900	43,600	42,400	40,800	43,900	43,200	38,800	43,000			80,000	Will not Permit if cargo is divisible		see [11] below
Arkansas	53-6	38,200			43,500	43,900	43,600	42,400	40,800	43,900	43,200	38,800	44,200	Reference Bridge Law Formula		80,000	Will not Permit		permit within a county
California	48-0 *	38,200			43,500	43,900	43,600	42,400	40,800	43,900	43,200	38,800	43,000			80,000	Will not Permit if cargo is divisible		see [11] below
Colorado	57-4	38,200			43,500	43,900	43,600	42,400	40,800	43,900	43,200	38,800	44,200	Reference Bridge Law Formula		80,000		$15. + $5./axle	
Connecticut	48-0	38,200			43,500	43,900	43,600	42,400	40,800	43,900	43,200	38,800	44,200	Reference Bridge Law Formula		80,000	Will not Permit		n/a
Delaware	53-0	38,200			43,500	43,900	43,600	42,400	40,800	43,900	43,200	38,800	44,200	Reference Bridge Law Formula		80,000	90,000		see [1] below
District of Columbia	48-0	38,200			43,400	39,500	39,200	38,000	36,400	39,500	38,000	34,400	39,600	Reference Bridge Law Formula		80,000	Will not Permit		n/a
Florida	48-0	38,200			43,500	43,900	43,600	42,400	40,800	43,900	43,200	38,800	44,200	Reference Bridge Law Formula		80,000	95,000	$0.2?/mile	
Georgia	48-0	38,200			43,500	43,900	43,600	42,400	40,800	43,900	43,200	38,800	44,200	Reference Bridge Law Formula		80,000	100,000	$20	$20
Hawaii	48-0	38,200			43,500	43,600	43,600	42,400	40,800	43,900	43,200	38,800	44,200	Reference Bridge Law Formula		80,000	Will not Permit		n/a
Idaho	48-0	38,200			43,500	43,900	43,600	42,400	40,800	43,900	43,200	38,800	44,200			80,000	Will not Permit if cargo is divisible		see [11] below
Illinois	53-0	38,200			38,700	40,500	40,200	39,100	37,500	40,500	39,800	35,400	40,800	Reference Bridge Law Formula		80,000	Will not Permit if cargo is divisible		see [2,11] below
Indiana	48-6 **	38,200			43,500	43,900	43,600	42,400	40,800	43,900	43,200	38,800	44,200	Reference Bridge Law Formula		80,000	Will not Permit		n/a
Iowa	53-0	38,200			43,500	43,900	43,600	42,400	40,800	43,900	43,200	38,800	44,200	Reference Bridge Law Formula		80,000	Will not Permit		n/a
Kansas	57-6	38,200			43,500	43,900	43,600	42,400	40,800	43,900	43,200	38,800	44,200	Reference Bridge Law Formula		80,000	Will not Permit		n/a
Kentucky	53-0	38,200			43,500	43,900	43,600	42,400	40,800	43,900	43,200	38,800	44,200	Reference Bridge Law Formula		80,000	Will not Permit		n/a
Louisiana	59-6	38,200			43,500	43,900	43,600	42,400	40,800	43,900	43,200	38,800	44,200	Reference Bridge Law Formula		80,000	100,000	$65-$85 +admin fee	
Maine	48-0	38,200			43,500	43,900	43,600	42,400	40,800	43,900	43,200	38,800	44,200	Reference Bridge Law Formula		80,000	Will not Permit		n/a
Maryland	48-0	38,200			43,500	43,900	43,600	42,400	40,800	43,900	43,200	38,800	44,200	Reference Bridge Law Formula		80,000	90,000		see [4] below
Massachusetts	48-0	38,200			43,500	43,900	43,600	42,400	40,800	43,900	43,200	38,800	44,200	Reference Bridge Law Formula		80,000	Will not Permit		n/a
Michigan	48-0	38,200			43,500	43,900	43,600	42,400	40,800	43,900	43,200	38,800	44,200	Reference Bridge Law Formula		80,000	Will not Permit		n/a
Minnesota	48-0	38,200			43,500	43,900	43,600	42,400	40,800	43,900	43,200	38,800	44,200	Reference Bridge Law Formula		80,000			see [5] below
Mississippi	53-0	38,200			43,500	43,900	43,600	42,400	40,800	43,900	43,200	38,800	44,200	Reference Bridge Law Formula		80,000	95,000	$10. + $5./1klbs over	
Missouri	53-0	37,600			43,400	37,400	37,100	35,900	34,300	37,400	36,700	32,300	37,700	Reference Bridge Law Formula		80,000	Will not Permit if cargo is divisible		see [11] below
Montana	53-0	38,200			43,500	43,900	43,600	42,400	40,800	43,900	43,200	38,800	44,200			80,000	Will not Permit if cargo is divisible		see [11] below
Nebraska	53-0	38,200			43,500	43,900	43,600	42,400	40,800	43,900	43,200	38,800	44,200	Reference Bridge Law Formula		80,000	80,000+	$10	
Nevada	53-0	38,200			43,500	43,900	43,600	42,400	40,800	43,900	43,200	38,800	44,200			80,000	Will not Permit if cargo is divisible		see [11] below
New Hampshire	48-0	38,200			43,500	43,900	43,600	42,400	40,800	43,900	43,200	38,800	44,200	Reference Bridge Law Formula		80,000			no set rule, per load base
New Jersey	48-0	38,200			43,500	43,900	43,600	42,400	40,800	43,900	43,200	38,800	44,200	Reference Bridge Law Formula		80,000	Will not Permit		n/a
New Mexico	57-6	38,200			43,400	43,200	42,900	41,700	40,100	43,200	42,500	38,100	43,500	Reference Bridge Law Formula		80,000	Will not Permit if cargo is divisible		see [11] below
New York	48-0	38,200			43,400	43,400	43,100	41,700	40,300	43,400	42,700	38,300	43,700	Reference Bridge Law Formula		80,000	Will not Permit		n/a
North Carolina	48-0	38,200			43,500	43,900	43,600	42,400	40,800	43,900	43,200	38,800	44,200	Reference Bridge Law Formula		80,000	94,500	$10	
North Dakota	53-0	38,200			43,500	43,900	43,600	42,400	40,800	43,900	43,200	38,800	44,200	Reference Bridge Law Formula		80,000	Will not Permit if cargo is divisible		see [11] below
Ohio	53-0	38,200			43,500	43,900	43,600	42,400	40,800	43,900	43,200	38,800	44,200	Reference Bridge Law Formula		80,000	Will not Permit		n/a
Oklahoma	59-6	38,200			43,500	43,900	43,600	42,400	40,800	43,900	43,200	38,800	44,200	Reference Bridge Law Formula		80,000		$20. + $5./1klbs over	
Oregon	53-0	38,200			43,500	43,900	43,600	42,400	40,800	43,900	43,200	38,800	44,200			80,000	Will not Permit if cargo is divisible		see [11] below
Pennsylvania	53-0	38,200			43,500	43,900	43,600	42,400	40,800	43,900	43,200	38,800	44,200	Reference Bridge Law Formula		80,000	95,000	$100.00 annually	
Puerto Rico	48-0	38,200			43,500	43,900	43,600	42,400	40,800	43,900	43,200	38,800	44,200	Reference Bridge Law Formula		50,000			
Rhode Island	48-6	38,200			43,500	43,900	43,600	42,400	40,800	43,900	43,200	38,800	44,200	Reference Bridge Law Formula		80,000	Will not Permit		n/a
South Carolina	48-0	38,200			43,500	43,900	43,600	42,400	40,800	43,900	43,200	38,800	44,200	Reference Bridge Law Formula		80,000	90,000	$20	
South Dakota	53-0	38,200			43,500	43,900	43,600	42,400	40,800	43,900	43,200	38,800	44,200	Reference Bridge Law Formula		80,000			see [7] below
Tennessee	50-0	38,200			43,500	43,900	43,600	42,400	40,800	43,900	43,200	38,800	44,200	Reference Bridge Law Formula		80,000	90,000	$16. + $.05/1ton/mile over	
Texas	59-0	38,200			43,500	43,900	43,600	42,400	40,800	43,900	43,200	38,800	44,200	Reference Bridge Law Formula		80,000			permit per county
Utah	48-0	38,200			43,500	43,900	43,600	42,400	40,800	43,900	43,200	38,800	44,200			80,000	Will not Permit if cargo is divisible		see [11] below
Vermont	48-0	38,200			43,500	43,900	43,600	42,400	40,800	43,900	43,200	38,800	44,200	Reference Bridge Law Formula		80,000	90,000		see [8] below
Virginia	48-0	38,200			43,500	43,900	43,600	42,400	40,800	43,900	43,200	38,800	44,200	Reference Bridge Law Formula		80,000	90,000	no cost	
Washington	48-0	38,200			43,500	43,900	43,600	42,400	40,800	43,900	43,200	38,800	44,200			80,000	Will not Permit if cargo is divisible		see [11] below
West Virginia	48-0	38,200			43,500	43,900	43,600	42,400	40,800	43,900	43,200	38,800	44,200	Reference Bridge Law Formula		80,000	110,000		see [9] below
Wisconsin	48-0 ***	38,200			43,500	43,900	43,600	42,400	40,800	43,900	43,200	38,800	44,200	Reference Bridge Law Formula		80,000	Will not Permit if cargo is divisible		see [10,11] below
Wyoming	57-4	38,200			43,500	43,900	43,600	42,400	40,800	43,900	43,200	38,800	44,200	Reference Bridge Law Formula		80,000	Will not Permit if cargo is divisible		see [11]

HAZMAT Freight

Hazmat - Hazardous Materials

Hazardous Materials, which is also known as HAZMAT and Dangerous Goods, is any liquid, solid, or gas which can be harmful and dangerous for public health, property, or the environment. Each person who transports or offers to transport hazardous materials (hazmat) is known as a hazmat employer or employee. The Federal Hazardous Materials Regulations (HMR) [located in Title 49, Code of Federal Regulations (49 CFR)] require hazmat employers to train, test, and maintain records of this training for all their hazmat employees. This includes any employee that has responsibility for preparing hazmat for shipment or for transporting the shipment.

Freight Brokers' Regulations

Hazardous materials are regulated by various federal agencies including the Department of Transportation (DOT), the Occupational Safety and Health Administration (OSHA), and the Environmental Protection Agency (EPA). Freight brokers and forwarding agents are both as liable for hazmat as the shipper. Therefore, you must have adequate knowledge of DOT's HMR to make sure that your operation complies with the HMR. You must carry the same HAZMAT certifications as a carrier if you want to move this type of freight. You should also be sure that the carrier has sufficient <u>Primary Liability coverage</u> for hazmat.

- **Know Your Shipper** - Do they ship hazmats? If so, what kind and in what quantity? A broker must know when hazmat is being shipped. This involves more than just examination of documents. Is the material in DOT/UN authorized packages?

- **Verify Hazmat Descriptions** - Does it match the proper shipping name, hazard class or division, identification number, and packaging group listed in the Hazardous Material Table (HMT) in 172.101? Is there a conflict between the documentation and the package marking? Is there an emergency response telephone number on the shipping paper? Does emergency response information accompany the shipping paper?

- Advise the Shipper of Discrepancies.

- **Make a Visual Inspection of Shipments** -Has the hazmat been damaged? Is it in conflict with the documentation? Is it improperly packaged? Other possible violations? To meet the requirements of the HMR, each hazmat shipment's packaging, marking, labeling, certification, and documentation should be seen and verified.

- **Provide Correct Documentation to the Carrier** –You are assuming shipper responsibility for a hazmat shipment that is made by another party. You must rely on the shipper for correct documentation and packaging. It is your responsibility to be sure that any discrepancies are corrected PRIOR to offering the shipment for movement. The documentation you give is the only information that the carrier receives.

Before you hire a carrier to transport a load of hazardous materials, there are two things that you must check. First, you should always check that the carrier has the "permission" to transport HAZMAT. You can do so quickly by entering the carrier's information into the SAFER system (Safety and Fitness Electronic Records System). This allows you to perform a "snapshot" of the potential motor carrier to be sure they are properly registered with the FMCSA. There are three methods to locate carriers in the SAFER database: by USDOT number, by MC/MX number, or by Company Name. Typically, you should ask the carrier for their MC number. Once you have arrived at the carrier's "snapshot," you should look for confirmation that the carrier has on file either MCS-150A or MCS-150B, depending on the shipment. Do NOT confuse these forms with the standard form MCS-150, which is a Motor Carrier Identification Report (Application for USDOT Number).

Attached in Appendix D is a separate PDF that explains in detail the many Hazmat Classifications.

Intermodal Freight

Intermodal freight transport means the transportation of freight in an intermodal container or vehicle using multiple modes of transportation (rail, ship, and truck), without any handling of the freight itself when changing modes. The method reduces cargo handling, and so improves security. It reduces damages and losses, and allows freight to be transported faster. It also reduces costs versus over-the-road trucking, which is its key benefit for intra-continental use.

Rail Transport

Rail transportation burns less fuel than over-the-road (OTR) trucking, which means the impact on the environment is significantly less. By taking advantage of an intermodal shipping route, your company not only saves a great deal of money, but it also does its part to contribute to a green supply chain. Shipping your freight over-the-road (OTR) is not always the optimal choice for your company. The costs associated with long-distance trucking can be unnecessarily high, especially if you are shipping high volume freight. Intermodal shipping, a combination of OTR trucking and rail transportation for a single shipment, can produce significant savings for your company, regardless of freight type or destination.

In North America, containers are often shipped by rail in container well cars. These cars resemble flatcars but the newer ones have a container-sized depression in the middle (between the bogies or "trucks") of the car. This depression allows sufficient clearance for two containers to be loaded in the car in a "double stack" arrangement. The newer container cars also are specifically built as a small articulated "unit," most commonly in components of three or five, whereby two components are connected by a single bogie as opposed to two bogies, one on each car.

It is also common in North America to transport semi-trailers on railway flatcars or spine cars, which is an arrangement called "piggyback" or TOFC (trailer on flatcar) to distinguish it from container on flatcar (COFC). Some flatcars are designed with collapsible trailer hitches so they can be used for trailer or container service. Such designs allow trailers to be rolled on from one end, though lifting trailers on and off flatcars by specialized loaders is more common. TOFC terminals typically have large areas for storing trailers pending loading or pickup.

Equipment of Handling

Handling equipment is designed to assist in transferring containers between rail, road and sea. These can include:

- Transtainers for transferring containers from sea-going vessels onto either trucks or rail wagons. A transtainer extends on rails with a large boom spanning the distance between the ship's cargo hold and the quay, moving parallel to the ship's side.

- Gantry cranes, also known as straddle carriers, which are able to straddle rail and road vehicles allowing for quick transfer of containers. A spreader beam moves in several directions allowing accurate positioning of the cargo.

- Grappler Lift, which is very similar to a straddle carrier

- Reach Stackers are fitted with lifting arms as well as spreader beams and lifts containers to swap bodies or stack containers on top of each other.

Intermodal Carriers - Click link below on pdf to go to their website.

- Union Pacific Railroad

- Pacific Container, Inc.

- Norfolk Southern Corp.

- CSX Intermodal Inc.

- BNSF Railway

DOD – Department of Defense - Military Freight

Military Surface Deployment and Distribution Command Freight Carrier Registration Program

Welcome to the Military Surface Deployment and Distribution Command's (SDDC) Freight Carrier Registration Program (FCRP). In order to transport DOD freight, carriers must comply with the requirements of the FCRP as well as requirements of Department of Transportation Title 49, Code of Federal Regulations (DOT 49 CFR) and SDDC Freight Traffic Rules Publications (MFTRP).

The link for **MFTRP** is http://www.sddc.army.mil/sddc/Content/Pub/8188/MFTRP1C.pdf

You will need a performance certificate in order to transfer military freight, or become an agent for an approved broker who is already established with the DOD. (However, these loads must be tendered under the authority of that broker.) The performance certificate for DOD freight is separate from and additional to the surety bond necessary to obtain your freight broker authority. Carriers must complete the following prior to approval.

(Note: in these instructions, "carrier" refers to all Transportation Service Providers):

1. All carriers wanting to do business with DOD must have a valid Standard Carrier Alpha Code (**SCAC**). The **SCAC** is a unique two-to-four letter code issued through the National Motor Freight Traffic Association (**NMFTA**) that is used in order to identify transportation companies.

If you do not have a SCAC, use website www.nmfta.org or contact NMFTA at 2200 Mill Road, Alexandria, VA 22314, Telephone # (703)838-1831. **Note:** Each mode of transportation (motor, air, barge, ocean, pipeline, and rail) requires a separate SCAC for filing tenders and submitting spot bid quotes.

2. **US Bank** – All companies must have an agreement with US Bank and be **Power Track** certified in order to receive electronic payment for transportation services. Power Track is available on the Internet at www.usbank.com/powertrack or by contacting US Bank Power Track, 1010 South Seventh St., Minneapolis, MN 55415, (800) 417-1844.

3. Complete the Carrier Registration Form at https://akita.eta.sddc.army.mil/ccp/jsp/CCPScac.jsp and then click the **SUBMIT** button. You must fill Power Track certification first. SDDC will review your registration form and then send an e-mail notification of your status within three (3) working days. At this time you are responsible for obtaining your performance bond as outlined below in item #4. The amount of the bond depends on how you register and whether you're a small or large business.

4. **Bond Performance**– Instruct your bond surety company to forward your bond information only to: mtfecarrierregistration@sddc.army.mil by email. The subject line of the email must contain your company name and SCAC; in the body, you should provide the bond number, amount and effective date, Surety Company name, agent's name, address and telephone number. SDDC does not require the original or a copy of the bond form. The requests of bond cancellation must be sent to the same e-mail address.

Once all requirements are ready, SDDC will send an e-mail notification of your approval. In this approval, you will receive instructions for obtaining an Electronic Transportation Acquisition (ETA) password that will allow you to access DOD transportation programs including tutorials and on-line training for help with Tender Entry and Spot Bid on the Web.

For questions on training:

- e-mail: gfm-training@sddc.army.mil

- Additionally, upon approval, contact by e-mail (mtfenegotiations@sddc.army.mil) SDDC's Negotiations Group and request for inclusion on their e-mail solicitations for volume moves and special services. Remember to include your SCAC in all correspondence.

Performance Bond

Carriers will be required to submit a performance bond. The cost of the bond is based on the size of your company and the number of states you intend to serve. Large companies may select one (1) state for bond that may cost you about $25,000; 2 to 3 states for $50,000; 4 or more states for $100,000.

Carriers registered with the Small Business Administration (SBA), http://pro-net.sba.gov/, may select up to 3 states with a performance bond of $25,000, up to10 states with a performance bond of $50,000, and 11 or more states for $100,000.

Note: Movements must begin and end in one of the selected states.

- Carriers that have conducted business in their own name with DOD for three years or more must submit a performance bond with 2.5% of their total DOD revenue for the previous 12 months, not to exceed $100,000 and not less than $25,000.

- Bulk fuel carriers must pay $25,000 performance bond.

- The bond amount is set at $100,000 for surface freight forwarders, shipper agents, brokers, and air freight forwarders due to the volume of traffic handled by these modes.

- Local drayage, commercial zone, barge, rail, sealift and pipeline carriers are free from the bond requirements.

The performance bond secures performance and fulfillment of carrier obligations that ensures that the DOD freight is delivered. It will cover any instance where a carrier cannot or will not deliver DOD freight tendered to them. This includes default, abandoned shipments, and bankruptcy by the carrier. The bond is not utilized for operational problems such as late pickup or delivery, excessive transit times, refusals, no shows, improper/inadequate equipment. or claims for lost or damaged cargo.

Here is a listing of approved surety companies:

- http://www.fms.treas.gov/c570/index.html.

Under "quick links" select "Treasury Listing of Approved Sureties"

- http://www.sddc.army.mil/sddc/Content/Pub/14712/CarrierRegInstructions.pdf

Note: Trust funds are not accepted instead of the bond.

Please be aware that you cannot conduct business with the government if you or your company is on the Excluded Parties List (EPL). The EPL is a list of contractors who have been debarred, suspended or declared ineligible by ANY government agency. If you or your company are on that list, you will be ineligible to work with the Department of Defense.

Operating Authority

The carrier agrees to maintain valid operating certificates for its scope of operations. USDOT# is a mandatory field on the registration form. Your company's SCAC will automatically populate your DOT/MC number. You will be responsible for filling in your operating identification number in case you are not operating as a motor carrier. The below websites can assist in this matter:

- Motor - www.safersys.org

- Pipeline - http://ops.dot.gov/index.htm

- Barge - www.fmc.gov

- Air - http://nasdac.faa.gov/main.htm

- Rail - http://safetydata.fra.dot.gov/officeofsafety

Inspections

The carrier agrees to permit unannounced safety and security inspections of its facilities, terminals, employees, and operational procedures by DOD civilian or military personnel, or DOD contract employees. Furthermore, the carrier agrees to have visitor control procedures in place to verify individuals requesting access to, or information of, DOD shipments.

The verification processes can be initiated by contacting SDDC's hotline at (800)526-1465. The carrier must not reveal any information to unauthorized persons concerning the nature, kind, quantity, destination, consignee, or routing of any protected commodities tendered to them.

Transportation Protective Services (TPS) and Arms, Ammunition and Explosives:

The carriers must have approval of not less than twelve consecutive months and have satisfactory performance in order to transport materials designated by DOD as protected or sensitive that require a TPS.

Additionally, a "satisfactory" safety rating must be on file and maintained with the Federal Highway Administration, Department of Transportation, and/or the appropriate state agency or commission in the case of intrastate transportation.

Some safety ratings are not accepted, such as "unsatisfactory," "conditional," "insufficient information," "not rated," or "none."

Keep in consideration that brokers, freight forwarders, shipper agents, and logistic companies are restricted from handling shipments requiring a TPS.

Trading Partner Agreement

Following approval by SDDC, a carrier should sign a Trading Partner Agreement (TPA) in order to send or receive electronic data interchange (EDI) transactions with any DOD system. You can obtain a copy of the TPA from: http://www.sddc.army.mil .

Click on Freight Cargo, then New Visitor, then Carrier Qualification and then Trading Partner Guide. For assistance, please call 703-428-2933.

EDI -Electronic Data Interchange

Electronic Data Interchange (EDI) is the computer-to-computer exchange of business information using a public standard format. EDI is a central part of Electronic Commerce (EC), as it enables faster electronic exchange of information between business partners. Moreover, it is cheaper and more accurate than paper-based systems.

EDI is used by...

Nearly 50,000 private companies that operate in the United States currently use EDI. Companies such as Federal Express, Eastman Kodak, American Airlines, Nike, Staples, Nations-Bank, JC Penney, and Prudential Insurance are just a few.

EDI is widely used in various fields including manufacturing, shipping, warehousing, utilities, pharmaceuticals, construction, petroleum, metals, food processing, banking, insurance, retailing, government, health care, and textiles among other industries. According to a recent study, the number of companies using EDI is expected to quadruple within the next six years.

EDI's Origins

EC/EDI wasn't invented by the government; simply, it is taking advantage of an established technology that has been widely used in the private sector for the last few decades. EDI's first usage dates back to more than twenty years ago as it was used in the transportation industry by that time.

It was used by ocean, motor, air, and rail carriers and the associated shippers, brokers, customs, freight forwarders, and bankers. The development of the first set of industry EDI standards was done by the Transportation Data Coordinating Committee (TDCC) and consisted of 45 transaction sets for the transportation industry. ANSI X12 standards, the system currently used, were developed later and are based upon the TDCC syntax and format.

Military Freight

Once all the required procedures for moving Department of Defense freight are performed, then you will need to do the following before officially moving any freight as a freight broker or trucking company.

First of all you will need to **"Propose Your Freight Rates"** to Military Transportation Officers so they can view and contact you for moving loads. To learn how to submit these rates according to Department of Defense standards, you will need to download the following: Publication of Revision and Consolidation of Military Freight Traffic Rules Publications (MFTRP) 1C-R (Motor), 10 (Rail), 30 (Barge), 6A (Pipeline), 4A (Tank Truck), Military Standard Tender Instruction Publication (MSTIP) 364D, Spot Bid Business Rules, and SDDC Military Class Rate Publication No. 100A to a Consolidation of Procurement Requirements for the Purchase of Commercial Transportation Services into the Military Freight Traffic Unified Rules Publication (MFTURP) No. 1.

You can access it here: http://www.sddc.army.mil/sddc/Content/Pub/12706/364d.pdf

This publication will guide you on how to successfully submit your freight rates to the Department of Defense and also provide general information to answer your questions. The publication provides a listing of commodity codes necessary to propose your rates.

1. As soon as your freight has been tendered to the Department of Defense, you are ready to go. You will then **"Log In"** with your User Name and Password as provided by the GFM Administrator.

2. Once you log into the system on the SDDC website, you will then scroll to the bottom of the screen and select **"CAVS"** and then choose the option **"Costed Shipment Query."** Then enter your **SCAC** code, **Date of Movement** and, **Trailer Type** to view available freight.

3. Now it is time to get freight. If you see a load that suits your required lane and rate criteria, go ahead and contact the Transportation Officer to see if the load is available. If it is and your tender

is competitive, he will then award you the load.

4. You will then have to provide the Transportation Officer your **Driver Information, Truck** and **Trailer** number, and **SCAC** Code.

5. You will then give the Transportation Officer an email address or FAX number so he can send you a "**CBL**" or Certified Bill of Lading, which contains the information you will need to create your rate confirmation sheet for the carrier.

6. Ask the "Transportation Officer" to set your company as a "**Trading Partner**" within his perspective base. You will just need to provide him your company's information again such as billing info and "**SCAC**" code and the process will be completed once he enters it into the SDDC system.

7. Once your load has been delivered and you have a "**Signed CBL**," you can now bill it to "**PowerTrack.**" You will need the "**GBLOC ID**" codes from the Base of Origin and Destination. Once all this information has been gathered, simply submit the information requested and payment will be processed if all required information has been met.

Attached in Appendix E is a list of 2010 Intercoms.

Cross Border - Canadian Shipping Cross Border

To move freight into Canada, you need to find a motor carrier that has Canadian Authority. You will also need documentation from Customs Brokers of the load you are carrying. Canadian officials will also require proper PARS documentation.

Pre-Arrival Review System (PARS)

The Pre-Arrival Review System (PARS) is a Canada Border Services Agency (CBSA) (formerly the Canada Customs Revenue Agency or CCRA) border cargo release mechanism for those importers with RMD (Release on Minimum Documentation) privileges to expedite the release of commercial shipments to Canada.

The Canadian PARS system is the same as the U.S. Pre-Arrival Processing System (PAPS), but where PAPS applies to shipments from Canada to the U.S., PARS applies to shipments from the U.S. to Canada.

The main document for PARS is a barcoded cargo control number, which the carrier or U.S. ex-porter applies to the top right-hand corner of the original CBSA invoice for each shipment. All other required documents must also be provided, including:

- Certificate(s) of origin

- Invoices

- Shippers export declarations, etc.

The PARS can handle goods that require permits or certificates. A copy of the complete set of documents, including the bill of barcoded label, are sent to the Canadian importer or broker by fax before the arrival of the shipment in Canada. The importer or broker then submits a request for import CBSA. PARS must be clearly laid down by the importer or customs broker to release pack-ages.

When the documentation is received by the CBSA, a customs officer enters data into the automated CBSA computer system. A recommendation is made in the Customs Commercial System (CCS), which remains in force for a limited period of time.

The carrier/driver offers the original version of the barcoded release documentation to a CBSA inspector, who scans the bar code in an automated system at the time of arrival of a shipment at the point of import. The system displays the status of the shipment as "release" or "review." If the status of the shipment is "release," the CCRA inspector releases the goods to the driver. The customs inspector date-stamps copies of the invoice and returns the stamped invoice photocopy to the carrier as proof of clearance. If the status in the system is set to "review," the load will be referred to the cargo inspector who will follow the normal examination procedures.

For more information, go to the Canada Border Services Agency website at: www.cbsa-asfc.gc.ca

The Profit

Developing a relationship with your carrier base will lead to a better understanding of which carriers will move your loads for the rates you want. When moving a load, a carrier looks at the lane in which the load is traveling. For instance, if you have a load going from California to Wisconsin and you carrier is from Illinois, the carrier is more likely to give you a better rate to move the load because it is traveling in the general direction of his yard. This is known as a backhaul.

One of the main benefits of having a relationship with your carrier is that it enables you to create a separate income stream for your brokerage. If you know where your carriers are located and when loads become available from other brokers, you can enter into a co-broker agreement with them and simply dispatch the carrier to the load. Freight will find you as long as you have the trucks, so it is extremely important to have a firm hold on where your favorite carrier's equipment is located at all times.

Lane Management

- Having a good knowledge of lane rates and its frequent changes on loads is important for efficiently negotiating the freight rate of the line haul with the carrier. Lane rates are determined by fuel rates, equipment availability, seasonal changes, and backhauls. Using load boards and their provided tools such as Carrier Depot will allow you to simply input the pertinent data for the load and generate a rate for that lane based upon current market trends.

Market Price & Carrier Rate Negotiations

The Price will be paid...

Suppose a shipper has a load of products leaving Salinas, CA in June, and has six (6) pickups and three (3) deliveries in Jessup, MD. The shipper provides you with a marginal rate in order to get the load moved and you are getting no action from carriers for the load.

- One problem with this load is related to seasonal trends. June is a busy season for produce in Salinas, CA, and getting a backhaul into Jessup, MD, would be very difficult.

- Another problem is the number of pickups and deliveries on the load. When lanes are tight, such as the peak of the produce season, carriers become picky about the loads they take.

Let's say your shipper is offering you a rate on this load of $6,000. This is an unrealistic rate as during this time of year it is not unusual for the carrier to command a rate of $2.60 per mile.

- Salinas, CA – Jessup, MD is 2,869 practical miles, so if you do your math you will come up with a general rate of $7459.40.

There are other variables to take into consideration, such as pickup and delivery, but the overall rate of extra points is $50.00 for each stop, so you're looking at secondary charges of $400.00 to stop. Carriers will also probably ask for fees of a few extra hundred dollars because of the inconveniences involved.

So the rate you should get will be around $8,200. After spending some time talking with the carrier, you might get him to reduce the rate of a mile by about $2.35. This would allow you to make a potential profit of $717.25 on this load.

This is lower than the 10% recommended average, but still a good margin because of high gross on the load. You will earn every penny on this load because of all pickup and delivery, but you will work almost as hard as the carrier.

Final Settlements to Carriers & Advances

Fuel Advances

Refers to advance partial payments. A fuel advance is a portion of the payment amount given to the driver in the form of a T-check, COM check, or wire transfer. This advance is given only when you have received verifiable proof that the load has been picked up. To verify this information ask the driver to fax in the signed BOLs or scanned EDI copies to your company.

Usually, amount given for a fuel advance is 35%-40% of the gross amount of the load.

ComData- http://www.comdata.com

Comdata offers a simple, cost-effective alternative to paper checks for distributing funds to both banked and unbanked employees. Paying employees with the Comdata Card or Security Numbers provides the convenience and flexibility of electronic payroll in a secure, card-based solution without the need for the cardholder to have a bank account.

T-Chek- http://www.tchek.com

T-Chek Systems, Inc., now known as EFS, is a leading provider of payment and information services to transportation-related organizations. Whether you are an owner-operator, a small, medium, or large carrier, a truck stop, c-store, or freight broker, T-Chek can help you measure your business performance, make informed decisions, and manage your daily operations. T-Chek's products and services give you the productivity, purchasing control, negotiating power, and information management you need to increase your bottom line.

Net 30

Net 30 is another alternative, which is a form of trade credit which specifies payment is expected to be received in full 30 days after the goods are delivered. Net 30 terms are often coupled with a credit for early payment; for example, the notation "2% 10, net 30" indicates that a 2% discount is provided if payment is received within 10 days of the delivery of goods, and that full payment is expected within 30 days.

Final Payments

Final payments to carriers should only be made after all issues on the load have been resolved. There are many factors to be considered before issuing payments. These include:

- Are the BOLs clean and free of discrepancies?

- Are there any claims against the load?

- Are all lumper receipts turned in?

- Are all weight tickets turned in?

- Did the carrier use pallets from the shipper and was he charged for them?

- Have all fuel advances been subtracted from the balance of payment?

Co-Brokering & Double Brokering

Contrary to popular belief, double brokering is completely legal. Unfortunately, a number of transportation brokers have received improper training concerning this issue. The majority of transportation brokers will not knowingly double broker a load unless a co-broker agreement is on file. Double brokering may be prohibited by the originating shipper. It is best to establish the terms and conditions with all parties before co-brokering or double brokering any freight. Here are the drawbacks of double brokering or co-brokering a load.

- You have no control over the actions of the other broker. For example, suppose you pay the second broker for the line haul, but he fails to pay the carrier. Now the carrier is seeking compensation from your brokerage and shipper. Although your payment has been made to the second broker, the carrier of record listed on the bill of lading has not been paid by the second broker. The carrier responsible for the line haul can place a lien on the freight until compensated or he can file against your bond.

- Your brokerage may be liable for any damages incurred during the load if a carrier is in an accident. This happens when the second broker uses carriers that are unreliable, have expired insurance or authorities, or use faulty equipment.

What should I do if I have been double brokered?

Here are the steps to take if you have ever been the victim of double brokering. This is rampant in the industry and it will likely happen with you at some point.

- First and foremost, it is very important to have this clearly spelled out in your carrier broker agreement and also your rate confirmation that if a load has been double brokered, the rate for the load is null and void. You can opt to use the carrier broker agreement that is contained within our manual to address this issue.

- If you suspect that your load has been double brokered, contact the consignee and have the receiver of the load place the information of the carrier responsible for the line haul on the original bill of lading when he unloads. He will need to provide the name of the carrier, MC authority number, and also the driver's signature. If a carrier is legally leased to another company, he is required to have carrier paperwork to that effect in his truck and also display signage on the cab and trailer.

- Once you have taken these steps, you then re-negotiate the rate of the load with the carrier responsible for the line haul. You are not responsible to pay this carrier, but it is a good way to build a loyal carrier following and also provide your shipper with secondary coverage against possible repercussions.

Once you have begun negotiations of the rate with the carrier that actually moved the freight, follow the same steps as setting up a new carrier, by having him complete a "Set Up" package and signing a new rate confirmation sheet, carrier broker agreement, and also lien waiver against the load.

Fuel Surcharges

Do They Go To The Carrier?

A fuel surcharge is an additional charge imposed by motor carriers due to the increasing price of diesel. The charge is a percentage added to each load based upon the U.S. National Average Diesel Fuel Index published weekly by the U.S. Department of Energy. Fuel surcharges will fluctuate accordingly as diesel prices rise or lower.

Hidden Profit

A Fuel Surcharge (FSC) is a great way to make additional profits for your brokerage. When a shipper is providing you with a freight rate for the line haul, occasionally they will include a fuel surcharge in addition to the base rate. If the base rate is a decent rate for the haul, just pocket the fuel surcharge on the load. It is a great way to increase the gross profit. Most major companies will include a fuel surcharge, but the smaller companies will not.

Nearly every dispatcher will ask you if there is a fuel surcharge on the load. You should mostly give them a flat rate, depending on how hard the load is to cover in a specific lane.

Links

Energy Information Administration - http://tonto.eia.doe.gov/oog/info/wohdp/diesel.asp

This is the website where the Department of Energy publishes weekly diesel prices across the country. Shippers use this data to determine the base rate of the fuel surcharge.

Ancillary Ways to Make Money

In addition to being a freight broker agent, you can also apply your trade to major trucking companies as a truck agent/dispatcher. The role is basically the same with exception to the fact that you have access to many more trucks that are not normally available to the normal freight broker agent.

How It Works

As a truck agent, you will be paid a commission of typically 8.5% to 9.0% for loading trucks. Many carrier groups have intranet truck boards that you can access. You can simply match available freight to their fleet and get paid a commission for doing so.

Independent Truck Dispatcher

An independent truck dispatcher works the same was as a truck agent with exception to the fact that they represent multiple trucking entities at once. Owner Operators are independently owned trucking companies that often do not have dispatchers to keep them loaded. This is where you can get paid.

They are in need of your services to find freight and to keep them rolling. In addition to finding freight for their company, you will also be in charge of communication with the shipper, invoicing the load, and other miscellaneous services that the driver might need.

You will find loads on internet load boards from shippers, freight brokers, and logistics companies. Since you represent the carrier directly, you are not double brokering the freight. You simply transfer all of the Owner-Operator's paperwork for him, sign the rate confirmation on his behalf, and transfer the load details to him. Once he has accepted the load and it has been delivered, you will bill him for a previously agreed-upon percentage.

Insurance & Claims

Liability Insurance

Liability insurance has two components that are always included together: Bodily Injury coverage and Property Damage coverage. Liability insurance is the basic insurance coverage that covers injuries or damage to other people or property if you're at fault for an accident. If you cause an accident that injures or even kills another person, the Bodily Injury (BI) portion of your liability insurance will pay for the related expenses. Bodily Injury (BI) will cover hospital and medical bills, rehabilitation, long-term nursing care, funeral expenses, lost earnings, pain and suffering, and other expenses, up to the limits you select.

If you cause an accident that damages another person's property, the Property Damage (PD) portion of your liability insurance will pay for the related expenses. Property Damage (PD) will cover the expense to repair or replace damaged items, including other vehicles, lamp posts, houses, or even a pet, up to the limits you select. Liability insurance will also pay for your legal defense costs if you are sued as a result of your involvement with the accident.

Carrier Requirements:

- BMC-91 or Public Liability Insurance (Bodily Injury/ Motor Common Carrier)

- Freight: $750,000–$5,000,000, depending on commodities transported; $300,000 for non-hazardous freight moved only in vehicles weighing under 10,001 lbs.

- Passengers: $5,000,000; $1,500,000 for registrants operating only vehicles with seating capacity of 15 or fewer passengers.

- BMC-34 Cargo insurance: $5,000 per vehicle; Motor Common Carrier

Contingent Cargo Insurance

As a freight broker, you should carry contingent cargo insurance to pay for shipper loss or damage claims if the carrier and its insurance company refuse to pay. Contingent cargo coverage provides you and the shippers with a second level of protection, as long as a claim is valid.

Contingent cargo insurance is available only to freight brokers. It is not cargo insurance; it is insurance **"contingent"** upon the motor carrier's insurance not paying a claim that has been made. A freight broker is typically never liable for cargo damage. The higher your shipper's or client's insurance requirements are, the more difficult it will be to find a carrier to transport their freight. Therefore, you will need to have contingent cargo to make up for the difference in coverage.

The only exceptional scenario in which a freight broker might be held liable is when they are negligent in their duties. A freight broker never takes possession of the cargo and can never be legally liable for cargo damage. Contingent cargo coverage provides indemnity and defense to a freight broker for third-party cargo claims.

As an example of where such coverage applies, consider a scenario where the broker relies upon a trucker's certificate of insurance to be valid but it turns out to be bogus. A claim ensues and the freight broker is brought into the fracas. The contingent policy provides for indemnity and defense.

Example: Your carrier allowed his policy to lapse due to non-payment, and his insurance company assumes no responsibility for this loss. YOUR contingent cargo liability insurance will certainly come in handy in this predicament.

How Do I Know if a Carrier Has Allowed their Policy to Lapse?

FreightBrokersCourse.com offers a monitoring service enabling you to monitor and qualify carriers for insurance policy changes, safety ratings, and more. Registry Monitoring Insurance Service Inc. (RMIS) offers brokers the following: Carrier Insurance Tracking, Contingent Cargo Insurance, Claims Assistance, DOT Reporting, and Insurance Verification. Therefore, RMIS offers both insurance and monitoring under one roof, so you can be confident that your carrier is in compliance prior to dispatching them under a load.

Errors & Omissions Insurance

Errors & Omissions covers a financial loss incurred by your customer resulting from your failure to perform, wholly or in part, your contractual obligations.

Could it happen to you?

Freight brokers are more vulnerable than ever to actions brought against them by their clients due to errors made, or errors that the client perceives were made. Mistakes can be extremely costly to a shipper, and very frequently, it is the freight broker who is asked to pay for the mistake. Even if there is no mistake, the cost to defend your company can create a substantial expense. It is highly recommended that your business should carry this insurance.

Claims

What Constitutes a Claim?

A claim against a carrier is a legal demand for the payment of money arising from the breach of the contract of carriage (usually the bill of lading). Therefore, the rules governing the filing of claims are founded in law and must be followed strictly. Claims are also governed by government regulations, whether intrastate or interstate commerce is involved. If an international movement is involved, the claim may also be governed by international treaties.

Claims rules will be found either in carriers' tariffs, in their bills of lading, or both. Court decisions interpret these regulations, laws, and tariffs, and determine the rights and obligations of the parties. If a claim shipment is governed by a contract, the terms of that agreement will govern the carrier's liability. Often contracts will adopt common carrier tariff rules, as described herein.

No specific claim form is prescribed by law, but four elements are essential:

- the shipment must be identified to enable the carrier to conduct an investigation

- the type of loss or damage must be stated

- the amount of the claim must be stated or estimated

- a demand for payment by the carrier must be made

The shipment identification information must include the carrier's "pro number," shipper's number, vehicle number, origin date, delivery date, and commodity description.

The claimant's name must be either:

- the entity having title to the goods in transit

- the entity assuming the risk of loss in transit

- an assignee of either (1) or (2)

The carrier against whom the claim may be filed is either the originating carrier or the delivering carrier. It is not recommended that claims be filed against intermediate connecting carriers, although it is permissible to do so if it is definitely known which carrier caused the loss or damage.

The claim must be delivered to the carrier within the time period specified in the carrier's contract and/or tariff, or in the time prescribed by law (usually 9 months from delivery). Since the date of receipt by the carrier determines whether or not the claim is timely filed, claims should be filed via delivery methods which give some type of confirmation of receipt and guarantee as to length of time for delivery, such as: facsimile transmission (FAX), registered or certified mail, Return Receipt Requested (RRR), express mail, express courier services, or Electronic Data Interchange (EDI).

Claims

Also referred to in the logistics industry as OS&D (Overage, Shortage, or Damage). There are generally 3 types of freight claims: Freight Lost in Transit, Freight Damaged In Transit, and Concealed Damage. A freight claim is essentially made when there is a payment that has not been fulfilled and must be addressed immediately. This holds true even if you are in doubt if the claim is reputable. Depending on the freight and carrier, freight claims are handled in a variety of ways. The act of response could depend on specific state, federal, or international laws. Claims should be addressed to the carrier's claims manager at the carrier's home office. Personal delivery to a carrier's representative may be effective if the claim is actually delivered in time, but an acknowledgment should be obtained in writing, and a copy sent to the carrier's claims manager.

Receipt by the carrier is deemed to be notice to all connecting carriers as well!

The names and addresses of the consignor (shipper) and consignee (receiver) must be stated, including all stop-off locations for completion of loading and/or unloading. Information on who is liable for the freight charges should be included in the claim.

Information on any liability limitations (e.g., collect, prepaid, C.O.D., etc.) must be noted on the BOL.

Details of a Claim

A detailed description of the loss, damage, or delay must be stated, setting forth the specific commodities, number of units of each type, extent of loss suffered, the value of each unit, the amount of salvage realized, the net loss, and a description of the events which caused the loss.

Supporting Documentation

- The original bill of lading

- The paid freight bill

- Proof of the value of the commodities

- Inspection reports, if made

- Copies of request for inspection

- Notification of loss

- Waiver of inspection by carrier

- Photographs

- Temperature reports

- Impact records

- Dumping certificates

- Laboratory analysis

- Quality control reports

- Package certifications

- Loading diagrams

- Weight certificates

- Affidavits

- Carrier's passing reports

- Loading and unloading tallies

A **"Bond of Indemnity"** may be filed with the claim indemnifying the carrier for any loss it may suffer as a result of improperly paying the claim on the basis of the claimant's furnishing a copy of the original document.

Every claim should be numbered by the claimant and recorded in a claim log or computer system. The carrier should also assign its claim number and acknowledge receipt of the claim within 30 days, pursuant to D.O.T. regulations. Both claim numbers should be shown on all correspondence and checks.

Claims

You may encounter three different types of freight claims:

1) Freight Damaged In Transit:

1. This claim is filed when freight is damaged at the time the carrier had claim over it. This includes dents or cuts to the container holding the freight or the actual load itself. The damage must be visual and apparent. If there is damage to the container holding the load, there may be additional damage that will not be discovered until it is opened. This is known as hidden loss.

2. Damage could also include freight alteration because of non-compliance to temperature regulations during the trip. This may result in the spoiling of food, also considered damaged freight. This damage is noted on the Bill of Lading by the customer when they receive the load.

2) Freight Lost in Transit:

1. This claim is filed when a shipment cannot be located due to misdirection. It is then impossible to deliver the load within a suitable time frame. Lost freight due to hijacking or criminal activity can also be described as being lost in transit. An extended delay can also lead to a freight loss in transit claim.

3) Concealed Damage:

1. If freight is defined as damaged after the time of delivery, it is called concealed damage.

A separate file should be kept on each claim. Important deadlines and dates should be recorded in the claim log and systematically reviewed. Violations of government regulations should be notified in the following cases:

- If a claim is not acknowledged within 30 days, or;

- If a claim is not paid, compromised, or disallowed within 120 days, or;

- If the carrier does not provide status reports every 60 days thereafter.

Repeated violations of D.O.T claim regulations should be reported to the Surface Transportation Board, 1201 Constitution Ave. NW, Washington, DC, 20423-0001.

Suit Deadlines

If a carrier denies liability for a loss for which the claimant has reason to believe the carrier is lawfully liable, the claimant has the right to institute a lawsuit. However, such suits must be instituted within strict time limits.

The most commonly applicable suit time limit is two years and one day from the date the carrier disallowed the claim. See the **"Carmack Amendment"** governing regulated truck **(49 U.S.C. § 14706)** and rail traffic **(§ 11706)**. The date of mailing the carrier's disallowance letter usually governs the lawsuit, not the date of its receipt by the claimant.

However, some traffic is not subject to the **"Carmack Amendment"** and therefore, the time limits vary. For instance;

- On some piggyback traffic, the suit must be instituted within one year from the date of delivery.

- On ocean traffic, the suit must be instituted within one year of delivery, but the carrier may extend that date provided such a request is received before the expiration of one year.

- Airline claim limits vary for each carrier.

- A system must be implemented to periodically review the status of pending claims to prevent the expiration of the suit-filing deadlines.

Note: Only a written statement declining payment of a claim in whole or in part flags the start of the time period for filing suits.

Note: An offer to settle or compromise a claim is deemed a declination, but it must also state that the remainder of the claim is disallowed. (See 49 U.S.C. § 14706(e)(2)(A))

Note: Don't wait until the last day to request your attorneys to institute a suit. Set your review schedule to allow at least 30 days' lead time.

Who Files the Freight Claim?

Freight claims are filed by either

1. The shipper who sends the freight.

2. The consignee who receives the freight.

This depends on the F.O.B. (free on board) designation. The F.O.B designation helps by placing the responsibility on to one party for the freight at the time of transportation. The Bill of Lading will determine and tell you who has ownership of the freight so you can contact the correct person.

Two terms that should be focused on are **destination** and **origin** which define who had control of the freight. F.O.B., free on board, means that the price for the commodity being transported includes delivery only to a certain point. These terms are then associated with one another as "F.O.B. Destination" or "F.O.B. Origin." The distinction between these two terms depends on who is bearing the risk of transportation. F.O.B destination designates the seller or shipper as bearing the risk of transportation. They are in control and held responsible for filing claims until delivery. However, F.O.B origin shows that the consignee or receiver is taking that risk of transportation. They are given the title once the freight is loaded and are the ones who file the claim.

Prepaid & Add, Prepaid & Allow, or Collect are the most common payment terms that are used when dealing with freight claims.

1. **Prepaid & Add** - The shipper pays shipping costs beforehand, and then later adds additional charges to the invoice. The consignee can be reimbursed for these charges later on.

2. **Prepaid & Allow** - The shipper prepays shipping costs (already included in price).

3. **Collect** – The consignee gives the shipping charges to the carrier at the time of delivery.

What defines a freight claim and how are they filed?

Specific aspects must be communicated to the carrier in order for a legal claim to be made. An investigation is overseen by the carrier and they must be able to identify the carrier's "Pro number," the shipper's number, the vehicle number, the date the shipment was originated, and the final delivery date. Along with these, there needs to be a full description of the discrepancy including:

1. The specific kind of loss or damage (visible damage, lost in transit, concealed damage) incurred.

2. An actual or good faith estimate of the amount of loss incurred.

3. A formal demand for payment by the carrier

The claim must be filed with the carrier within the specific time frame set out in the carrier's tariff or any authorized contract for cartage.

Once the claim is filed, it should include a descriptive summary of the damage to the freight including an approximate estimate. Documentation is also needed to support the claim. These include:

- An original or certified copy of the bill of lading

- Proof that the freight bill was paid

- Loading/unloading count sheets or inspection reports

- Evidence, such as photos of damage

- Driver's temperature reports (for climate-controlled shipments)

- Freight claim tracking & investigation

You must also include an internal tracking number and record the claimant's tracking number. You have 30 days to acknowledge you have received this receipt. This is vital and could have serious consequences such as fines if neglected. After documentation is done, the claim will be investigated to decide its credibility. These investigations will be conducted in compliance with the NMFC "Principles and Practices" dealing with the Investigation of Freight Claims.

Consignee Options for Addressing Damaged Freight

The consignee has the power to either reject the whole delivery, or accept the delivery by simply recording damage on the delivery paperwork. This is dependent on the severity of the claim and the amount of damage visible. Drivers need to be trained on how to react to a damage claim and collect enough information, such as pictures of damage, so that the claim can be processed. In the event of the consignee rejecting the whole shipment, the driver must notify his office. The office staff then will contact those who authorized the shipment to receive more information on what to do. If the load is sent to a different location, this may include more freight payments to cover repacking and re-routing.

Although insurance claims for lost or damaged freight do not happen that often, they are a scenario that you must be prepared for. The most common type of claim will be Freight Damaged in Transit and this will more than likely be caused by the carrier. The legal owner of the freight at the time files the claim, either the shipper or the consignee.

This is why it's important to obtain a copy of the motor carrier's insurance certificate prior to dispatching them and to make sure they have the proper coverage to haul the freight. However, it is also important that you, as a broker, obtain **Contingent Cargo Insurance.** This will cover any claims or loss that the <u>carrier's insurance cannot or does not cover.</u>

Claims – Frequently Asked Questions

Q. How do I find the time limits for filing claims against carriers?

a) The carriers' tariff or bills of lading will specify the various time limits, but they could be different for each mode, or different for carriers within the same mode, particularly on traffic which is exempt from government regulations. The best procedure is to draw up a time limit chart listing these key periods for each carrier in your routing guide. This will also help you to select the carriers with the most favorable liability terms and conditions.

Q. Must we notify our own insurance company of a claim against a carrier?

a) Yes, under most shippers' cargo insurance policies, the insurer stipulates that it must be given notice of claims promptly, or within a reasonable time. If you are not able to recover from a carrier, you may be time-barred from claiming against the insurer if you have not given them prompt notice of your claim against the carrier.

Q. Must I use a specific claim form?

a) No, any written notice containing the basic elements of a claim will suffice.

Q. May I include interest, administrative costs, freight charges, loss of profits, attorney's fees, etc. in my claim?

a) Yes and No. The measure of damage is governed by common law. "Freight Claims in Plain English" reviews the case law on this issue as well as all other legal issues affecting claims.

Q. Can I recover a claim from a carrier after it files for bankruptcy?

a) Yes. Call the D.O.T. for the name and address of the carrier's cargo insurer at **(202) 927-7600.** Get the cargo policy number in effect on the date of the loss. Then write to the insurer and demand payment under the BMC 32 Endorsement.

Standard Carrier Alpha Code (SCAC)

The Standard Carrier Alpha Code (SCAC) is a unique two- to- four-letter code used to identify transportation companies. NMFTA developed the SCAC identification codes in the mid-1960s to facilitate computerization in the transportation industry. The Standard Carrier Alpha Code is the recognized transportation company identification code used in the American National Standards Institute (ANSI) Accredited Standards Committee (ASC) and United Nations EDIFACT approved electronic data interchange (EDI) transaction sets such as the 856 Advance Ship Notice, the 850 Purchase Order, and all motor, rail, and water carrier transactions where carrier identification is required. The SCAC is required on tariffs filed with the Surface Transportation Board (STB).

The United States Bureau of Customs and Border Protection has mandated the use of the SCAC for their Automated Manifest (AMS) and Pre-Arrival Processing Systems (PAPS). SCACs are required when doing business with all U.S. Government agencies and with many commercial shippers including, but not limited to, those in the automobile, petroleum, forest products, and chemical industries as well as suppliers to retail businesses and carriers engaged in railroad piggyback trailer and ocean container drayage.

Carriers who use the Uniform Intermodal Interchange Agreement (UIIA) are required to maintain a valid SCAC. The petroleum industry uses SCACs in their integrated software programs that expedite the movement of bills of lading, pipeline tickets, product transfer orders, and inventory data. Many commercial shippers and receivers utilize SCACs in their freight bill audit and payment systems.

Certain groups of SCACs are reserved for specific purposes. Codes ending with the letter "U" are reserved for the identification of freight containers. Codes ending with the letter "X" are reserved for the identification of privately owned railroad cars. Codes ending with the letter "Z" are reserved for the identification of truck chassis and trailers used in intermodal service.

To apply for your SCAC code with the NMFTA, visit:

https://secure.nmfta.org/Welcome.aspx

Transportation to U.S. Ports

TWIC Cards

What is TWIC™?

A Transportation Worker Identification Credential (TWIC™) is a biometric credential that ensures only vetted workers are eligible to enter a secure area of a Maritime Transportation Security Act-regulated port or vessel unescorted.

Port security procedures, rules, and laws affecting the delivery of cargo can and do change over time and have a direct impact on the cost of transporting cargo. In major US ports, "unescorted access" to secure areas is no longer possible.

At major US ports, what areas are deemed "secure" or sensitive are subject to change without notice. New rules and regulations require that transportation workers making delivery of cargo to secure areas have a TWIC card—**"Transportation Worker Identification Credential."** This is issued by the US Federal Government, Transportation Security Agency (TSA). The TWIC card is a "biometric" ID card that costs money to obtain, involves going through a security check, has a biometric chip and photo identification, and lasts up to five years. In certain US ports, since the last part of 2008, this is required of all drivers delivering cargo "directly" to the seaport.

Most FCL (full container load) container haulers are "up to speed" with this ID requirement. However, many vehicle and heavy equipment truckers coming from the US interior—far from the ports where these rules have gone into effect—do not have this required TWIC card. Likewise, many private people looking to make direct delivery of their vehicles to effected ports do not have this card.

History

Congress mandated the Transportation Worker Identification Credential in the Maritime Transportation Security Act of 2002 (MTSA) as amended by the Security and Accountability for Every Port Act of 2006 (SAFE Port Act).

MTSA directed the secretary of the Department of Homeland Security to prescribe regulations that would prohibit an individual from gaining unescorted access to a secure area as designated in an approved security plan of a regulated facility unless that individual holds a duly-issued transportation security card and is otherwise authorized by the owner or operator to be in such a secure area.

TWIC Escorts

In some US ports, TWIC escorts are available to provide secure access to ports of call. These escorts are paid at the time of service by the carrier. Some of these escorts are listed with contact information below. You will need to contact the local TSA office at the specific port your truck is delivering to for TWIC escorts that are available.

What is the enrollment process?

The enrollment process consists of the following components: optional pre-enrollment, in-person enrollment, security threat assessment and notification of the results, and issuance of the TWIC to the applicant. Applicants may pre-enroll online to enter all of the biographic information required for the threat assessment and make an appointment at the enrollment center to complete the process (although appointments are not required). Then applicants must visit the enrollment center where they will pay the enrollment fee, complete a **TWIC Application Disclosure Form**, provide biographic information and a complete set of fingerprints, and sit for a digital photograph. The applicant must bring identity verification documents to enrollment and, in the case of aliens, immigration documents that verify their immigration status so that the documents can be scanned into the electronic enrollment record.

What documents do I need to enroll?

All applicants are required to bring appropriate documentation to the enrollment center in order to verify their identity (click **here** for a list of approved documents). Applicants can provide any one document from List A or two documents from List B, one of which must be a government-issued photo ID. A good example of appropriate documentation from List B is a state-issued driver's license and a social security card.

What documentation is an applicant required to bring to the enrollment center if he/she is a U.S. citizen, but was not born in the United States?

Applicants should bring one of the following documents:

1. Department of State - Certificate of Report of Birth (Form DS-1350);

2. Department of State - Consular Report of Birth Abroad (Form FS-240); or

3. U.S. Passport.

Note: If the Certificate of Birth Abroad, Consular Report of Birth Abroad, or an expired U.S. Passport are presented, additional documents will be required to verify identity; see list of acceptable identity documents. If a current (unexpired) U.S. Passport is presented, it is the only identity verification document required.

How much does a TWIC cost?

The fee for a TWIC card is $132.50 and the credential is valid for five years. Those who hold a valid MMD issued after February 3, 2003, MML issued after January 13, 2006, HME issued after May 31, 2005, or a FAST card, may pay a reduced fee of $105.25. Those applicants choosing to pay the reduced fee must present an MML, MMD, HME, or FAST card at the time of enrollment. If the reduced fee is paid, the TWIC expiration date will be five years from the date of the supporting MML, MMD, HME, or FAST card.

What are the methods of payment?

Payment must be made with money order, certified/cashier's check, corporate check, or credit card (Visa or MasterCard only). Checks should be made payable to Lockheed Martin. Two additional payment options are available for companies to pay for their employees: company purchased pre-paid debit cards or bulk payments. For companies choosing to use the pre-paid option, additional information can be found at http://www.twiccard.com. For additional information on bulk payments please click here for Lockheed Martin's policy document. In all cases, payment is to be made at the enrollment center at the beginning of the enrollment process.

What is the pre-paid debit card for the TWIC Program?

This method of payment is a prepaid Visa® card and is intended for employers who wish to purchase TWICs for their employees. They may be purchased in bulk and are redeemable at any TWIC enrollment center. The website for additional information or purchasing them is at http://www.twiccard.com.

What is the fee for a replacement card?

The card replacement fee (for lost, stolen, or damaged TWICs) is $60.

What is the deployment schedule?

Click **here** to view the latest TWIC deployment schedule, which provides monthly or quarterly time frames. As the start of the enrollment period for each grouping of ports nears, specific enrollment start dates and addresses will be posted, so stay tuned.

Where can I enroll?

The current listing of enrollment locations is available on this website, under the **Schedule** tab.

Where can I get more information on mobile enrollment?

Click **here** to view a document that provides background information, requirements, and contact information for requesting and hosting a mobile enrollment facility.

What is pre-enrollment?

The pre-enrollment process allows applicants to provide much of the biographic information required for enrollment, to select an enrollment center where they wish to complete enrollment, and to make an appointment to complete enrollment at the enrollment center of their choosing. Applicants are encouraged, but not required, to pre-enroll. Pre-enrollment is available by clicking **here**.

Are appointments required for enrollment?

No. Appointments are encouraged to save applicants' time but are not required and walk-ins are welcome.

How can I make an appointment for enrollment?

To make an appointment for TWIC enrollment, an applicant must first **pre-enroll**. If pre-enrolling on the website, an applicant may use his/her address to search for nearby enrollment centers and set an appointment time for the location of his/her choice. If pre-enrolling via the Help Desk (1-866-DHS - TWIC), an operator will help the applicant set an appointment time at the enrollment center of his/her choice.

How long does enrollment take?

The enrollment process for a pre-enrolled applicant is expected to take approximately 10 minutes. The enrollment process for an individual who has chosen not to pre-enroll is expected to take approximately 15 minutes.

How will the cards be issued?

The applicant will be notified by email or phone, as specified during enrollment, when his/her credential is available at the enrollment center. The applicant must return to the same enrollment center to pick up his/her TWIC.

How long does it take to receive a TWIC?

Currently, there is typically three- to four-week turnaround from enrollment until card activation. Eligibility issues or insufficient paperwork may increase the turnaround time.

Where can I get additional information on TWIC?

The **TSA website** for the TWIC program provides additional information on the program, supporting policies, and regulation (information on waivers and appeals), etc. Additionally, the Coast Guard's website contains information on U.S. Coast Guard policies and contains specific documents, such as the Coast Guard Navigation and Vessel Inspection Circular (NVIC) and small entity guides for TWIC applicants and owners/operators.

Carrier Qualification - Setup with New Carrier's

FMCSA's Compliance, Safety, Accountability (CSA) program—formerly known as Comprehensive Safety Analysis (CSA 2010) initiative, has changed the way carrier and driver performance are "measured." CSA replaces SafeStat with a new Safety Measurement System (SMS) that measures the roadside violations and crash data of the previous two years. With SMS, every inspection counts, not just out-of-service violations, and both driver and carrier safety performance are monitored using seven new Behavior Analysis Safety Improvement Categories knows as BASICs. CSA means more contact between FMCSA and the carrier. As a household goods broker, you may do business only with a motor carrier that has a valid USDOT number and valid household goods motor carrier authority. You may not arrange transportation with motor carriers having only property motor carrier authority or household goods authority that is under suspension or has been revoked. You are encouraged to regularly verify the authority status of motor carriers that you do business with.

You can check the status of a motor carrier's operating authority by going to the FMCSA Licensing and Insurance website at http://li-public.fmcsa.dot.gov.

This process of checking if a motor carrier has valid operating authority has been replaced with new CSA methodology. As a freight broker you will need to understand how to do your due diligence in selecting motor carriers with CSA scores in the seven BASICS categories that are in the thresholds required to be considered a "safe" motor carrier. Unsatisfactory, Conditional, and Satisfactory, will be replaced by CSA 2010 SFDs.

General Overview of

CSA 1. What is CSA 2010?

Comprehensive Safety Analysis 2010, or CSA 2010, is a high-impact Federal Motor Carrier Safety Administration (FMCSA) safety program to improve large truck and bus safety and ultimately reduce crashes. It introduces a new enforcement and compliance model that allows FMCSA and its state partners to contact a larger number of carriers earlier in order to address safety problems before crashes occur.

2. Why was CSA 2010 implemented?

FMCSA's mission is to improve safety by reducing crashes. Prior to 2010, the rate of crash reduction had slowed, prompting FMCSA to take a fresh look at how the agency evaluates the safety of motor carriers and drivers and to explore ways to improve its safety monitoring, evaluation, and intervention processes. CSA 2010 is the result of this comprehensive examination. CSA 2010 enables FMCSA and its state partners to assess the safety performance of a greater segment of the industry and to intervene with more carriers to change unsafe behavior early.

3. What is the CSA 2010 Operational Model?

The CSA 2010 Operational Model is how FMCSA and its state partners carry out the compliance and enforcement programs. The CSA 2010 Operational Model is characterized by (1) a more comprehensive measurement system, (2) a proposed safety fitness determination methodology that is based on performance data, and (3) a comprehensive intervention process designed to more efficiently and effectively correct safety problems

4. What are the BASICs and how are they used in CSA 2010?

The Behavioral Analysis and Safety Improvement Categories, or BASICs, are seven categories of safety behaviors measured in the Safety Measurement System (SMS). The BASICs represent behaviors that can lead to crashes: unsafe driving, fatigue (hours-of-service), driver fitness, controlled substances and alcohol, vehicle maintenance, and cargo related; and crash history. The Carrier SMS uses a motor carrier's data from roadside inspections, including all safety-based violations, State reported crashes, and the Federal motor carrier census to score and rank carriers in each BASIC.

5. Where can I find more specific information about measurements for specific BASICs?

For a detailed look at the safety measurement system methodology including in-depth information on how data is categorized and scored for the BASICs, please read the Safety Measurement System (SMS) Methodology.

How will CSA 2010 affect freight dispatchers and 3PLs?

Carrier qualification criteria. Most brokers and 3PLs will need to adapt their carrier qualification processes to CSA 2010, because the program includes significant changes in the measurement of carrier performance:

- The new Safety Measurement System (SMS) emphasizes on-road performance, compared to SafeStat's reliance on out-of-service and moving violations.

- Instead of the four Safety Evaluation Area (SEA) categories in the SafeStat system, the CSA divides carrier and driver safety performance data into seven categories called BASICs: Behavioral Analysis Safety Improvement Categories.

1. Unsafe driving

2. Fatigued driving, based on Hours of Service (HOS) compliance

3. Driver fitness

4. Controlled substance or alcohol

5. Vehicle maintenance

6. Improper loading of cargo

7. Crash indicators (Note: The Crash indicator will not be available to the public.)

Safety Measurement System SMS Website

For the most current information please visit:

https://csa.fmcsa.dot.gov/whatsnew.aspx

Safety Ratings Explained

Safety Ratings

A compliance review results in a safety rating for the motor carrier. This rating can be satisfactory, conditional, or unsatisfactory.

Satisfactory Rating

A motor carrier that receives a satisfactory rating is found to be in compliance with the applicable FMCSA agencies, state regulations, and hazardous materials regulations, if applicable. Carriers with a satisfactory rating also are found to have adequate safety management controls. The FMSCA will administer a satisfactory rating no later than 60 days following the completion of the compliance review.

Unsatisfactory Rating

If a carrier is found to be unsatisfactory, the FMCSA will issue the notification no later than 45 days following the compliance review. Motor carriers receiving an unsatisfactory rating have their operating authority suspended 15 days after the date of the unsatisfactory notice. An out-of-service order is imposed, which prohibits the carrier from operating any motor vehicles in the United States, unless the carrier can prove errors in the compliance review within 10 days of the date of the notice.

Within 30 days of receiving the suspension order, the motor carrier must make the necessary corrections specified in the order to prevent the provisional operating authority from being revoked. A follow-up review may take place to ensure that all necessary corrective actions were taken.

Conditional Rating

A conditional rating is issued by the FMCSA no later than 45 days following a compliance review. When a conditional rating is issued, the motor carrier's operating authority is revoked and an out-of-service order is imposed unless the carrier takes the necessary corrective action within 30 days of receiving the order. A follow-up review takes place to ensure that corrective actions have been made by the motor carrier.

You can check the rating here: http://safer.fmcsa.dot.gov/CompanySnapshot.aspx

Company Snapshot

The Company Snapshot is a concise electronic record of a company's identification, size, commodity information, and safety record, including the safety rating (if any), a roadside out-of-service inspection summary, and crash information. The Company Snapshot is available via an ad-hoc query (one carrier at a time) free of charge.

Search Criteria

Users can search by DOT Number, MC/MX Number or Company Name

The rating below is current as of 06/30/2013

Review Information

Rating Date			Review Date	
Rating			Type	

Things to Remember about CSA 2010

The SMS is updated monthly.

Enforcement includes progressive measures. CSA2010 measurement system will trigger progressive interventions for any carrier whose performance falls below the required threshold on one or more of the seven BASICs. When dealing with a carrier that has one or more BASICs that require intervention, brokers may wish to get a copy of the carrier's corrective action plan.

Carrier safety ratings provide information on the safety performance of carriers to shippers, insurance companies, and the public and allow for more informed marketplace decisions. The FMCSA maintains the SAFERSYS website where complete information may be obtained instantly on any licensed motor carrier.

How to Check Carrier Safety Ratings and Insurance Coverage

http://www.safersys.org

Before you move any load with a carrier, or set them as a potential carrier to move your loads, a safety check should always be performed through the FMCSA database.

To check these ratings, simply type in the MC number the carrier has provided you and wait for the results. The website will provide you with the carrier safety record, insurance coverage, etc. Always check that the information provided to you by the carrier is listed on the ICC Authority.

- Check Valid Authority Information here - http://www.safersys.org/CompanySnapshot.aspx

- Check Valid Insurance here –

http://li-public.fmcsa.dot.gov/LIVIEW/pkg_carrquery.prc_carrlist

The Golden Rule

- Use only carriers with a satisfactory rating or above.

- Liability insurance of minimum $1,000,000

- Cargo insurance of minimum $100,000

- Check to make sure the carrier has some recent inspections and the correct number of available trucks on fleet.

Occasionally, you will find a motor carrier that will contact you regarding a shipment that has been listed as a "conditional" or "none" rotated carrier on the SAFERSYS website. These can be used to move your loads but discretion is advised.

CERTIFICATE OF LIABILITY INSURANCE

ACORD

DATE (MM/DD/YYYY)

PRODUCER	CONTACT NAME:	
BIN Insurance Holdings, LLC	PHONE (A/C, No, Ext):	FAX (A/C, No):
insureon	E-MAIL ADDRESS:	
1301 Central Expy. South, Suite 115		
Allen, TX 75013	INSURER(S) AFFORDING COVERAGE	NAIC #
	INSURER A :	
INSURED	INSURER B :	
	INSURER C :	
	INSURER D :	
	INSURER E :	
	INSURER F :	

COVERAGES   CERTIFICATE NUMBER: REVISION NUMBER:

THIS IS TO CERTIFY THAT THE POLICIES OF INSURANCE LISTED BELOW HAVE BEEN ISSUED TO THE INSURED NAMED ABOVE FOR THE POLICY PERIOD INDICATED. NOTWITHSTANDING ANY REQUIREMENT, TERM OR CONDITION OF ANY CONTRACT OR OTHER DOCUMENT WITH RESPECT TO WHICH THIS CERTIFICATE MAY BE ISSUED OR MAY PERTAIN, THE INSURANCE AFFORDED BY THE POLICIES DESCRIBED HEREIN IS SUBJECT TO ALL THE TERMS, EXCLUSIONS AND CONDITIONS OF SUCH POLICIES. LIMITS SHOWN MAY HAVE BEEN REDUCED BY PAID CLAIMS.

INSR LTR	TYPE OF INSURANCE	ADDL INSR	SUBR WVD	POLICY NUMBER	POLICY EFF (MM/DD/YYYY)	POLICY EXP (MM/DD/YYYY)	LIMITS	
	GENERAL LIABILITY						EACH OCCURRENCE	$
	COMMERCIAL GENERAL LIABILITY						DAMAGE TO RENTED PREMISES (Ea occurrence)	$
	☐ CLAIMS-MADE ☐ OCCUR						MED EXP (Any one person)	$
							PERSONAL & ADV INJURY	$
							GENERAL AGGREGATE	$
	GEN'L AGGREGATE LIMIT APPLIES PER:						PRODUCTS - COMP/OP AGG	$
	☐ POLICY ☐ PRO-JECT ☐ LOC							$
	AUTOMOBILE LIABILITY						COMBINED SINGLE LIMIT (Ea accident)	$
	☐ ANY AUTO						BODILY INJURY (Per person)	$
	☐ ALL OWNED AUTOS ☐ SCHEDULED AUTOS						BODILY INJURY (Per accident)	$
	☐ HIRED AUTOS ☐ NON-OWNED AUTOS						PROPERTY DAMAGE (Per accident)	$
								$
	☐ UMBRELLA LIAB ☐ OCCUR						EACH OCCURRENCE	$
	☐ EXCESS LIAB ☐ CLAIMS-MADE						AGGREGATE	$
	☐ DED ☐ RETENTION $							$
	WORKERS COMPENSATION AND EMPLOYERS' LIABILITY						☐ WC STATU-TORY LIMITS ☐ OTH-ER	
	ANY PROPRIETOR/PARTNER/EXECUTIVE OFFICER/MEMBER EXCLUDED? (Mandatory in NH) ☐ Y/N ☐ N/A						E.L. EACH ACCIDENT	$
							E.L. DISEASE - EA EMPLOYEE	$
	If yes, describe under DESCRIPTION OF OPERATIONS below						E.L. DISEASE - POLICY LIMIT	$

DESCRIPTION OF OPERATIONS / LOCATIONS / VEHICLES (Attach ACORD 101, Additional Remarks Schedule, if more space is required)

CERTIFICATE HOLDER	CANCELLATION
	SHOULD ANY OF THE ABOVE DESCRIBED POLICIES BE CANCELLED BEFORE THE EXPIRATION DATE THEREOF, NOTICE WILL BE DELIVERED IN ACCORDANCE WITH THE POLICY PROVISIONS.
	AUTHORIZED REPRESENTATIVE

ACORD 25 (2010/05)

HOW TO VERIFY INSURANCE

Motor Carrier Details

US DOT:	1228268		Docket Number:		MC455455	
Legal Name:	R A STEPHENS					
Doing Business As Name:	STEPHENS' TRUCK LINE					

Business Address	Business Telephone and Fax	Mail Address	Mail Telephone and Fax	Undeliverable Mail
109 S. DOOLY ST. MONTEZUMA, GA 31063	(229) 815-9657	P O BOX 457 MONTEZUMA GA 31063		NO

Authority Type	Authority Status	Application Pending
Common	INACTIVE	NO
Contract	NONE	NO
Broker	NONE	NO

Property	Passenger	Household Goods	Private	Enterprise
YES	NO	NO	NO	NO

Insurance Type	Insurance Required	Insurance on File
BIPD	$750,000	$0
Cargo	NO	NO
Bond	NO	NO

BOC-3: YES
Blanket Company: OWNER OPERATOR SERVICES, INC.
Web Site Content and BOC-3 Information Clarification

| Active/Pending Insurance | Rejected Insurance | Insurance History | Authority History | Pending Application | Revocation |

Changes for CSA 2020

The changes are the largest since it was launched in 2010. Its focus has shifted from predicting accidents, to prevention and creating a safety culture. This includes analyzing new categories of data, such as driver turnover, driver compensation, and cargo type.

The new scoring system is aiming to be easier to understand. As you might expect, there is a new acronym involved. Item Response Theory (IRT) is replacing the old SMS. IRT is the new math that will replace the old weighting system in SMS that was found to be lacking.

What this means is:

A single CSA BASIC score will replace all the complicated weights, points, and BASIC measures.

Percentile ratings are expected to go away.

Violations will not be weighted by how recent they are.

Different state enforcement levels will be taken into account (if you drive in a tough enforcement area, you won't be rated below someone who is less safe but drives where enforcement is less strict).

If you have excellent marks in all but a couple of areas, your fleet's overall score won't be as bad as under the old system.

Things like power units, driver count, inspection count, and miles traveled will be taken into account to make a more level playing field between carriers. It should even consider the fact that northern carriers drive in icy winter weather.

Full-scale testing has not started, so this is not final.

California Air Resources Board (CARB) - Rules for Freight Brokers

On October 21, 2011, the California Air Resources Board (CARB) approved a package of amendments ("2011 Amendments") to the Transport Refrigeration Unit (TRU) Airborne Toxic Control Measure (ATCM). Included in this package was an amendment affecting brokers, freight forwarders, shippers, receivers, motor carriers, and their drivers. CARB staff investigations had found a greater frequency of noncompliance among carriers hired by brokers, freight forwarders, shippers, and receivers compared to private fleets. These new requirements were put into effect starting January 1, 2013.

What is the requirement for brokers?

If a broker or forwarder arranges, hires, contracts for, or dispatches reefer-equipped trucks, tractor-trailers, shipping containers, or rail cars for the transport of perishable goods on California highways or railways, the broker or forwarder must:

- Require the carriers they hire or contract with to only dispatch reefers that comply with the Air Resources Board TRU ATCM in-use performance standards; and

- Provide contact information to the carrier so that dispatched drivers can present it to authorized enforcement personnel upon request. Contact information must include the broker's company name, street address, state, and zip code and a contact person's name and business phone number. If a broker is not involved in arranging the transport of the load, then broker contact information is not required on bills of lading or related documents. CARB staff has indicated that as long as the broker provides their contact information to the driver, the requirement will be met.

The requirement applies to any broker that hires a carrier that will travel on a California highway or railway, regardless of where the broker or forwarder is based or conducting business. CARB staff indicates that brokers are not responsible if a driver chooses to enter California by choice if the origin and destination are outside of California, but if the route the load in question is traveling on typically includes travel in California (i.e., AZ to OR), the broker should ensure compliance.

Brokers are not required to physically inspect TRUs to determine compliance or turn away non-compliant TRUs at docks. However, brokers must take steps to comply with the requirements.

What are the guidelines for demonstration of due diligence?

According to the guidelines disseminated by CARB, brokers and forwarders should be able to verify compliance by asking carriers to provide proof of compliance and reference the Air Resources Board Equipment Registration (ARBER) system for 100%-compliant carriers. Through the ARBER data system, brokers and forwarders can check carrier's compliance status.

Furthermore, the CARB "suggest" the following strategies that a broker or forwarder could use to ensure hiring a compliant carrier:

- Businesses should consider sending an annual notice to their carrier base indicating that only carriers listed in the CARB's 100%-compliant database will be considered for hire or contract when arranging freight that travels on California highways and railways;

- Businesses (shippers) should include contract language in agreements between the shipper and broker or forwarder, or receiver and broker or forwarder, that clearly requires only CARB-compliant TRUs to be dispatched on California highways and railways;

- When advertising a load on an on-line load board, brokers should specify that the load requiring refrigerated transport equipment will travel on California highways or railways and the TRU used for the load must by CARB compliant;

- A broker should document the steps during hiring and contract negotiations with the carrier, showing that the carrier was notified that a CARB-compliant TRU is required and that the carrier confirmed the contractual obligation to only dispatch CARB-compliant TRUs on California highways and railways;

- A broker should include contract language that clearly states that only CARB-compliant reefers will be dispatched on California highways and railways. For example, "Carrier or its agent certifies that any TRU equipment furnished will be in compliance with the in-use requirements of California's TRU regulations." This language should be highlighted and bolded with a space provided for a signature of acknowledgment; and

- The carrier must provide the ARBER certification page to the broker to show that the dispatched unit is compliant. This document may be used to show that there was a reasonable expectation that only certified/compliant reefer equipment would be used for a specific job, if the specific IDN is called out in the contract.

Are there certain exemptions?

There are certain exemptions, including any trailer TRU housing that remains attached to a trailer van, but the fuel tank and battery have been removed and a label with the word "NONOPERA-TIONAL" has been affixed or attached to the housing in letters that contrast sharply with the color of the TRU housing and can be seen from 50 feet away during daylight hours when the vehicle is stationary. For the full list of exemptions, please reference Section 2477.3 of the CARB Final Regulation Order.

The regulation does apply to dry good loads being hauled on a reefer unit, unless it meets one of the statutory exemptions.

What are the penalties?

All persons found be to in violation of this regulation may be cited and subject to the penalty provisions set forth in the California Health and Safety Code. The penalty is $1,000 for each occurrence. If a carrier is found to have violated the requirement to dispatch only CARB-compliant TRUs on California highways or railways, the broker should take preventive steps to ensure no further hiring of that non-compliant carrier will happen.

On April 25, 2014 the California Air Resources Board adopted amendments to its Truck and Bus Regulation that will provide new flexible compliance options to owners of aging diesel fleets and recognize fleet owners that have made investments to comply, while also protecting air quality.

The changes approved at the Board hearing provide additional regulatory flexibility to small fleets, lower use vehicles, and fleets in rural areas that have made substantial progress towards cleaner air. Fleets that have invested in cleaner, compliant equipment and trucks will be able to use credits longer and any vehicles retrofit by 2014 do not have to be replaced until 2023.

"We recognize the enormous investments that many businesses have already made to clean up their equipment and abide by the terms of the regulation," said ARB Chairman Mary D. Nichols, "but we are also aware that, particularly for many rural areas of the state, economic recovery has been painfully slow and funding for improvements scarce.

"By providing limited additional time for certain fleets to comply, we believe that we'll have higher compliance rates overall. It's a difficult balance but we believe that this is a fair approach that offers flexibility to those who need it, while also rewarding those business owners who have already upgraded their vehicles to meet the requirements of the regulation."

Nichols also said that the amendments, while potentially delaying compliance for some, will still protect air quality, preserving 93% of the NOx (oxides of nitrogen) and diesel particulate matter (PM) benefits of the original regulation.

The amendments include:

- A longer phase-in period for diesel PM requirements for trucks that operate exclusively in certain rural areas with cleaner air;

- Additional time and incentive funding opportunities for small fleets;

- A new compliance option for owners who cannot currently afford compliance;

- Expansion of the low-use exemption and the construction truck extension;

- Recognition of fleet owners who have already complied by providing additional "useable life" for retrofit trucks and reducing near-term compliance requirements.

The amendments will still ensure that, by 2020, nearly every truck in California will have a PM filter, consistent with the goals of the Diesel Risk Reduction Plan.

On November 15, 2018 The California Air Resources Board adopted a new emissions tracking program that will help regulators identify vehicles with excess smog-related and greenhouse gas emissions and propel California further towards its goal of meeting state and federal air quality standards in the decades ahead.

Real Emissions Assessment Logging (REAL) is part of the amendments to the OBD (On-board Diagnostic) Regulations approved by the Board at the hearing. OBD systems are mainly comprised of software designed into a vehicle's on-board computer to detect emission control system malfunctions as they occur by monitoring virtually every component that can cause increased emissions. When the OBD system detects a malfunction, it alerts the driver by illuminating an indicator light on the instrument panel, and stores information that helps identify the faulty equipment, enabling technicians to quickly fix the problem.

While the OBD system currently notifies drivers when emissions components are malfunctioning, the REAL program would require the OBD system to do more than that. It would require OBD systems to collect and store emissions data from NOx (oxides of nitrogen, a pre-curser to smog) on medium- and heavy-duty diesel vehicles in-use starting in the 2022 model year. It would also require OBD systems to collect and store fuel consumption data that would be used to characterize CO_2 emissions on all heavy-duty vehicles in-use. Storage of similar data for greenhouse gas emissions is already required on light-duty and medium-duty vehicles starting in model year 2019. The REAL data will be retrieved from the vehicle by plugging a scan tool or data reader into the vehicle.

Currently, to get a snapshot of how vehicles are performing in terms of emissions, CARB either brings them to laboratories for testing or equips a handful of vehicles with Portable Emissions Measurement Systems (PEMS) equipment to find high emitters on the road.

"REAL will provide the ability to monitor all vehicles for emissions performance, and allow us to spot trouble faster. Had this program been available sooner, we would likely have recognized widespread, serious problems with manufacturers such as Volkswagen and Cummins much earlier," said CARB Executive Officer Richard Corey. "California's vehicle fleet is getting cleaner every year but we still have a lot of work to do to reach our air quality and climate change goals. The REAL program is yet another way to utilize the OBD system and help ensure that engines and vehicles maintain low emissions throughout their full lives."

The REAL program will require no new technology since it will take advantage of existing sensors to track the necessary data. Older vehicles will not be part of the REAL program and will not require any new equipment.

"For decades, while the automobile has grown cleaner and more efficient, the other half of our transportation system has barely moved the needle on clean air," said CARB Chair Mary D. Nichols.

"Diesel vehicles are the workhorses of the economy, and we need them to be part of the solution to persistent pockets of dirty air in some of our most disadvantaged communities. Now is the time – the technology is here and so is the need for investment."

Trucks are the largest single source of air pollution from vehicles, responsible for 70 percent of the smog-causing pollution and 80 percent of carcinogenic diesel soot even though they number only 2 million among the 30 million registered vehicles in the state.

This requirement to shift to zero-emission trucks, along with the ongoing shift to electric cars, will help California meet its climate goals and federal air quality standards, especially in the Los Angeles region and the San Joaquin Valley – areas that suffer the highest levels of air pollution in the nation. Statewide, the Advanced Clean Truck regulation will lower related premature deaths by 1,000.

The rule drives technology and investment, phasing in available heavy-duty zero-emission technology starting in 2024 with full transformation over the next two decades. This sends a clear signal to manufacturers, fleet owners and utilities that the time to invest in zero-emission trucks – and the economy – is now. It builds on California's leadership as a manufacturer of zero-emission transportation.

In the coming months, CARB will also consider two complementary regulations to support today's action. The first sets a stringent new limit on NOx (oxides of nitrogen), one of the major precursors of smog. This will require that new trucks that still use fossil fuels include the most effective exhaust control technology during the transition to electric trucks. There is also a proposed requirement for larger fleets in the state to transition to electric trucks year over year.

June 25, 2020 The California Air Resources Board adopted a first-in-the-world rule requiring truck manufacturers to transition from diesel trucks and vans to electric zero-emission trucks beginning in 2024. By 2045, every new truck sold in California will be zero-emission.

This bold and timely move sets a clean-truck standard for the nation and the world, and marks the Newsom administration's most important air pollution regulation to date. It zeroes in on air pollution in the state's most disadvantaged and polluted communities.

"California is an innovation juggernaut that is going electric. We are showing the world that we can move goods, grow our economy and finally dump dirty diesel," said Jared Blumenfeld, California's Secretary for Environmental Protection.

Many California neighborhoods, especially Black and Brown, low-income and vulnerable communities, live, work, play and attend schools adjacent to the ports, railyards, distribution centers, and freight corridors and experience the heaviest truck traffic. This new rule directly addresses disproportionate risks and health and pollution burdens affecting these communities and puts California on the path for an all zero-emission short-haul drayage fleet in ports and railyards by 2035, and zero-emission "last-mile" delivery trucks and vans by 2040.

Freight Factoring

What Is Freight Factoring?

Factoring is all about cash flow. The process of factoring is selling your accounts receivable so that you can get paid immediately for the work you have performed. Factoring is often used synonymously with accounts receivable financing. Factoring is a form of commercial finance whereby a business sells its accounts receivable **(in the form of invoices)** at a discount. Effectively, the business is no longer dependent on the conversion of accounts receivable to cash from the actual payment from their customers, which takes place on typical 30- to 90-day terms. Businesses benefit from the acceleration of cash flow. Factoring is considered off-balance sheet financing in that it is not a form of debt or a form of equity. This makes factoring more attainable than traditional bank and equity financing.

There are usually three parties involved when an invoice is factored:

1. Seller of the product or service who originates the invoice.

2. Debtor is the recipient of the invoice for services rendered who promises to pay the balance within the agreed payment terms (the customer).

3. Factor company.

Factor companies come in all sizes and many different models. A trucking company using a factor does it for a reason or a variety of reasons. First and foremost, freight factoring is the ability to obtain a line of credit from a bank. Factoring is an easy method of financing. Truckers have invoices and under the Uniform Commercial Code (UCC), invoices are freely assignable. Think of it as a truck purchase. You go to the dealer and buy a truck, but you need financing. The contract you make with the truck dealer is assigned to the bank. IF you have a long-standing mortgage, you have your mortgage assigned a number of times as companies merge or your mortgage is sold from one company to another. The UCC provides that this "commercial paper" is freely assignable, meaning it can be done without the consent of the party making the payment.

Almost always, along with the purchase of the invoice, the factor requires a party to execute a UCC form, which constitutes a lien upon the invoice and may state that it is a lien upon all receivables of the trucking company UNTIL RELEASED. The UCC form is then registered in the home state of the trucking company or the state in which they are incorporated. Without going into a very detailed further explanation, the first registered UCC is in the first position just like the first mortgage on a house. Until your first is paid off, should the first foreclose, any second mortgage must buy out the first to protect their interest. Failure to file a UCC form does not affect the ability to assign the invoice or the obligations of the party assigned. Failure to file a UCC form does, however, cause a factoring company to run the risk of UCC form filing by another factoring company, causing the first factor to fall behind the right of the filer even though the non-filer (first factor) obligation was incurred first in time. Think of it as similar to patent rights. First to file for the patent is the holder of the right to receive royalties. All factoring companies that know what they are doing file UCC forms, which are usually furnished to the company responsible for paying the invoice.

Types of Factors

1. Purchase with Non-Recourse

In a purchase of an invoice by a non-recourse factor, the purchaser of the invoice receives the right to payment of the invoice. That right to payment becomes binding on the company owning the payment upon receipt of notice that the right to payment has been assigned. The trucker no longer has any right to receive payment and the factoring company assumes the risk of collecting. Stated plainly, when the notice has been given and receive under the UCC, payment to the trucker by the broker becomes what is known as a Payment over Notice. When a Payment over Notice occurs, the right to receive payment by the factoring company is not discharged if payment is made to the trucker rather than the factor, and may make the broker liable for paying twice for the transportation cost.

2. Purchase with Recourse

A recourse factor is a company that maintains a right to return unpaid invoices to the trucker for payment. Usually, a percentage of each load is maintained in a client's account until a certain total amount is reached to ensure that payment for unpaid invoices can be deducted from the client's account. These agreements vary in terms and content, but are essentially the same in how they work. Stated plainly, the recourse factor can collect from the client account or the client when an invoice is not paid. A non-recourse factor takes the risk of non-payment.

Factoring Basics

1. Are Factors Licensed?

There are no permits or licenses required for factors (or other purchasers or lenders) when the business is standard commercial credit through Article 9 of the Uniform Commercial Code (UCC).

2. Am I Bound by a Notice of Assignment?

If you have received a Notice of Assignment, you are bound by it even if you do not acknowledge the notice.

3. How Can I be Sure the Assignment is Real?

If you are suspicious of the notice that you have received, you can request additional proof of the assignment (UCC 9-406©) which reads, "Subject to inspection (h), if requested by the account debtor, an assignee shall reasonably furnish reasonable proof that the assignment has been made. Unless the assignee complies, the account debtor may discharge its obligation by paying the assignor, even if the account debtor has received a notification under subsection (a)."

Reasonable proof would be a signed Notice of Assignment letter, a redacted security agreement, proof of the creditor's purchase of the account in question, or a UCC financing statement.

4. Should I Sign a Notice of Assignment?

Since you are bound by a Notice of Assignment once received, whether you sign it or not, it is probably better not to sign such notices so that you do not inadvertently agree to new terms or conditions. By simply filing the Notice of Assignment and following its payment instructions, you have not agreed to any new conditions.

5. Do Factors Have to Abide by the Terms of the Broker–Carrier Contract?

Factors buy receivables from carriers for a discounted rate. This results in a subrogation of the carrier's receivables. By doing so, they also inherit the terms and conditions related to those receivables (i.e., if the carrier agreed to 60-day terms, then the factor must respect those terms). Factors should be aware of the terms the carriers have with their clients before factoring. If the factor does not agree with the pre-established terms, they should turn back to the carrier to resolve the issue. The factor should not negatively affect the payer's credit rating in attempting to collect with agreed terms.

6. Where can I Get Additional Information

The International Factoring Association (www.factoring.org) has a great deal of information on its website.

TIA Recommended Best Practices for Factors

1. The carrier must provide the broker with documentation indicating that the load has been factored, and to whom payment is to be made.

2. The factoring information should not be changed during the payment terms agreed to for the shipment.

3. A factor should not subrogate receivables that are already assigned. The carrier should not re-assign its receivables to a new factor without having received a release from the initial factor.

4. The broker should establish procedures for being contacted by the factor and should make said procedures known during carrier set-up; factors should abide by the broker's procedures.

1. Factors should confirm, within the parameters of the broker's established procedures, that the broker has been advised of the assignment of the receivables and is aware to whom the payables should be made.

2. Payment terms and conditions should be agreed upon between the broker and the carrier by written contract.

3. Factoring loads does not free the receivables from any legal lien due to the non-performance of the carrier as defined in the broker-carrier contract. If funds are being held due to the non-performance of the carrier, the factor should not negatively affect the broker's credit in an attempt to collect, but should address the issue back to the carrier for resolution.

4. All information gathered by the factor should be considered confidential and not be transmitted to any party other than as required to ensure their receivables.

5. There should be a clear and arm's-length separation between the factor and any related businesses to avoid the appearance of impropriety or conflict of interest.

6. Factors should disclose information about any brokerages, freight forwarders, carriers, or other transportation-related businesses they own or operate, or with whom they are associated.

Carrier Qualification - Setup with New Carriers

New changes are being made as how to verify and qualify new carriers as a broker. To stay up to date with the latest information, please visit: https://csa.fmcsa.dot.gov/WhatsNew/Index

On December 4, 2015, the FAST Act came into effect, prohibiting the display of a property carrier's relative percentile, so on December 4, 2015, FMCSA removed the information prohibited from display, and also removed the absolute measures to allow time to modify the SMS website to be compliant. **As of 2016, brokers CANNOT use the CSA 2010 methodology to verify carriers, as there are no CSA scores available to the public.**

As a household goods broker, you may do business only with a motor carrier that has a valid USDOT number and valid *household goods motor carrier authority*. You may not arrange transportation with motor carriers having only property motor carrier authority or household goods authority that is under suspension or has been revoked. You are encouraged to regularly verify the authority status of motor carriers that you do business with.

You can check the status of a motor carrier's operating authority by going to the FMCSA Licensing and Insurance website at http://li-public.fmcsa.dot.gov .

Appendix

Appendix - Hazmat

Class 1: Explosives.

Subclass 1.1

Consists of explosives that have a mass explosion hazard. A mass explosion is one which affects almost the entire load instantaneously.

Subclass 1.2

Consists of explosives that have a projection hazard but not a mass explosion hazard.

Subclass 1.3

Consists of explosives that have a fire hazard and either a minor blast hazard or a minor projection hazard or, both but not a mass explosion hazard.

Subclass 1.4

Consists of explosives that present a minor explosion hazard. The explosive effects are largely confined to the package and no projection of fragments of appreciable size or range is to be expected. An external fire must not cause virtually instantaneous explosion of almost the entire contents of the package.

Subclass 1.5

Consists of very insensitive explosives. This division is comprised of substances which have a mass explosion hazard but are so insensitive that there is very little probability of initiation or of transition from burning to detonation under normal conditions of transport

Subclass 1.6

Consists of extremely insensitive articles, which do not have a mass explosive hazard. This division is comprised of articles which contain only extremely insensitive detonating substances and which demonstrate a negligible probability of accidental initiation or propagation.

Class 2: Gases.

Subclass 2.1 - Flammable Gas

454 kg (1001 lbs.) of any material which is a gas at 20°C (68°F) or less and 101.3 kPa (14.7 psi) of pressure (a material which has a boiling point of 20°C (68°F) or less at 101.3 kPa (14.7 psi)) which:

1.Is ignitable at 101.3 kPa (14.7 psi) when in a mixture of 13 percent or less by volume with air; or

2.Has a flammable range at 101.3 kPa (14.7 psi) with air of at least 12 percent regardless of the lower limit.

Subclass 2.2 - Non-flammable, Non-poisonous Gas

This division includes compressed gas, liquefied gas, pressurized cryogenic gas, compressed gas in solution, asphyxiant gas and oxidizing gas. A non-flammable, nonpoisonous compressed gas (Division 2.2) means any material (or mixture) which:

1. Exerts in the packaging an absolute pressure of 280 kPa (40.6 psia) or greater at 20°C (68°F), and

2. Does not meet the definition of Division 2.1 or 2.3.

Subclass 2.2 - Oxygen Gas

This is an optional placard to the 2.2 Non-flammable Gas placard for compressed Oxygen in either the gas or liquid state. Oxygen is considered a non-flammable because it in and of itself does not burn. It is, however, required for combustion to take place. High concentrations of oxygen greatly increases the rate and intensity of combustion.

Subclass 2.3 - Poison Gas

Gas poisonous by inhalation means a material which is a gas at 20°C or less and a pressure of 101.3 kPa (a material which has a boiling point of 20°C or less at 101.3kPa (14.7 psi)) and which:

1. is known to be so toxic to humans as to pose a hazard to health during transportation, or

2. in the absence of adequate data on human toxicity, is presumed to be toxic to humans because when tested on laboratory animals it has an LC50 value of not more than 5000 ml/m3.

Class 3: Flammable Liquids.

Flammable Liquid

A flammable liquid (Class 3) means a liquid having a flashpoint of not more than 60.5°C (141°F), or any material in a liquid phase with a flashpoint at or above 37.8°C (100°F) that is intentionally heated and offered for transportation or transported at or above its flashpoint in a bulk packaging, with the following exceptions:

1. Any liquid meeting one of the definitions specified in 49CFR 173.115.

2. Any mixture having one or more components with a flashpoint of 60.5°C (141°F) or higher, that make up at least 99 percent of the total volume of the mixture, if the mixture is not offered for transportation or transported at or above its flashpoint.

3. Any liquid with a flash point greater than 35°C (95°F) which does not sustain combustion according to ASTM 4206 or the procedure in Appendix H of this part.

4. Any liquid with a flash point greater than 35°C (95°F) and with a fire point greater than 100°C (212°F) according to ISO 2592.

5. Any liquid with a flash point greater than 35°C (95°F) which is in a water-miscible solution with a water content of more than 90 percent by mass.

Class 4.1: Flammable Solids or Substances.

Flammable Solids or Substances

Desensitized explosives that when dry are explosives of Class 1 and are specifically authorized by name or have been assigned a shipping name and hazard class by the Associate Administrator.

Self-reactive materials, which are thermally unstable and that can undergo a strongly exothermic decomposition even without participation of air.

Readily combustible solids that can cause a fire through friction and show a burning rate faster than 2.2 mm (0.087 inches) per second, or metal powders that can be ignited and react over the whole length of a sample in 10 minutes or less.

Class 4.2: Flammable solids.

Flammable Solids

Spontaneously Combustible material is a pyrophoric material, which is a liquid or solid that can ignite within five (5) minutes after coming in contact with air or a self-heating material that when in contact with air and without an energy supply is liable to self-heat.

Class 4.3: Substances, which, in contact with water, emit flammable gases.

Substances, which, in contact with water, emit flammable gases

Dangerous When Wet material is a material that when it makes contact with water is liable to become spontaneously flammable or give off flammable or toxic gas at a rate greater than 1 L per kilogram of the material per hour.

Class 5.1: Oxidizing substances (agents) by yielding oxygen increase the risk and intensity of fire.

Oxidizing substances (agents) by yielding oxygen increase the risk and intensity of fire

Oxidizer (Division 5.1) means a material that may, generally by yielding oxygen, cause or enhance the combustion of other materials.

1. A solid material is classed as a Division 5.1 material if, when tested in accordance with the UN Manual of Tests and Criteria, its mean burning time is less than or equal to the burning time of a 3:7 potassium bromate/cellulose mixture.

2. A liquid material is classed as a Division 5.1 material if, when tested in accordance with the UN Manual of Tests and Criteria, it spontaneously ignites or its meantime for a pressure rise from 690 kPa to 2070 kPa gauge is less than the time of a 1:1 nitric acid (65

percent)/cellulose mixture.

Class 5.2: Organic peroxides - most will burn rapidly and are sensitive to impact or friction.

Organic peroxides - most will burn rapidly and are sensitive to impact or friction

Organic peroxide (Division 5.2) means any organic compound containing oxygen (O) in the bivalent - O-O-structure and which may be considered a derivative of hydrogen peroxide, where one or more of the hydrogen atoms have been replaced by organic radicals, unless any of the following paragraphs applies:

1. The material meets the definition of an explosive as prescribed in subpart C of this part, in which case it must be classed as an explosive;

2. The material is forbidden from being offered for transportation according to 49CFR 172.101 of this subchapter or 49CFR 173.21;

3. The Associate Administrator for Hazardous Materials Safety has determined that the material does not present a hazard which is associated with a Division 5.2 material; or

4. The material meets one of the following conditions:

   a. For materials containing no more than 1.0 percent hydrogen peroxide, the available oxygen, as calculated using the equation in paragraph (a)(4)(ii) of this section, is not more than 1.0 percent, or

   b. For materials containing more than 1.0 percent but not more than 7.0 percent hydrogen peroxide

Class 6.1: Toxic substances.

Toxic, poison substances

Known to be toxic to humans so as to afford a hazard to health during transportation or is presumed to be toxic to humans because it falls within a toxic category when tested on laboratory animals.

An irritating material such as tear gas that causes extreme irritation, especially in confined spaces.

Class 6.2: Infectious substances.

Infectious Substance material is known to contain or suspected of containing a pathogen

3.6.2.1 Definitions

For the purposes of these Regulations:

3.6.2.1.1 Infectious substances are substances which are known or are reasonably expected to contain pathogens. Pathogens are defined as microorganisms (including bacteria, viruses, rickettsiae, parasites, fungi) and other agents such as prions, which can cause disease in humans or animals.

Note: Toxins from plant, animal or bacterial sources which do not contain any infectious substances or toxins that are not contained in substances which are infectious substances should be considered for classification in Division 6.1 and assigned to UN3172.

3.6.2.1.2 Biological products are those products derived from living organisms, which are manufactured and distributed in accordance with the requirements of appropriate national authorities, which may have special licensing requirements, and are used either for prevention, treatment, or diagnosis of disease in humans or animals, or for development, experimental or investigational purposes related thereto. They include, but are not limited to, finished or unfinished products such as vaccines.

3.6.2.1.3 Cultures are the result of a process by which pathogens are intentionally. This definition does not include patient specimens as defined in 3.6.2.1.4.

3.6.2.1.4 Patient specimens are those collected directly from humans or animals, including, but not limited to, excreta, secreta, blood and its components, tissue and tissue fluid swabs, and body parts being transported for purposes such as research, diagnosis, investigational activities, disease treatment and prevention.

3.6.2.1.5 Medical or clinical wastes are wastes derived from the medical treatment of animals or humans or from bioresearch.

3.6.2.2 Classification of Infectious Substances

3.6.2.2.1 Infectious substances must be classified in Division 6.2 and assigned to UN2814, UN2900, UN 3291 or UN3373, as appropriate.

3.6.2.2.2 Infectious substances are divided into the following categories.

3.6.2.2.2.1 Category A:

An infectious substance, which is transported in a form, that, when exposure to it occurs, is capable of causing permanent disability, life-threatening or fatal disease in otherwise healthy humans or animals. Indicative examples of substances that meet these criteria are given in Table 3.6.D.

Note: An exposure occurs when an infectious substance is released outside of the protective packaging, resulting in physical contact with humans or animals.

(a) Infectious substances meeting these criteria which cause disease in humans or both in humans and animals must be assigned to UN 2814. Infectious substances which cause disease only in animals must be assigned to UN 2900.

(b) Assignment to UN 2814 or UN 2900 must be based on the known medical history and symptoms of the source human or animal, endemic local conditions, or professional judgment concerning individual circumstances of the source human or animal.

Notes:

1. The proper shipping name for UN 2814 is Infectious substance, affecting humans. The proper shipping name for UN 2900 is Infectious substance, affecting animals only.

2. The following table is not exhaustive. Infectious substances, including new or emerging pathogens, which do not appear in the table, but which meet the same criteria must be assigned to Category A. In addition, if there is doubt as to whether or not a substance meets the criteria it must be included in Category A.

3. In the following list, the microorganisms written in italics are bacteria, mycoplasma, rickettsia or fungi.

Bacillus anthracis (cultures only)

Infectious substance

Brucella abortus (cultures only)

Brucella melitensis (cultures only)

Brucella suis (cultures only)

Burkholderia mallei – Pseudomonas mallei – Glanders (cultures only)

Burkholderia pseudomallei – Pseudomonas pseudomallei (cultures only)

Chlamydia psittaci – avian strains (cultures only)

Clostridium botulinum (cultures only)

Coccidioides immitis (cultures only)

Coxiella burnetii (cultures only)

Crimean-Congo hemorrhagic fever virus

Dengue virus (cultures only)

Eastern equine encephalitis virus (cultures only)

Escherichia coli, verotoxigenic (cultures only)

Ebola virus

Flexal virus

Francisella tularensis (cultures only)

Guanarito virus

Hantaan virus

Hantavirus causing hemorrhagic fever with renal syndrome

Hendra virus

Hepatitis B virus (cultures only)

Herpes B virus (cultures only)

Human immunodeficiency virus (cultures only)

Highly pathogenic avian influenza virus (cultures only)

Japanese Encephalitis virus (cultures only)

Junin virus

Kyasanur Forest disease virus

Lassa virus

Machupo virus

Marburg virus

Monkeypox virus

Mycobacterium tuberculosis (cultures only)

Nipah virus

Omsk hemorrhagic fever virus

Poliovirus (cultures only)

Rabies virus

Rickettsia prowazekii (cultures only) Rickettsia rickettsii (cultures only) Rift Valley fever virus

Russian spring-summer encephalitis virus (cultures only) Sabia virus

Shigella dysenteriae type 1 (cultures only)

Tick-borne encephalitis virus (cultures only) Variola virus

Venezuelan equine encephalitis virus

West Nile virus (cultures only)

Yellow fever virus (cultures only)

Yersinia pestis (cultures only)

African swine fever virus (cultures only)

Avian paramyxovirus Type 1 – Velogenic Newcastle disease virus (cultures only) Classical swine fever virus (cultures only) Foot and mouth disease virus (cultures only)

Goatpox virus (cultures only)

Lumpy skin disease virus (cultures only)

Mycoplasma mycoides – Contagious bovine pleuropneumonia (cultures only)

Peste des petits ruminants virus (cultures only)

Rinderpest virus (cultures only)

Sheep-pox virus (cultures only)

Swine vesicular disease virus (cultures only)

Vesicular stomatitis virus (cultures only)

3.6.2.2.2.2 Category B:

An infectious substance which does not meet the criteria for inclusion in Category A. Infectious substances in Category B must be assigned to UN 3373.

Note: The proper shipping name of UN 3373 is Diagnostic specimens or Clinical specimens or Biological substance, category B. On 1 January 2007, it is anticipated that the use of the shipping names Diagnostic specimens and Clinical specimens will no longer be permitted.

3.6.2.2.3 Exemptions

3.6.2.2.3.1 Substances which do not contain infectious substances or substances which are unlikely to cause disease in humans or animals are not subject to these Regulations unless they meet the criteria for inclusion in another class.

3.6.2.2.3.2 Substances containing microorganisms which are non-pathogenic to humans or animals are not subject to these Regulations unless they meet the criteria for inclusion in another class.

3.6.2.2.3.3 Substances in a form that any present pathogens have been neutralized or inactivated such that they no longer pose a health risk are not subject to these Regulations unless they meet the criteria for inclusion in another class.

3.6.2.2.3.4 Environmental samples (including food and water samples) which are not considered to pose a significant risk of infection are not subject to these Regulations unless they meet the criteria for inclusion in another class.

3.6.2.2.3.5 Dried blood spots, collected by applying a drop of blood onto absorbent material, or faecal occult blood screening tests and blood or blood components which have been collected for the purposes of transfusion or for the preparation of blood products to be used for transfusion or transplantation and any tissues or organs intended for use in transplantation are not subject to these Regulations.

3.6.2.2.3.6 Patient specimens for which there is minimal likelihood that pathogens are present are not subject to these Regulations if the specimen is packed in a packaging which will prevent any leakage and which is marked with the words "Exempt human specimen" or "Exempt animal specimen", as appropriate. The packaging must meet the following conditions:

(a) The packaging must consist of three components:

(i) a leak-proof primary receptacle(s);

(ii) a leak-proof secondary packaging; and

(iii) an outer packaging of adequate strength for its capacity, mass and intended use, and with at least one surface having minimum dimensions of 100 mm × 100 mm;

(b) For liquids, absorbent material in sufficient quantity to absorb the entire contents must be placed between the primary receptacle(s) and the secondary packaging so that, during transport, any release or leak of a liquid substance will not reach the outer packaging and will not compromise the integrity of the cushioning material;

(c) When multiple fragile primary receptacles are placed in a single secondary packaging, they must be either individually wrapped or separated to prevent contact between them..

NOTE: In determining whether a patient specimen has a minimum likelihood that pathogens are present, an element of professional judgment is required to determine if a substance is exempt under this paragraph. That judgment should be based on the known medical history, symptoms and individual circumstances of the source, human or animal, and endemic local conditions.

Examples of specimens which may be transported under this paragraph include the blood or urine tests to monitor cholesterol levels, blood glucose levels, hormone levels, or prostate specific antigens (PSA); those required to monitor organ function such as heart, liver or kidney function for humans or animals with non-infectious diseases, or therapeutic drug monitoring; those conducted for insurance or employment purposes and are intended to determine the presence of drugs or alcohol; pregnancy test; biopsies to detect cancer; and antibody detection in humans or animals.

3.6.2.3 Biological Products

3.6.2.3.1 For the purposes of these Regulations, biological products are divided into the following groups:

(a) those which are manufactured and packaged in accordance with the requirements of appropriate national authorities and transported for the purposes of final packaging or distribution, and use for personal health care by medical professionals or individuals. Substances in this group are not subject to these Regulations

(b) those which do not fall under paragraph (a) and are known or reasonably believed to contain infectious substances and which meet the criteria for inclusion in Category A or Category B. Substances in this group must be assigned to UN2814, UN2900 or UN3373, as appropriate.

Note: Some licensed biological products may present a biohazard only in certain parts of the world. In that case, competent authorities may require these biological products to be in compliance with local requirements for infectious substances or may impose other restrictions.

3.6.2.4 Genetically Modified Microorganisms and Organisms

3.6.2.4.1 Genetically modified microorganisms not meeting the definition of an infectious substance must be classified according to Subsection 3.9.

3.6.2.5 Medical or Clinical Wastes

3.6.2.5.1 Medical or clinical wastes containing Category A infectious substances must be assigned to UN2814 or UN2900, as appropriate. Medical or clinical wastes containing infectious substances in Category B, must be assigned to UN3291.

3.6.2.5.2 Medical or clinical wastes which are reasonably believed to have a low probability of containing infectious substances must be assigned to UN3291. Note: The proper shipping name for UN3291 is Clinical waste, unspecified, n.o.s. or (Bio) Medical waste, n.o.s. or Regulated medical waste, n.o.s..

3.6.2.5.3 Decontaminated medical or clinical wastes which previously contained infectious substances arc not subject to these Regulations unless they meet the criteria for inclusion in another class.

3.6.2.6 Infected Animals

3.6.2.6.1 A live animal that has been intentionally infected and is known or suspected to contain an infectious substance must not be transported by air unless the infectious substance contained cannot be consigned by any other means. Infected animals may only be transported under terms and conditions approved by the appropriate national authority.

3.6.2.6.2 Unless an infectious substance cannot be consigned by any other means, live animals must not be used to consign such a substance.

3.6.2.6.3 Animal carcasses affected by pathogens of category A or which would be assigned to category A in cultures only, must be assigned to UN 2814 or UN 2900 as appropriate. Other animal carcasses affected by pathogens included in Category B must be transported in accordance with provisions determined by the competent authority.

3.6.2.7 Patient Specimens Patient specimens must be assigned to UN 2814, UN 2900 or UN 3373 as appropriate except if they comply with 3.6.2.2.3

Class 7: Radioactive Substances.

Radioactives

Any quantity of packages bearing the RADIOACTIVE YELLOW III label (LSA-III). Some radioactive materials in "exclusive use" with low specific activity radioactive materials will not bear the label, however, the RADIOACTIVE placard is required.

Closed transport vehicle means a transport vehicle or conveyance equipped with a securely attached exterior enclosure that during normal transportation restricts the access of unauthorized persons to the cargo space containing the Class 7 (radioactive) materials. The enclosure may be either temporary or permanent, and in the case of packaged materials may be of the "see-through" type, and must limit access from top, sides, and bottom.

Containment system means the assembly of components of the packaging intended to retain the radioactive contents during transportation.

Conveyance means:

1. For transport by public highway or rail: any transport vehicle or large freight container;

2. For transport by water: any vessel, or any hold, compartment, or defined deck area of a vessel including any transport vehicle on board the vessel; and

3. For transport by aircraft, any aircraft.

Design means the description of a special form Class 7 (radioactive) material, a package, packaging, or LSA-III, that enables those items to be fully identified. The description may include specifications, engineering drawings, reports showing compliance with regulatory requirements, and other relevant documentation.

Exclusive use (also referred to in other regulations as "sole use" or "full load") means sole use by a single consignor of a conveyance for which all initial, intermediate, and final loading and unloading are carried out in accordance with the direction of the consignor or consignee. The consignor and the carrier must ensure that any loading or unloading is performed by personnel having radiological training and resources appropriate for safe handling of the consignment. The consignor must issue specific instructions in writing, for maintenance of exclusive use shipment controls, and include them with the shipping paper information provided to the carrier by the consignor.

Fissile material means plutonium-238, plutonium-239, plutonium-241, uranium-233, uranium-235, or any combination of these radionuclides. The definition does not apply to unirradiated natural uranium and depleted uranium, and natural uranium or depleted uranium that has been irradiated in a thermal reactor. Certain additional exceptions are provided in 49CFR 173.453.

Fissile material, controlled shipment means any shipment that contains one or more packages that have been assigned, in accordance with 49CFR 173.457, nuclear criticality control transport indices greater than 10.

Freight container means a reusable container having a volume of 1.81 cubic meters (64 cubic feet) or more, designed and constructed to permit its being lifted with its contents intact and intended primarily for containment of packages in unit form during transportation. A "small freight container" is one which has either one outer dimension less than 1.5 meters (4.9 feet) or an internal volume of not more than 3.0 cubic meters (106 cubic feet). All other freight containers are designated as "large freight containers."

Highway route controlled quantity means a quantity within a single package which exceeds:

1. 3,000 times the A1 value of the radionuclides as specified in 49CFR 173.435 for special form Class 7 (radioactive) material;

2. 3,000 times the A2 value of the radionuclides as specified in 49CFR 173.435 for normal form Class 7 (radioactive) material; or

3. 1,000 TBq (27,000 Ci), whichever is least.

Limited quantity of Class 7 (radioactive) material means a quantity of Class 7 (radioactive) material not exceeding the materials package limits specified in 49CFR 173.425 and conforming with requirements specified in 49CFR 173.421.

Low Specific Activity (LSA) material means Class 7 (radioactive) material with limited specific activity which satisfies the descriptions and limits set forth below. Shielding materials surrounding the LSA material may not be considered in determining the estimated average specific activity of the package contents.

Class 8: Corrosives.

Corrosives

1. For the purpose of this subchapter "corrosive materials" (Class 8) means a liquid or solid that causes full thickness destruction of human skin at the site of contact within a specified period of time. A liquid that has a severe corrosion rate on steel or aluminum is also a corrosive material.

2. If human experience or other data indicate that the hazard of a material is greater or less than indicated by the results of the tests specified in paragraph (a) of this section, RSPA may revise its classification or make the determination that the material is not subject to the requirements of this subchapter.

3. Skin corrosion test data produced no later than September 30, 1995, using the procedures of 49CFR 173, Appendix A, in effect on September 30, 1995 (see 49CFR Part 173, Appendix A, revised as of October 1, 1994) for appropriate exposure times may be used for classification and assignment of packing group for Class 8 materials corrosive to skin.

454 kg (1001 lbs.) or more gross weight of a corrosive material. Although the corrosive class includes both acids and bases, the hazardous materials load and segregation chart does not make any reference to the separation of various incompatible corrosive materials from each other. In spite of this, however, when shipping corrosives care should be taken to ensure that incompatible corrosive materials cannot become mixed as many corrosives react very violently if mixed. If responding to a transportation incident involving corrosive materials (especially a mixture of

corrosives), caution should be exercised.

Class 9: Miscellaneous dangerous substances and articles.

Miscellaneous

A material which presents a hazard during transportation but which does not meet the definition of any other hazard class. This class includes:

1. Any material which has an anesthetic, noxious or other similar property which could cause extreme annoyance or discomfort to a flight crew member so as to prevent the correct performance of assigned duties; or

2. Any material for an elevated temperature material, a hazardous substance, a hazardous waste, or a marine pollutant.

Appendix D - INCO Terms

What are INCO Terms? How and why are they used?

When negotiating an international sales contract, the Terms of Sale can be just as important as the sale price. Language barriers could complicate this point. Since 1936 the INCO Terms created by the International Chamber of Commerce (ICC) have been used to break down these barriers.

INternational **CO**mmerce Terminology (**INCO** Terms) defines exactly the shipping responsibilities of both the buyer and the seller. This table illustrates the cost responsibilities for each party –

WHAT INCOTERMS DO

INCOTERMS inform the sales contract by defining the respective obligations, costs and risks involved in the delivery of goods from the seller to the buyer.

WHAT INCOTERMS DO NOT DO

INCOTERMS by themselves DO NOT:

Constitute a contract;

Supersede the law governing the contract;

Define where title transfers; nor,

Address the price payable, currency or credit terms.

These items are defined by the express terms in the sales contract and by the governing law.

INCOTERMS ® 2020 Rules Responsibility Quick Reference Guide

Groups	Freight Collect Terms						Freight Prepaid Terms				
	Anymode or Modes of transport		Sea and Inland Waterway Transport				Any Mode or Modes of Transport				
Incoterm ®	EXW	FCA	FAS	FOB	CFR	CIF	CPT	CIP	DAP	DPU	DDP
	Ex Works (Place)	Free Carrier (Place)	Free Alongside Ship (Port)	Free on Board (Port)	Cost and Freight (Port)	Cost, Insurance & Freight (Port)	Carriage Paid to (Place)	Carriage & Insurance Paid to (Place)	Delivered at Place (Place)	Delivered at Place Unloaded (Place)	Delivered Duty Paid (Place)
Transfer of Risk	At buyers Disposal	On Buyer's Transport	Alongside Ship	On Board Vessel	On Board Vessel	On Board Vessel	At Carrier	At Carrier	At Named Place	At Named Placed Unloaded	At Named Place
Obligations & Charges:											
Export Packaging	Seller	Seller	Seller	Seller	Seller	Seller	Seller	Seller	Seller	Seller	Seller
Loading Charges	Buyer	Seller	Seller	Seller	Seller	Seller	Seller	Seller	Seller	Seller	Seller
Delivery to Port/Place	Buyer	Seller	Seller	Seller	Seller	Seller	Seller	Seller	Seller	Seller	Seller
Export Duty, Taxes & Customs Clearance	Buyer	Seller	Seller	Seller	Seller	Seller	Seller	Seller	Seller	Seller	Seller
Original Terminal Charges	Buyer	Buyer	Seller	Seller	Seller	Seller	Seller	Seller	Seller	Seller	Seller
Loading on Carriage	Buyer	Buyer	Buyer	Seller	Seller	Seller	Seller	Seller	Seller	Seller	Seller
Carriage Charges	Buyer	Buyer	Buyer	Buyer	Seller	Seller	Seller	Seller	Seller	Seller	Buyer
Insurance	Negotiable	Negotiable	Negotiable	Negotiable	Negotiable	*Seller	Negotiable	**Seller	Negotiable	Negotiable	Negotiable
Destination Terminal Charges	Buyer	Buyer	Buyer	Buyer	Buyer	Buyer	Seller	Seller	Seller	Seller	Seller
Delivery to Destination	Buyer	Buyer	Buyer	Buyer	Buyer	Buyer	Buyer	Buyer	Seller	Seller	Seller
Unloading at Destination	Buyer	Buyer	Buyer	Buyer	Buyer	Buyer	Buyer	Buyer	Buyer	Seller	Buyer
Import Duty, Taxes & Customs Clearance	Buyer	Buyer	Buyer	Buyer	Buyer	Buyer	Buyer	Buyer	Buyer	Buyer	Seller

*CIF requires at least an Insurance with the minimum cover of the Institute Cargo Clause (C) (Number of listed risks, subject to itemized exclusions)

**CIP now requires at least an Insurance with the minimum cover of the Institute Cargo Clause (A) (All risk, subject to itemized exclusions)

Appendix D - INCO Terms

THE ELEVEN INCOTERMS® 2020 RULES—
"SEA AND INLAND WATERWAY" AND "ANY MODE(S) OF
TRANSPORT": GETTING IT RIGHT

The main distinction introduced in the Incoterms® 2010 rules, that between Rules for any Mode or Modes of Transport (comprising EXW, FCA, CPT, CIP, DAP, the newly named INCOTERMS® 2020

10 | INTERNATIONAL CHAMBER OF COMMERCE (ICC) DPU—the old DAT—and DDP), and Rules for Sea and Inland Waterway Transport, (comprising FAS, FOB, CFR and CIF) has bccn retained.

The four so-called "maritime" Incoterms® rules are intended for use where the seller places the goods on board (or in FAS alongside) a vessel at a sea or river port. It is at this point that the seller delivers the goods to the buyer. When these rules are used, the risk of loss of or damage to those goods is on the buyer's shoulders from that port.

The seven Incoterms® rules for any mode or modes of transport (so-called "multi-modal"), on the other hand, are intended for use where:

a)   the point at which the seller hands the goods over to, or places them at the disposal of, a carrier, or
b)   the point at which the carrier hands the goods over to the buyer, or the point at which they are placed at the disposal of the buyer, or
c)   both points (a) and (b) are not on board (or in FAS alongside) a vessel.

Where delivery happens and risk transfers in each of these seven Incoterms® rules will depend on which particular rule is used. For example, in CPT, delivery happens at the seller's end when the goods are handed over to the carrier contracted by the seller. In DAP, on the other hand, delivery happens when the goods are placed at the buyer's disposal at the named place or point of destination.

The order in which the Incoterms® 2010 rules were presented has, as we have said, been largely retained in Incoterms® 2020 and it is important to underline the distinction between the two families of Incoterms® rules so that the right rule is used for the contract of sale depending on the means of transport used.

One of the most frequent problems in the use of the Incoterms® rules is the choice of the wrong rule for the particular type of contract.

Thus, for example, an FOB inland point (for example an airport or a warehouse) sale contract makes little sense: what type of contract of carriage must the buyer make? Does the buyer owe the seller an obligation to make a contract of carriage under which the carrier is bound to take over the goods at the named inland point or at the nearest port to that point?

Again, a CIF named sea port sale contract where the buyer expects the goods to be brought to an inland point in the buyer's country makes little sense. Must the seller procure a contract of carriage and insurance cover to the eventual inland destination intended by the parties or to the seaport named in the sale contract?

INCOTERMS® 2020
11 | INTERNATIONAL CHAMBER OF COMMERCE (ICC)

Gaps, overlaps and unnecessary costs are likely to arise—and all this because the wrong Incoterms® rule has been chosen for the particular contract. What makes the mismatch "wrong" is that insufficient regard has been given to the two most important features of the Incoterms® rules, features which are mirrors of each other, namely the port, place or point of delivery and the transfer of risks.

The reason for the frequent misuse of the wrong Incoterms® rule is that Incoterms® rules are frequently regarded exclusively as price indicators: this or that is the EXW, FOB, or DAP price. The initials used in the Incoterms® rules are doubtless handy abbreviations for the formula used in the calculation of the price. Incoterms® rules are not, however, exclusively, or even primarily, price indicators. They are a list of general obligations that sellers and buyers owe each other under well-recognized forms of sale contract—and one of their main tasks is to indicate the port, place or point of delivery where the risk is transferred.

VIII. ORDER WITHIN THE INCOTERMS® 2020 RULES

All the ten A/B articles in each of the Incoterms® rules are important—but some are more important than others.

There has, indeed, been a radical shake-up in the internal order in which the ten articles within each Incoterms® rule have been organized. In Incoterms® 2020, the internal order within each Incoterms® rule now follows this sequence:

A1/B1 General obligations
A2/B2 Delivery/Taking delivery
A3/B3 Transfer of risks
A4/B4 Carriage
A5/B5 Insurance
A6/B6 Delivery/transport document
A7/B7 Export/import clearance
A8/B8 Checking/packaging/marking
A9/B9 Allocation of costs
A10/B10 Notices

It will be noticed that concerning the Incoterms® 2020 rules, after recording in A1/B1 the basic goods/payment obligations of the parties, Delivery and the Transfer of risks are moved to a more prominent location, namely to A2 and A3 respectively.

The broad sequence thereafter goes:
 ancillary contracts (A4/B4 and A5/B5, carriage and insurance); transport documents (A6/B6);

` export/import clearance (A7/B7);
` packaging (A8/B8);
` costs (A9/B9); and
` notices (A10/B10).

It is appreciated that this change in the order of the A/B articles will take some time—and cost—to become familiar. It is hoped that with delivery and risk now made more prominent, traders will find it easier to identify the differences among the various Incoterms® rules, i.e. the different points in time and place at which the seller "delivers" the goods to the buyer with risk transferring to the buyer from that time and point.

For the first time, the Incoterms® rules are published both in the traditional format setting out the eleven Incoterms® rules and in a new "horizontal" format setting out the ten articles within each Incoterms® rule under each of the headings listed above in paragraph 53, first for the seller and then for the buyer.

Traders can therefore now far more easily see the difference, for example, between the place of delivery in FCA and the place of delivery in DAP; or the items of cost which fall on a buyer in CIF when compared with the items of cost which fall on a buyer in CFR. It is hoped that this "horizontal" representation of the Incoterms® 2020 rules will further assist traders in choosing the Incoterms® rule most appropriate to their commercial requirements.

IX. DIFFERENCES BETWEEN INCOTERMS® 2010 AND 2020

The most important initiative behind the Incoterms® 2020 rules has been to focus on how the presentation could be enhanced to steer users towards the right Incoterms® rule for their sale contract. Thus:

a)   a greater emphasis in this Introduction on making the right choice;
b)   a clearer explanation of the demarcation and connection between the sale contract and its ancillary contracts;
c)   upgraded Guidance Notes presented now as Explanatory Notes to each Incoterms® rule; and
d)   a re-ordering within the Incoterms® rules giving delivery and risk more prominence.

All these changes, though cosmetic in appearance, are in reality substantial attempts on the part of ICC to assist the international trading community towards smoother export/ import transactions.

Apart from these general changes, there are more substantive changes in the Incoterms® 2020 rules when compared with Incoterms® 2010. Before looking at those changes, mention
must be made of a particular development in trade practice

INCOTERMS® 2020

INTERNATIONAL CHAMBER OF COMMERCE (ICC) |
13 | Which occurred since 2010 and which ICC has decided should not lead to a change in the Incoterms® 2020 rules, namely
Verified Gross Mass (VGM).

Note on Verified Gross Mass (VGM)—Since 1 July 2016, Regulation 2 under the International Convention for the Safety of Life at Sea (SOLAS) imposed on shippers in the case of the shipment of containers the obligation either to weigh the packed container using calibrated and certified equipment, or to weigh the contents of the container and add the weight
of the container when empty. In either case, the VGM is to be recorded with the carrier. A failure to comply bears the sanction under the SOLAS Convention that the container "should not be loaded onto a ship": see paragraph 4.2, MSC1/Circ.1475, 9 June 2014.

These weighing operations obviously incur expense and failure may lead to delay in loading. As this happened after 2010, it is unsurprising that there was some pressure in the consultations
leading to Incoterms® 2020 for a clear indication to be given as to who, as between seller and buyer, should bear such obligations.

It was felt by the Drafting Group that obligations and costs relating to VGM were too specific and complex to warrant explicit mention in the Incoterms® 2020 rules.

Returning to the changes made by ICC to the Incoterms® 2010 rules in the Incoterms® 2020 rules, these are:

[a] Bills of lading with an on-board notation and the FCA Incoterms® rule
[b] Costs, where they are listed
[c] Different levels of insurance cover in CIF and CIP
[d] Arranging for carriage with seller's or buyer's own
means of transport in FCA, DAP, DPU and DDP
[e] Change in the three-letter initials for DAT to DPU
[f] Inclusion of security-related requirements within carriage obligations and costs
[g] Explanatory Notes for Users
[a] Bills of lading with an on-board notation and the FCA Incoterms® rule

Where goods are sold FCA for carriage by sea, sellers or buyers (or more likely their banks where a letter of credit is in place) might want a bill of lading with an on-board notation.

However, delivery under the FCA rule is completed before the loading of the goods on board the vessel. It is by no means certain that the seller can obtain an on-board bill of lading from the carrier. That carrier is likely, under its contract of carriage, to be bound and entitled to issue an on-board bill of lading only once the goods are actually on board.

INCOTERMS® 2020

14 | INTERNATIONAL CHAMBER OF COMMERCE (ICC)

To cater for this situation, FCA A6/B6 of Incoterms® 2020 now provides for an additional option. The buyer and the seller can agree that the buyer will instruct its carrier to issue an on-board bill of lading to the seller after the loading of the goods, the seller then being obliged to tender that bill of lading to the buyer, typically through the banks. ICC recognises that, despite
this somewhat unhappy union between an on-board bill of lading and FCA delivery, this caters for a demonstrated need in the marketplace. Finally, it should be emphasised that even where this optional mechanism is adopted, the seller is under no obligation to the buyer as to the terms of the contract of carriage.

Does it remain true to say that where containerised goods are delivered by seller to buyer by handing over to a carrier before loading onto a ship, the seller is well advised to sell on FCA
terms rather than on FOB terms? The answer to that question is Yes. Where Incoterms® 2020 have made a difference, however, is that where such a seller still wants or needs a bill of lading with an on-board notation, the new additional option in the FCA term A6/B6 makes provision for such a document.

[b] Costs, where they are listed

In the new ordering of the articles within the Incoterms® 2020 rules, costs now appear at A9/B9 of each Incoterms® rule.
Apart from that re-location, however, there is another change that will become obvious to users early on. The various costs which fall to be allocated by various articles within the Incoterms® rules have traditionally appeared in different parts of each Incoterms® rule. Thus, for example, costs related to the obtaining of a delivery document in FOB 2010 were mentioned in A8, the article under the heading "Delivery Document", but not in A6, the article under the heading "Allocation of Costs".

In the Incoterms® 2020 rules, however, the equivalent of A6/B6, namely A9/B9, now lists all the costs allocated by each particular Incoterms® rule. A9/B9 in the Incoterms® 2020 rules
are consequently longer than A6/B6 in the Incoterms® 2010 rules.

The purpose is to provide users with a one-stop list of costs, so that the seller or buyer can now find in one place all the costs for which it would be responsible under that particular Incoterms® rule. Items of cost are also mentioned in their home article: thus, for example, the costs involved in obtaining documents in FOB still also appear at A6/B6 as well as at A9/B9. The thinking here was that users interested in discovering the specific allocation of documentary costs might be more inclined to go to the specific article dealing with delivery documents rather than to the general article listing all the costs.

INCOTERMS® 2020

15 | INTERNATIONAL CHAMBER OF COMMERCE (ICC)

[c] Different levels of insurance cover in CIF and CIP

In the Incoterms® 2010 rules, A3 of both CIF and CIP imposed on the seller the obligation to "obtain at its own expense cargo insurance complying at least with the minimum cover as provided by Clauses (C) of the Institute Cargo Clauses (Lloyd's Market Association/International Underwriting Association 'LMA/IUA') or any similar clauses." Institute Cargo Clauses (C) provide cover for a number of listed risks, subject to itemised exclusions; Institute Cargo Clauses (A), on the other hand, cover "all risks", again subject to itemized exclusions. During the consultations leading to the Incoterms® 2020 rules, the case was made for moving from Institute Cargo Clauses (C) to Institute Cargo Clauses (A), thus increasing the cover obtained by the seller for the benefit of the buyer. This could, of course, also involve an additional cost in premium. The contrary case, namely to stay with Institute Cargo Clauses (C), was equally strongly put, particularly by those involved in the maritime trade of commodities. After considerable discussion within and beyond the Drafting Group, the decision was made to provide for different minimum cover in the CIF Incoterms® rule and in the CIP Incoterms® rule. In the first, which is much more likely to be used in the maritime commodity trades, the status quo has been retained, with Institute Cargo Clauses (C) as the default position, although it is, of course, open to the parties to agree to higher cover. In the second, namely the CIP Incoterms® rule, the seller must now obtain insurance cover complying with Institute Cargo Clauses (A), although it is, of course, again open to the parties to agree on a lower level of cover.

[d] Arranging for carriage with seller's or buyer's own means of transport in FCA, DAP, DPU and DDP

In the Incoterms® 2010 rules, it was assumed throughout that where the goods were to be carried from the seller to the buyer, they would be carried by a third-party carrier engaged for the purpose either by the seller or the buyer, depending on which Incoterms® rule was used.

It became clear in the deliberations leading to Incoterms® 2020, however, that there were some situations where, although the goods were to be carried from the seller to the buyer, they could be so carried without any third-party carrier being engaged at all. Thus, for example, there was nothing stopping a seller on a D rule from arranging for such carriage without outsourcing that function to a third party, namely by using its own means of transportation. Likewise, with an FCA purchase, there was nothing to stop the buyer from using its own vehicle for the collection of the goods and for their transport to the buyer's premises.

INCOTERMS® 2020

16 | INTERNATIONAL CHAMBER OF COMMERCE (ICC)

The rules appeared not to take account of these eventualities.

The Incoterms® 2020 rules now do, by expressly allowing not only for the making of a contract of carriage, but also for simply arranging for the necessary carriage.

[e] Change in the three-letter initials for DAT to DPU

The only difference between DAT and DAP in the Incoterms® 2010 rules was that in DAT the seller delivered the goods once unloaded from the arriving means of transport into a "terminal"; whereas in DAP, the seller delivered the goods when the goods were placed at the disposal of the buyer on the arriving means of transport for unloading. It will also be recalled that the Guidance Note for DAT in Incoterms® 2010 defined the word "terminal" broadly to include "any place, whether covered or not…".

ICC decided to make two changes to DAT and DAP. First, the order in which the two Incoterms® 2020 rules are presented has been inverted, and DAP, where delivery happens before unloading, now appears before DAT. Secondly, the name of the rule DAT has been changed to DPU (Delivered at Place Unloaded), emphasizing the reality that the place of destination could be any place and not only a "terminal". However, if that place is not in a terminal, the seller should make sure that the place where it intends to deliver the goods is a place where it is able to unload the goods.

[f] Inclusion of security-related requirements within carriage obligations and costs

It will be recalled that security-related requirements made a rather subdued entry into the Incoterms® 2010 rules, through A2/B2 and A10/B10 in each rule. The Incoterms® 2010 rules were the first revision of the Incoterms® rules to come into force after security-related concerns became so prevalent in the early part of this century. Those concerns, and the associated shipping practices which they have created in their wake, are now much more established. Connected as they are to carriage requirements, an express allocation of security-related obligations has now been added to A4 and A7 of each Incoterms® rule. The costs incurred by these requirements are also now given a more prominent position in the costs article, namely A9/B9.

[g] Explanatory Notes for Users

The Guidance Notes appearing at the start of each Incoterms® rule in the 2010 version now appear as "Explanatory Notes for Users". These Notes explain the fundamentals of each Incoterms® 2020 rule, such as when it should be used, when risk transfers and how costs are allocated between seller and buyer. The Explanatory Notes are intended (a) to help the user accurately and efficiently steer towards the appropriate

INCOTERMS® 2020
17 | INTERNATIONAL CHAMBER OF COMMERCE (ICC)
Incoterms® rule for a particular transaction; and (b) to provide those deciding or advising on disputes or contracts governed by Incoterms® 2020 with guidance on matters which might require interpretation.

CFR - Cost and Freight (... named port of destination)

«Cost and Freight» means that the seller delivers when the goods pass the ship's rail in the port of shipment. The seller must pay the costs and freight necessary to bring the goods to the named port of destination BUT the risk of loss of or damage to the goods, as well as any additional costs due to events occurring after the time of delivery, are transferred from the seller to the buyer.

The CFR term requires the seller to clear the goods for export. This term can be used only for sea and inland waterway transport. If the parties do not intend to deliver the goods across the ship's rail, the **CPT** term should be used.

THE SELLER'S OBLIGATIONS	THE BUYER'S OBLIGATIONS

A1 Provision of goods in conformity with the contract

The seller must provide the goods and the commercial invoice, or its equivalent electronic message, in conformity with the contract of sale and any other evidence of conformity which may be required by the contract.

A2 Licenses, authorizations and formalities

The seller must obtain at his own risk and expense any export license or other official authorization and carry out, where applicable (Refer to Introduction paragraph 14) , all customs formalities necessary for the export of the goods.

A3 Contracts of carriage and insurance

a) Contract of carriage

The seller must contract on usual terms at his own expense for the carriage of the goods to the named port of destination by the usual route in a seagoing vessel (or inland waterway vessel as the case may be) of the type normally used for the transport of goods of the contract description.

b) Contract of insurance

No obligation (Refer to Introduction paragraph 10)

A4 Delivery

The seller must deliver the goods on board the vessel at the port of shipment on the date or within the agreed period.

A5 Transfer of risks

B1 Payment of the price

The buyer must pay the price as provided in the contract of sale.

B2 Licenses, authorizations and formalities

The buyer must obtain at his own risk and expense any import license or other official authorization and carry out, where applicable (Refer to Introduction paragraph 14), , all customs formalities for the import of the goods and for their transit through any country.

B3 Contracts of carriage and insurance

a) Contract of carriage

No obligation (Refer to Introduction paragraph 10)

b) Contract of insurance

No obligation (Refer to Introduction paragraph 10)

B4 Taking delivery

The buyer must accept delivery of the goods when they have been delivered in accordance with A4 and receive them from the carrier at the named port of destination.

B5 Transfer of risks

The seller must, subject to the provisions of B5, bear all risks of loss of or damage to the goods until such time as they have passed the ship's rail at the port of shipment.

The buyer must bear all risks of loss of or damage to the goods from the time they have passed the ship's rail at the port of shipment.

The buyer must, should he fail to give notice in accordance with B7, bear all risks of loss of or damage to the goods from the agreed date or the expiry date of the period fixed for shipment provided, however, that the goods have been duly appropriated to the contract, that is to say, clearly set aside or otherwise identified as the contract goods.

A6 Division of costs

The seller must, subject to the provisions of B6, pay

- all costs relating to the goods until such time as they have been delivered in accordance with A4; and

- the freight and all other costs resulting from A3 a), including the costs of loading the goods on board and any charges for unloading at the agreed port of discharge which were for the seller's account under the contract of carriage;

- where applicable (Refer to Introduction paragraph 14), the costs of customs formalities necessary for export as well as all duties, taxes and other charges payable upon export, and for their transit through any country if they were for the seller's account under the contract of carriage.

B6 Division of costs

The buyer must, subject to the provisions of A3 a), pay

all costs relating to the goods from the time they have been delivered in accordance with A4; and

- all costs and charges relating to the goods whilst in transit until their arrival at the port of destination, unless such costs and charges were for the seller's account under the contract of carriage; and

- unloading costs including lighterage and wharfage charges, unless such costs and charges were for the seller's account under the contract of carriage; and• all additional costs incurred if he fails to give notice in accordance with B7, for the goods from the agreed date or the expiry date of the period fixed for shipment, provided, however, that the goods have been duly appropriated to the contract, that is to say, clearly set aside or otherwise identified as the contract goods; and

- where applicable (Refer to Introduction paragraph 14) , all duties, taxes and other charges as well as the costs of carrying out customs formalities payable upon import of the goods and, where necessary, for their transit through any country unless included within the cost of the contract of carriage.

A7 Notice to the buyer

B7 Notice to the seller

The seller must give the buyer sufficient notice that the goods have been delivered in accordance with A4 as well as any other notice required in order to allow the buyer to take measures which are normally necessary to enable him to take the goods.

The buyer must, whenever he is entitled to determine the time for shipping the goods and/or the port of destination, give the seller sufficient notice thereof.

A8 Proof of delivery, transport document or equivalent electronic message

The seller must at his own expense provide the buyer without delay with the usual transport document for the agreed port of destination.

This document (for example a negotiable bill of lading, a non-negotiable sea waybill or an inland waterway document) must cover the contract goods, be dated within the period agreed for shipment, enable the buyer to claim the goods from the carrier at the port of destination and, unless otherwise agreed, enable the buyer to sell the goods in transit by the transfer of the document to a subsequent buyer (the negotiable bill of lading) or by notification to the carrier. When such a transport document is issued in several originals, a full set of originals must be presented to the buyer.

Where the seller and the buyer have agreed to communicate electronically, the document referred to in the preceding paragraphs may be replaced by an equivalent electronic data interchange (EDI) message.

B8 Proof of delivery, transport document or equivalent electronic message

The buyer must accept the transport document in accordance with A8 if it is in conformity with the contr

A9 Checking - packaging – marking

The seller must pay the costs of those checking operations (such as checking quality, measuring, weighing, counting) which are necessary for the purpose of delivering the goods in accordance with A4.

The seller must provide at his own expense packaging (unless it is usual for the particular trade to ship the goods of the contract description unpacked) which is required for the transport of the goods arranged by him. Packaging is to be marked appropriately.

B9 Inspection of goods

The buyer must pay the costs of any pre-shipment inspection except when such inspection is mandated by the authorities of the country of export.

A10 Other obligations

B10 Other obligations

The seller must render the buyer at the latter's request, risk and expense, every assistance in obtaining any documents or equivalent electronic messages (other than those mentioned in issued or transmitted in the country of rendering his assistance in acc shipment and/or of origin which the buyer may require for the import of the goods and, where necessary, for their transit through any country.

The seller must provide the buyer, upon request, with the necessary information for procuring insurance.

The buyer must pay all costs and charges incurred in obtaining the documents or equivalent electronic messages mentioned in A10 and reimburse those incurred by the seller in

CIF - Cost, Insurance and Freight (... named port of destination)

"Cost, Insurance and Freight" means that the seller delivers when the goods pass the ship's rail in the port of shipment. The seller must pay the costs and freight necessary to bring the goods to the named port of destination BUT the risk of loss of or damage to the goods, as well as any additional costs due to events occurring after the time of delivery, are transferred from the seller to the buyer.

CIF the seller also has to procure marine insurance against the buyer's risk of loss of or damage to the goods during the carriage.

Consequently, the seller contracts for insurance and pays the insurance premium. The buyer should note that under the CIF term the seller is required to obtain insurance only on minimum cover (Refer to Introduction paragraph 9.3). Should the buyer wish to have the protection of greater cover, he would either need to agree as much expressly with the seller or to make his own extra insurance arrangements.

The CIF term requires the seller to clear the goods for export. This term can be used only for sea and inland waterway transport. If the parties do not intend to deliver the goods across the ship's rail, the **CIP** term should be used.

THE SELLER'S OBLIGATIONS	THE BUYER'S OBLIGATIONS
A1 Provision of goods in conformity with the contract	**B1 Payment of the price**
The seller must provide the goods and the commercial invoice, or its equivalent electronic message, in conformity with the contract of sale and any other evidence of conformity which may be required by the contract.	The buyer must pay the price as provided in the contract of sale.

A2 Licenses, authorizations and formalities

The seller must obtain at his own risk and expense any export license or other official authorization and carry out, where applicable (Refer to Introduction paragraph 14) , all customs formalities necessary for the export of the goods.

A3 Contracts of carriage and insurance

a) Contract of carriage

The seller must contract on usual terms at his own expense for the carriage of the goods to the named port of destination by the usual route in a seagoing vessel (or inland waterway vessel as the case may be) of the type normally used for the transport of goods of the contract description.

b) Contract of insurance

No obligation (Refer to Introduction paragraph 10)

A4 Delivery

The seller must deliver the goods on board the vessel at the port of shipment on the date or within the agreed period.

A5 Transfer of risks

The seller must, subject to the provisions of B5, bear all risks of loss of or damage to the goods until such time as they have passed the ship's rail at the port of shipment.

or damage to the goods from the time they have passed the ship's rail at the port of shipment.

A6 Division of costs

B2 Licenses, authorizations and formalities

The buyer must obtain at his own risk and expense any import license or other official authorization and carry out, where applicable (Refer to Introduction paragraph 14), all customs formalities for the import of the goods and for their transit through any country.

B3 Contracts of carriage and insurance

a) Contract of carriage

No obligation (Refer to Introduction paragraph 10)

b) Contract of insurance

No obligation (Refer to Introduction paragraph 10).

B4 Taking delivery

The buyer must accept delivery of the goods when they have been delivered in accordance with A4 and receive them from the carrier at the named port of destination.

B5 Transfer of risks

The buyer must bear all risks of loss of The buyer must, should he fail to give notice in accordance with B7, bear all risks of loss of or damage to the goods from the agreed date or the expiry date of the period fixed for shipment provided, however, that the goods have been duly appropriated to the contract, that is to say, clearly set aside or otherwise identified as the contract goods.

B6 Division of costs

The seller must, subject to the provisions of B6, pay

- all costs relating to the goods until such time as they have been delivered in accordance with A4; and

- the freight and all other costs resulting from A3 a), including the costs of loading the goods on board; and

- the costs of insurance resulting from A3 b); and

- any charges for unloading at the agreed port of discharge which were for the seller's account under the contract of carriage; and

- where applicable (Refer to Introduction paragraph 14), the costs of customs formalities necessary for export as well as all duties, taxes and other charges payable upon export, and for their transit through any country if they were for the seller's account under the contract of carriage.

The buyer must, subject to the provisions of A3, pay

- all costs relating to the goods from the time they have been delivered in accordance with A4; and

- all costs and charges relating to the goods whilst in transit until their arrival at the port of destination, unless such costs and charges were for the seller's account under the contract of carriage; and

- unloading costs including lighterage and wharfage charges, unless such costs and charges were for the seller's account under the contract of carriage; and

- all additional costs incurred if he fails to give notice in accordance with B7, for the goods from the agreed date or the expiry date of the period fixed for shipment, provided, however, that the goods have been duly appropriated to the contract, that is to say, clearly set aside or otherwise identified as the contract goods; and

- where applicable (Refer to Introduction paragraph 14), all duties, taxes and other charges as well as the costs of carrying out customs formalities payable upon import of the goods and, where necessary, for their transit through any country unless included within the cost of the contract of carriage.

A7 Notice to the buyer

The seller must give the buyer sufficient notice that the goods have been delivered in accordance with A4 as well as any other notice required in order to allow the buyer to take measures which are normally necessary to enable him to take the goods.

B7 Notice to the seller

The buyer must, whenever he is entitled to determine the time for shipping the goods and/or the port of destination, give the seller sufficient notice thereof.

A8 Proof of delivery, transport document or equivalent electronic message

B8 Proof of delivery, transport document or equivalent electronic message

The seller must, at his own expense, provide the buyer without delay with the usual transport document for the agreed port of destination.

This document (for example a negotiable bill of lading, a non-negotiable sea waybill or an inland waterway document) must cover the contract goods, be dated within the period agreed for shipment, enable the buyer to claim the goods from the carrier at the port of destination and, unless otherwise agreed, enable the buyer to sell the goods in transit by the transfer of the document to a subsequent buyer (the negotiable bill of lading) or by notification to the carrier. When such a transport document is issued in several originals, a full set of originals must be presented to the buyer. Where the seller and the buyer have agreed to communicate electronically, the document referred to in the preceding paragraphs may be replaced by an equivalent electronic data interchange (EDI) message.

The buyer must accept the transport document in accordance with A8 if it is in conformity with the contract

A9 Checking - packaging - marking

The seller must pay the costs of those checking operations (such as checking quality, measuring, weighing, counting) which are necessary for the purpose of delivering the goods in accordance with A4.

The seller must provide at his own expense packaging (unless it is usual for the particular trade to ship the goods of the contract description unpacked) which is required for the transport of the goods arranged by him. Packaging is to be marked appropriately.

B9 Inspection of goods

The buyer must pay the costs of any pre-shipment inspection except when such inspection is mandated by the authorities of the country of export.

A10 Other obligations

The seller must render the buyer at the latter's request, risk and expense, every assistance in obtaining any documents or equivalent electronic messages (other than those mentioned in A8) issued or transmitted in the country of shipment and/or of origin which the buyer may require for the import of the goods and, where necessary, for their transit through any country.

The seller must provide the buyer, upon request, with the necessary information for procuring any additional insurance.

B10 Other obligations

The buyer must pay all costs and charges incurred in obtaining the documents or equivalent electronic messages mentioned in A10 and reimburse those incurred by the seller in rendering his assistance in accordance therewith.

The buyer must provide the seller, upon request, with the necessary information for procuring insurance.

CIP - Carriage and Insurance Paid To (... named place of destination)

Carriage and Insurance paid to... means that the seller delivers the goods to the carrier nominated by him but the seller must in addition pay the cost of carriage necessary to bring the goods to the named destination. This means that the buyer bears all risks and any additional costs occurring after the goods have been so delivered. However, in CIP the seller also has to procure insurance against the buyer's risk of loss of or damage to the goods during the carriage. Consequently, the seller contracts for insurance and pays the insurance premium. The buyer should note that under the CIP term the seller is required to obtain insurance only on minimum cover (Refer to Introduction paragraph 9.3).

the buyer wish to have the protection of greater cover, he would either need to agree as much expressly with the seller or to make his own extra insurance arrangements.

«Carrier» means any person who, in a contract of carriage, undertakes to perform or to procure the performance of transport, by rail, road, air, sea, inland waterway or by a combination of such modes.

If subsequent carriers are used for the carriage to the agreed destination, the risk passes when the goods have been delivered to the first carrier.

The CIP term requires the seller to clear the goods for export. This term may be used irrespective of the mode of transport including multimodal transport.

THE SELLER'S OBLIGATIONS	THE BUYER'S OBLIGATIONS
A1 Provision of goods in conformity with the contract	**B1 Payment of the price**
The seller must provide the goods and the commercial invoice, or its equivalent electronic message, in conformity with the contract of sale and any other evidence of conformity which may be required by the contract.	The buyer must pay the price as provided in the contract of sale.
A2 Licenses, authorizations and formalities	**B2 Licenses, authorizations and formalities**
The seller must obtain at his own risk and expense any export license or other official authorization and carry out, where applicable (54, all customs formalities necessary for the export of the goods.	The buyer must obtain at his own risk and expense any import license or other official authorization and carry out, where applicable (Refer to Introduction paragraph 10) , all customs formalities for the import of the goods and for their transit through any country.
A3 Contracts of carriage and insurance	**B3 Contracts of carriage and insurance**

a) Contract of carriage

The seller must contract on usual terms at his own expense for the carriage of the goods to the agreed point at the named place of destination by a usual route and in a customary manner. If a point is not agreed or is not determined by practice, the seller may select the point at the named place of destination which best suits his purpose.

b) Contract of insurance

The seller must obtain at his own expense cargo insurance as agreed in the contract, such that the buyer, or any other person having an insurable interest in the goods, shall be entitled to claim directly from the insurer and provide the buyer with the insurance policy or other evidence of insurance cover.

The insurance shall be contracted with underwriters or an insurance company of good repute and, failing express agreement to the contrary, be in accordance with minimum cover of the Institute Cargo Clauses (Institute of London Underwriters) or any similar set of clauses. The duration of insurance cover shall be in accordance with B5 and B4.

When required by the buyer, the seller shall provide at the buyer's expense war, strikes, riots and civil commotion risk insurances if procurable. The minimum insurance shall cover the price provided in the contract plus ten percent (i.e. 110 %) and shall be provided in the currency of the contract

a) Contract of carriage

No obligation (Refer to Introduction

A4 Delivery

The seller must deliver the goods to the carrier contracted in accordance with A3 or, if there are subsequent carriers to the first carrier, for transport to the agreed point at the named place on the date or within the agreed period.

B4 Taking delivery

The buyer must accept delivery of the goods when they have been delivered in accordance with A4 and receive them from the carrier at the named place.

A5 Transfer of risks

B5 Transfer of risks

The seller must, subject to the provisions of B5, bear all risks of loss of or damage to the goods until such time as they have been delivered in accordance with A4.

The buyer must bear all risks of loss of or damage to the goods from the time they have been delivered in accordance with A4.

The buyer must, should he fail to give notice in accordance with B7, bear all risks of the goods from the agreed date or the expiry date of the period fixed for delivery provided, however, that the goods have been duly appropriated to the contract, that is to say, clearly set aside or otherwise identified as the contract goods.

A6 Division of costs

The seller must, subject to the provisions of B6, pay

- all costs relating to the goods until such time as they have been delivered in accordance with A4 as well as the freight and all other costs resulting from A3 a), including the costs of loading the goods and any charges for unloading at the place of destination which were for the seller's account under the contract of carriage; and

- the costs of insurance resulting from A3 b); and

- where applicable (58, the costs of customs formalities necessary for export as well as all duties, taxes or other charges payable upon export, and for their transit through any country if they were for the seller's account under the contract of carriage.

B6 Division of costs

The buyer must, subject to the provisions of A3 a), pay

all costs relating to the goods from the time they have been delivered in accordance with A4; and

- all costs and charges relating to the goods whilst in transit until their arrival at the agreed place of destination, unless such costs and charges were for the seller's account under the contract of carriage; and

- unloading costs unless such costs and charges were for the seller's account under the contract of carriage; and

- all additional costs incurred if he fails to give notice in accordance with B7, for the goods from the agreed date or the expiry date of the period fixed for dispatch, provided, however, that the goods have been duly appropriated to the contract, that is to say, clearly set aside or otherwise identified as the contract goods; and

- where applicable (Refer to Introduction paragraph 14), all duties, taxes and other charges as well as the costs of carrying out customs formalities payable upon import of the goods and for their transit through any country unless included within the cost of the contract of carriage.

A7 Notice to the buyer

B7 Notice to the seller

The seller must give the buyer sufficient notice that the goods have been delivered in accordance with A4 as well as any other notice required in order to allow the buyer to take measures which are normally necessary to enable him to take the goods.

The buyer must, whenever he is entitled to determine the time for dispatching the goods and/or the destination, give the seller sufficient notice thereof.

A8 Proof of delivery, transport document or equivalent electronic message

The seller must provide the buyer at the seller's expense, if customary, with the usual transport document or documents (for example a negotiable bill of lading, a non-negotiable sea waybill, an inland waterway document, an air waybill, a railway consignment note, a road

Where the seller and the buyer have agreed to communicate electronically, the document referred to in the preceding paragraph may be replaced by an equivalent electronic data interchange (EDI) message.

B8 Proof of delivery, transport document or equivalent electronic message

consignment note, or a multimodal transport document) for the transport contracted in accordance with A3.

The buyer must accept the transport document in accordance with A8 if it is in conformity with the contract

A9 Checking - packaging - marking

The seller must pay the costs of those checking operations (such as checking quality, measuring, weighing, counting) which are necessary for the purpose of delivering the goods in accordance with A4.

The seller must provide at his own expense packaging (unless it is usual for the particular trade to send the goods of the contract description unpacked) which is required for the transport of the goods arranged by him. Packaging is to be marked appropriately.

B9 Inspection of goods

The buyer must pay the costs of any pre-shipment inspection except when such inspection is mandated by the authorities of the country of export.

A10 Other obligations

The seller must render the buyer at the latter's request, risk and expense, every assistance in obtaining any documents or equivalent electronic messages (other than those mentioned in A8) issued or transmitted in the country of dispatch and/or of origin which the buyer may require for the import of the goods and for their transit through any country.

The seller must provide the buyer, upon request, with the necessary information for procuring any additional insurance.

B10 Other obligations

The buyer must pay all costs and charges incurred in obtaining the documents or equivalent electronic messages mentioned in A10 and reimburse those incurred by the seller in rendering his assistance in accordance therewith.

The buyer must provide the seller, upon request, with the necessary information for procuring any additional insurance.

CPT - Carriage Paid To (... named place of destination)

«Carriage paid to...» means that the seller delivers the goods to the carrier nominated by him but the seller must in addition pay the cost of carriage necessary to bring the goods to the named destination. This means that the buyer bears all risks and any other costs occurring after the goods have been so delivered.

«Carrier» means any person who, in a contract of carriage, undertakes to perform or to procure the performance of transport, by rail, road, air, sea, inland waterway or by a combination of such modes. If subsequent carriers are used for the carriage to the agreed destination, the risk passes when the goods have been delivered to the first carrier.

The CPT term requires the seller to clear the goods for export. This term may be used irrespective of the mode of transport including multimodal transport.

THE SELLER'S OBLIGATIONS	THE BUYER'S OBLIGATIONS
A1 Provision of goods in conformity with the contract	**B1 Payment of the price**
The seller must provide the goods and the commercial invoice, or its equivalent electronic message, in conformity with the contract of sale and any other evidence of conformity which may be required by the contract.	The buyer must pay the price as provided in the contract of sale.
A2 Licenses, authorizations and formalities	**B2 Licenses, authorizations and formalities**
The seller must obtain at his own risk and expense any export license or other official authorization and carry out, where applicable (Refer to Introduction paragraph 14), all customs formalities necessary for the export of the goods.	The buyer must obtain at his own risk and expense any import license or other official authorization and carry out, where applicable (Refer to Introduction paragraph 14), all customs formalities for the import of the goods and for their transit through any country.
A3 Contracts of carriage and insurance	**B3 Contracts of carriage and insurance**

a) Contract of carriage

The seller must contract on usual terms at his own expense for the carriage of the goods to the agreed point at the named place of destination by a usual route and in a customary manner. If a point is not agreed or is not determined by practice, the seller may select the point at the named place of destination which best suits his purpose.

b) Contract of insurance

No obligation (Refer to Introduction paragraph 10).

a) Contract of carriage No obligation (Refer to Introduction paragraph 10).

b) Contract of insurance No obligation (Refer to Introduction paragraph 10).

A4 Delivery

The seller must deliver the goods to the carrier contracted in accordance with A3 or, if there are subsequent carriers to the first carrier, for transport to the agreed point at the named place on the date or within the agreed period.

B4 Taking delivery

The buyer must accept delivery of the goods when they have been delivered in accordance with A4 and receive them from the carrier at the named place.

A5 Transfer of risks

The seller must, subject to the provisions of B5, bear all risks of loss of or damage to the goods until such time as they have been delivered in accordance with A4.

B5 Transfer of risks

The buyer must bear all risks of loss of or damage to the goods from the time they have been delivered in accordance with A4.

The buyer must, should he fail to give notice in accordance with B7, bear all risks of the goods from the agreed date or the expiry date of the period fixed for delivery provided, however, that the goods have been duly appropriated to the contract, that is to say, clearly set aside or otherwise identified as the contract goods.

A6 Division of costs

B6 Division of costs

The seller must, subject to the provisions of B6, pay

- all costs relating to the goods until such time as they have been delivered in accordance with A4 as well as the freight and all other costs resulting from A3 a), including the costs of loading the goods and any charges for unloading at the place of destination which were for the seller's account under the contract of carriage; and

- where applicable (Refer to Introduction paragraph 14), the costs of customs formalities necessary for export as well as all duties, taxes or other charges payable upon export, and for their transit through any country if they were for the seller's account under the contract of carriage.

The buyer must, subject to the provisions of A3 a), pay

- all costs relating to the goods from the time they have been delivered in accordance with A4; and

- all costs and charges relating to the goods whilst in transit until their arrival at the agreed place of destination, unless such costs and charges were for the seller's account under the contract of carriage; and

- unloading costs unless such costs and charges were for the seller's account under the contract of carriage; and

- all additional costs incurred if he fails to give notice in accordance with B7, for the goods from the agreed date or the expiry date of the period fixed for dispatch, provided, however, that the goods have been duly appropriated to the contract, that is to say, clearly set aside or otherwise identified as the contract goods; and

- where applicable (Refer to Introduction paragraph 14), all duties, taxes and other charges as well as the costs of carrying out customs formalities payable upon import of the goods and for their transit through any country unless included within the cost of the contract of carriage.

A7 Notice to the buyer

The seller must give the buyer sufficient notice that the goods have been delivered in accordance with A4 as well as any other notice required in order to allow the buyer to take measures which are normally necessary to enable him to take the goods.

A8 Proof of delivery, transport document or equivalent electronic message

B7 Notice to the seller

The buyer must, whenever he is entitled to determine the time for the goods and/or the destination, give the seller sufficient notice thereof.

B8 Proof of delivery, transport document or equivalent electronic message

The seller must provide the buyer at the seller's expense, if customary, with the usual transport document or documents in (for example a negotiable bill of lading, a non-negotiable sea waybill, an inland waterway document, an air waybill, a railway consignment note, a road consignment note, or a multimodal transport document) for the transport contracted in accordance with A3. Where the seller and the buyer have agreed to communicate electronically, the document referred to in the preceding paragraph may be replaced by an equivalent electronic data interchange (EDI) message.

The buyer must accept the transport document in accordance with A8 if conformity with the contract.

A9 Checking - packaging - marking

The seller must pay the costs of those checking operations (such as checking quality, measuring, weighing, counting) which are necessary for the purpose of delivering the goods in accordance with A4.

The seller must provide at his own expense packaging (unless it is usual for the particular trade to send the goods of the contract description unpacked) which is required for the transport of the goods arranged by him. Packaging is to be marked appropriately.

B9 Inspection of goods

The buyer must pay the costs of any pre-shipment inspection except when such inspection is mandated by the authorities of the country of export.

A10 Other obligations

The seller must render the buyer at the latter's request, risk and expense, every assistance in obtaining any documents or equivalent electronic messages (other than those mentioned in A8) issued or transmitted in the country of dispatch and/or of origin which the buyer may require for the import of the goods and for their transit through any country.

The seller must provide the buyer, upon request, with the necessary information for procuring insurance.

B10 Other obligations

The buyer must pay all costs and charges incurred in obtaining the documents or equivalent electronic messages mentioned in A10 and reimburse those incurred by the seller in rendering his assistance in accordance therewith.

DAP - Delivered at Place (...named place of destination)

New Term - May be used for all transport modes

Seller delivers the goods when they are placed at the disposal of the buyer on the arriving means of transport ready for unloading at the named place of destination. Parties are advised to specify as clearly as possible the point within the agreed place of destination, because risks transfer at this point from seller to buyer. If the seller is responsible for clearing the goods, paying duties etc., consideration should be given to using the DDP term.

Responsibilities

- Seller bears the responsibility and risks to deliver the goods to the named place

- Seller is advised to obtain contracts of carriage that match the contract of sale

- Seller is required to clear the goods for export

- If the seller incurs unloading costs at place of destination, unless previously agreed they are not entitled to recover any such costs

- Importer is responsible for effecting customs clearance, and paying any customs duties

DDP - Delivered Duty Paid (... named place of destination)

Delivered duty paid» means that the seller delivers the goods to the buyer, cleared for import, and not unloaded from any arriving means of transport at the named place of destination. The seller has to bear all the costs and risks involved in bringing the goods thereto including, where applicable (Refer to Introduction paragraph 14), any «duty» (which term includes the responsibility for and the risk of the carrying out of customs formalities and the payment of formalities, customs duties, taxes and other charges) for import in the country of destination.

Whilst the **EXW** term represents the minimum obligation for the seller, DDP represents the maximum obligation. This term should not be used if the seller is unable directly or indirectly to obtain the import license.

However, if the parties wish to exclude from the seller's obligations some of the costs payable upon import of the goods (such as value-added tax : VAT), this should be made clear by adding explicit wording to this effect in the contract of sale (Refer to Introduction paragraph 11).

If the parties wish the buyer to bear all risks and costs of the import, the **DDU** term should be used. This term may be used irrespective of the mode of transport but when delivery is to take place in the port of destination on board the vessel or on the quay (wharf), the **DES** or **DEQ** terms should be used.

THE SELLER'S OBLIGATIONS	THE BUYER'S OBLIGATIONS

A1 Provision of goods in conformity with the contract

The seller must provide the goods and the commercial invoice, or its equivalent electronic message, in conformity with the contract of sale and any other evidence of conformity which may be required by the contract.

B1 Payment of the price

The buyer must pay the price as provided in the contract of sale.

A2 Licenses, authorizations and formalities

The seller must obtain at his own risk and expense any export and import license and other official authorization or other documents and carry out, where applicable (Refer to Introduction paragraph 14), all customs formalities necessary for the export of the goods, for their transit through any country and for their import.

B2 Licenses, authorizations and formalities

The buyer must render the seller at the latter's request, risk and expense, every assistance in obtaining, where applicable (Refer to Introduction paragraph 14), any import license or other official authorization necessary for the import of the goods.

A3 Contracts of carriage and insurance

a) Contract of carriage

The seller must contract at his own expense for the carriage of the goods to the named place of destination. If a specific point is not agreed or is not determined by practice, the seller may select the point at the named place of

destination which best suits his

purpose.

b) Contract of insurance

No obligation (Refer to Introduction paragraph 10)

B3 Contracts of carriage and insurance

a) Contract of carriage

No obligation (Refer to Introduction paragraph 10)

b) Contract of insurance

No obligation (Refer to Introduction paragraph 10)

A4 Delivery

The seller must place the goods at the disposal of the buyer, or at that of another person named by the buyer, on any arriving means of transport not unloaded at the named place of destination on the date or within the period agreed for delivery.

B4 Taking delivery

The buyer must take delivery of the goods when they have been delivered in accordance with A4.

A5 Transfer of risks

The seller must, subject to the provisions of B5, bear all risks of loss of or damage to the goods until such time as they have been delivered in accordance with A4.

B5 Transfer of risks

The buyer must bear all risks of loss of or damage to the goods from the time they have been delivered in accordance with A4.

The buyer must, should he fail to fulfill his obligations in accordance with B2, bear all additional risks of loss of or damage to the goods incurred thereby. The buyer must, should he fail to give notice in accordance with B7, bear all risks of loss of or damage to the goods from the agreed date or the expiry date of the agreed period for delivery provided, however, that the goods have been duly appropriated to the contract, that is to say, clearly set aside or otherwise identified as the contract goods.

A6 Division of costs

The seller must, subject to the provisions of B6, pay

- in addition to costs resulting from A3 a), all costs relating to the goods until such time as they have been delivered in accordance with A4; and

- where applicable (Refer to Introduction paragraph 14), the costs of customs formalities necessary for export and import as well as all duties, taxes and other charges payable upon export and import of the goods, and for their transit through any country prior to delivery in accordance with A4.

B6 Division of costs

The buyer must pay

- all costs relating to the goods from the time they have been delivered in accordance with A4; and

- all additional costs incurred if he fails to fulfill his obligations in accordance with B2, or to give notice in accordance with B7, provided, however, that the goods have been duly appropriated to the contract, that is to say, clearly set aside or otherwise identified as the contract goods.

A7 Notice to the buyer

The seller must give the buyer sufficient notice of the dispatch of the goods as well as any other notice required in order to allow the buyer to take measures which are normally necessary to enable him to take delivery of the goods.

B7 Notice to the seller

The buyer must, whenever he is entitled to determine the time within an agreed period and/or the point of taking delivery at the named place, give the seller sufficient notice thereof.

A8 Proof of delivery, transport document or equivalent electronic message

B8 Proof of delivery, transport document or equivalent electronic message

The seller must provide the buyer at the seller's expense with the delivery order and/or the usual transport document (for example a negotiable bill of lading, a non-negotiable sea waybill, an inland waterway document, an air waybill, a railway consignment note, a road consignment note, or a multimodal transport document) which the buyer may require to take delivery of the interchange (EDI) message.

goods in accordance with A4/B4. Where the seller and the buyer have agreed to communicate electronically, the document referred to in the preceding paragraph may be replaced by an equivalent electronic data

The buyer must accept the appropriate delivery order or transport document in accordance with A8.

A9 Checking - packaging - marking

The seller must pay the costs of those checking operations (such as checking quality, measuring, weighing, counting) which are necessary for the purpose of delivering the goods in accordance with A4.

The seller must provide at his own expense packaging (unless it is usual for the particular trade to deliver the goods of the contract description unpacked) which is required for the delivery of the goods. Packaging is to be marked appropriately.

B9 Inspection of goods

The buyer must pay the costs of any pre-shipment inspection except when such inspection is mandated by the authorities of the country of export.

A10 Other obligations

The seller must pay all costs and charges incurred in obtaining the documents or equivalent electronic messages mentioned in B10 and reimburse those incurred by the buyer in rendering his assistance herewith. The seller must provide the buyer, upon request, with the necessary information for procuring insurance.

B10 Other obligations

The buyer must render the seller, at the latter's request, risk and expense, every assistance in obtaining any documents or equivalent electronic messages issued or transmitted in the country of import which the seller may require for the purpose of making the goods available to the buyer in accordance therewith.

DAT - Delivered at Terminal (...named terminal at port or place of destination)

New Term - May be used for all transport modes

Seller delivers when the goods, once unloaded from the arriving means of transport, are placed at the disposal of the buyer at a named terminal at the named port or place of destination. "Terminal" includes quay, warehouse, container yard or road, rail or air terminal. Both parties should agree the terminal and if possible a point within the terminal at which point the risks will transfer from the seller to the buyer of the goods. If it is intended that the seller is to bear all the costs and responsibilities from the terminal to another point, DAP or DDP may apply.

Responsibilities

- Seller is responsible for the costs and risks to bring the goods to the point specified in the contract

- Seller should ensure that their forwarding contract mirrors the contract of sale

- Seller is responsible for the export clearance procedures

- Importer is responsible to clear the goods for import, arrange import customs formalities, and pay import duty

- If the parties intend the seller to bear the risks and costs of taking the goods from the terminal to another place then the DAP term may apply

EXW - EX Works (... named place)

«Ex works» means that the seller delivers when he places the goods at the disposal of the buyer at the seller's premises or another named place (i.e. works, factory, warehouse, etc.) not cleared for export and not loaded on any collecting vehicle.

This term thus represents the minimum obligation for the seller, and the buyer has to bear all costs and risks involved in taking the goods from the seller's premises However, if the parties wish the seller to be responsible for the loading of the goods on departure and to bear the risks and all the costs of such loading, this should be made clear by adding explicit wording to this effect in the contract of sale (Refer to Introduction paragraph 11.) .This term should not be used when the buyer cannot carry out the export formalities directly or indirectly. In such circumstances, the **FCA** term should be used, provided the seller agrees that he will load at his cost and risk.

A. THE SELLER'S OBLIGATIONS	B. THE BUYER'S OBLIGATIONS

A1 Provision of goods in conformity with the contract

The seller must provide the goods and the commercial invoice, or its equivalent electronic message, in conformity with the contract of sale and any other evidence of conformity which may be required by the contract.

B1 Payment of the price

The buyer must pay the price as provided in the contract of sale.

A2 Licenses, authorizations and formalities

The seller must render the buyer, at the latter's request, risk and expense, every assistance in obtaining, where applicable, (Refer to Introduction paragraph 14.), any export license or other official authorization necessary for the export of the goods.

B2 Licenses, authorizations and formalities

The buyer must obtain at his own risk and expense any export and import license or other official authorization and carry out, where applicable (Refer to Introduction paragraph 14.), all customs formalities for the export of the goods.

A3 Contracts of carriage and insurance

a) Contract of carriage

No obligation (Refer to Introduction paragraph 10).

b) Contract of insurance

No obligation (Refer to Introduction paragraph 10)

B3 Contracts of carriage and insurance

a) Contract of carriage

No obligation (Refer to Introduction paragraph 10).

b) Contract of insurance

No obligation (Refer to Introduction paragraph 10).

A4 Delivery

B4 Taking delivery

The seller must place the goods at the disposal of the buyer at the named place of delivery, not loaded on any collecting vehicle, on the date or within the period agreed or, if no such time is agreed, at the usual time for delivery of such goods. If no specific point has been agreed within the named place, and if there are several points available, the seller may select the point at the place of delivery which best suits his purpose.

The buyer must take delivery of the goods when they have been delivered in accordance with A4 and A7/B7.

A5 Transfer of risks

The seller must, subject to the provisions of B5, bear all risks of loss of or damage to the goods until such time as they have been delivered in accordance with A4.

B5 Transfer of risks

The buyer must bear all risks of loss of or damage to the goods

- from the time they have been delivered in accordance with A4;and

- from the agreed date or the expiry date of any period fixed for taking delivery which arise because he fails to give notice in accordance with B7, provided, however, that the goods have been duly appropriated to the contract, that is to say clearly set aside or otherwise identified as the contract goods.

A6 Division of costs

The seller must, subject to the provisions of B6, pay all costs relating to the goods until such time as they have been delivered in accordance with A4. 4.

B6 Division of costs

The buyer must pay

- all costs relating to the goods from the time they have been delivered in accordance with A4; and

- any additional costs incurred by failing either to take delivery of the goods when they have been placed at his disposal, or to give appropriate notice in accordance with B7 provided, however, that the goods have been duly appropriated to the contract, that is to say, clearly set aside or otherwise identified as the contract goods; and

- where applicable (Refer to Introduction paragraph 10), all duties, taxes and other charges as well as the costs of carrying out customs formalities payable upon export.

The buyer must reimburse all costs and charges incurred by the seller in rendering assistance in accordance with A2.

A7 Notice to the buyer

B7 Notice to the seller

The seller must give the buyer sufficient notice as to when and where the goods will be placed at his disposal.

The buyer must, whenever he is entitled to determine the time within an agreed period and/or the place of taking delivery, give the seller sufficient notice thereof.

A8 Proof of delivery, transport document or equivalent electronic message

No obligation (Refer to Introduction paragraph 10)

B8 Proof of delivery, transport document or equivalent electronic message

The buyer must provide the seller with appropriate evidence of having taken delivery.

A9 Checking - packaging - marking B9 Inspection of goods

The seller must pay the costs of those checking operations (such as checking quality, measuring, weighing, counting) which are necessary for the purpose of placing the goods at the buyer's disposal. The seller must provide at his own expense packaging (unless it is usual for the particular trade to make the goods of the contract description available unpacked) which is required for the transport of the goods, to the extent that the circumstances relating to the transport (for example modalities, destination) are made known to the seller before the contract of sale is concluded. Packaging is to be marked appropriately.

B9 Inspection of goods

The buyer must pay the costs of any pre-shipment inspection, including inspection mandated by the authorities of the country of export.

A10 Other obligations

The seller must render the buyer at the latter's request, risk and expense, every assistance in obtaining any documents or equivalent electronic messages issued or transmitted in the country of delivery and/or of origin which the buyer may require for the export and/or import of the goods and, where necessary, for their transit through any country. The seller must provide the buyer, upon request, with the necessary information for procuring insurance.

B10 Other obligations

The buyer must pay all costs and charges incurred in obtaining the documents or equivalent electronic messages mentioned in A10 and reimburse those incurred by the seller in rendering his assistance in accordance therewith.

FAS - Free Alongside Ship (... named port of shipment)

«Free Alongside Ship» means that the seller delivers when the goods are placed alongside the vessel at the named port of shipment. This means that the buyer has to bear all costs and risks of loss of or damage to the goods from that moment. The FAS term requires the seller to clear the goods for export. THIS IS A REVERSAL FROM PREVIOUS INCOTERMSVERSIONS WHICH REQUIRED THE BUYER TO ARRANGE FOR EXPORT CLEARANCE. However, if the parties wish the buyer to clear the goods for export, this should be made clear by adding explicit wording to this effect in the contract of sale.

This term can be used only for sea or inland waterway transport.

THE SELLER'S OBLIGATIONS	THE BUYER'S OBLIGATIONS
A1 Provision of goods in conformity with the contract	**B1 Payment of the price**
The seller must provide the goods and the commercial invoice, or its equivalent electronic message, in conformity with the contract of sale and any other evidence of conformity which may be required by the contract.	The buyer must pay the price as provided in the contract of sale.
A2 Licenses, authorizations and formalities	**B2 Licenses, authorizations and formalities**
The seller must obtain at his own risk and expense any export license or other official authorization and carry out, where applicable (Refer to Introduction paragraph 14.), all customs formalities necessary for the export of the goods.	The buyer must obtain at his own risk and expense any import license or other official authorization and carry out, where applicable (Refer to Introduction paragraph 14), all customs formalities for the import of the goods and for their transit through any country.
A3 Contracts of carriage and insurance	**B3 Contracts of carriage and insurance**
a) Contract of carriage	a) Contract of carriage
No obligation (Refer to Introduction paragraph 10).	The buyer must contract at his own expense for the carriage of the goods from the named port of shipment.
b) Contract of insurance	b) Contract of insurance
No obligation (Refer to Introduction paragraph 10).	No obligation (Refer to Introduction paragraph 10).
A4 Delivery	**B4 Taking delivery**

The seller must place the goods alongside the vessel nominated by the buyer at the loading place named by the buyer at the named port of shipment on the date or within the agreed period and in the manner customary at the port.

The buyer must take delivery of the goods when they have been delivered in accordance with A4.

A5 Transfer of risks

The seller must, subject to the provisions of B5, bear all risks of loss of or damage to the goods until such time as they have been delivered in accordance with A4.

B5 Transfer of risks

The buyer must bear all risks of loss of or damage to the goods

- from the time they have been delivered in accordance with A4;and formalities as well as all duties, taxes, and other charges payable upon export.

- from the agreed date or the expiry date of the agreed period for delivery which arise because he fails to give notice in accordance with B7, or because the vessel nominated by him fails to arrive on time, or is unable to take the goods, or closes for cargo earlier than the time notified in accordance with B7, provided, however, that the goods have been duly appropriated to the contract, that is to say, clearly set aside or otherwise identified as the contract goods.

A6 Division of costs

B6 Division of costs

The seller must, subject to the provisions of B6, pay

all costs relating to the goods until such time as they have been delivered in accordance with A4; and

where applicable(Refer to Introduction paragraph 14), the costs of customs

The buyer must pay

- all costs relating to the goods from the time they have been delivered in accordance with A4; and

- any additional costs incurred, either because the vessel nominated by him has failed to arrive on time, or is unable to take the goods, or closes for cargo earlier than the time notified in accordance with B7, or because the buyer has failed to give appropriate notice in accordance with B7 provided, however, that the goods have been duly appropriated to the contract, that is to say, clearly set aside or otherwise identified as the contract goods; and

- where applicable (Refer to Introduction paragraph 14), all duties, taxes and other charges as well as the costs of carrying out customs formalities payable upon import of the goods and for their transit through any country.

A7 Notice to the buyer

The seller must give the buyer sufficient notice that the goods have been delivered alongside the nominated vessel.

B7 Notice to the seller

The buyer must give the seller sufficient notice of the vessel name, loading point and required delivery time.

A8 Proof of delivery, transport document or equivalent electronic message

The seller must provide the buyer at the seller's expense with the usual proof of delivery of the goods in accordance with A4.

Unless the document referred to in the preceding paragraph is the transport document, the seller must render the buyer at the latter's request, risk and expense, every assistance in obtaining a transport document (for example a negotiable bill of lading, a non-negotiable sea waybill, an inland waterway document).

When the seller and the buyer have agreed to communicate electronically, the document referred to in the preceding paragraphs may be replaced by an equivalent electronic data interchange (EDI) message.

B8 Proof of delivery, transport document or equivalent electronic message

The buyer must accept the proof of delivery in accordance with A8.

A9 Checking - packaging - marking

B9 Inspection of goods

The seller must pay the costs of those checking operations (such as checking quality, measuring, weighing, counting) which are necessary for the purpose of delivering the goods in accordance with A4.

The seller must provide at his own expense packaging (unless it is usual for the particular trade to ship the goods of the contract description unpacked) which is required for the transport of the goods, to the extent that the circumstances relating to the transport (for example modalities, destination) are made known to the seller before the contract of sale is concluded. Packaging is to be marked appropriately.

The buyer must pay the costs of any pre-shipment inspection, except when such inspection is mandated by the authorities of the country of export.

A10 Other obligations

The seller must render the buyer at the latter's request, risk and expense, every assistance in obtaining any documents or equivalent electronic messages (other than those mentioned in A8) issued or transmitted in the country of shipment and/or of origin which the buyer may require for the import of the goods and, where necessary, for their transit through any country.

The seller must provide the buyer, upon request, with the necessary information for procuring insurance.

B10 Other obligations

The buyer must pay all costs and charges incurred in obtaining the documents or equivalent electronic messages mentioned in A10 and reimburse those incurred by the seller in re

FCA - Free Carrier (...named place)

«Free Carrier» means that the seller delivers the goods, cleared for export, to the carrier nominated by the buyer at the named place. It should be noted that the chosen place of delivery has an impact on the obligations of loading and unloading the goods at that place. If delivery occurs at the seller's premises, the seller is responsible for loading. If delivery occurs at any other place, the seller is not responsible for unloading.

This term may be used irrespective of the mode of transport, including multimodal transport.

«Carrier» means any person who, in a contract of carriage, undertakes to perform or to procure the performance of transport by rail, road, air, sea, inland waterway or by a combination of such modes.

If the buyer nominates a person other than a carrier to receive the goods, the seller is deemed to have fulfilled his obligation to deliver the goods when they are delivered to that person.

A. THE SELLER'S OBLIGATIONS	B. THE BUYER'S OBLIGATIONS
A1 Provision of goods in conformity with the contract	**B1 Payment of the price**
The seller must provide the goods and the commercial invoice, or its equivalent electronic message, in conformity with the contract of sale and any other evidence of conformity which may be required by the contract.	The buyer must pay the price as provided in the contract of sale.
A2 Payment of the price	**B2 Licenses, authorizations and formalities**
The buyer must pay the price as provided in the contract of sale.	The buyer must obtain at his own risk and expense any import license or other official authorization and carry out, where applicable (Refer to Introduction paragraph 14), all customs formalities for the import of the goods and for their transit through any country.
A3 Contracts of carriage and insurance	**B3 Contracts of carriage and insurance**

a) Contract of carriage

No obligation (Refer to Introduction paragraph 10). However, if requested by the buyer or if it is commercial practice and the buyer does not give an instruction to the contrary in due time, the seller may contract for carriage on usual terms at the buyer's risk and expense. In either case, the seller may decline to make the contract and, if he does, shall promptly notify the buyer accordingly. b) Contract of insurance

No obligation (Refer to Introduction paragraph 10)

a) Contract of carriage

The buyer must contract at his own expense for the carriage of the goods from the named place, except when the contract of carriage is made by the seller as provided for in A3 a).

b) Contract of insurance

No obligation (Refer to Introduction paragraph 10).

A4 Delivery

The seller must deliver the goods to the carrier or another person nominated by the buyer, or chosen by the seller in accordance with A3 a), at the named place on the date or within the period agreed for delivery. Delivery is completed;

a) If the named place is the seller's premises, when the goods have been loaded on the means of transport provided by the carrier nominated by A3 a) on the seller's means of transport not unloaded.

If no specific point has been agreed within the named place, and if there are several points available, the seller may select the point at the place of delivery which best suits his purpose.

Failing precise instructions from the buyer, the seller may deliver the goods for carriage in such a manner as the transport mode and/or the quantity and/or nature of the goods may require.

B4 Taking delivery

the buyer or another person acting on his behalf.

b) If the named place is anywhere other than a), when the goods are placed at the disposal of the carrier or another person nominated by the buyer, or chosen by the seller in accordance with

The buyer must take delivery of the goods when they have been delivered in accordance with A4.

A5 Transfer of risks

B5 Transfer of risks

The seller must, subject to the provisions of B5, bear all risks of loss of or damage to the goods until such time as they have been delivered in accordance with A4.

The buyer must bear all risks of loss of or damage to the goods

- from the time they have been delivered in accordance with A4; and

- from the agreed date or the expiry date of any agreed period for delivery which arise either because he fails to nominate the carrier or another person in accordance with A4, or because the carrier or the party nominated by the buyer fails to take the goods into his charge at the agreed time, or because the buyer fails to give appropriate notice in accordance with B7, provided, however, that the goods have been duly appropriated to the contract, that is to say, clearly set aside or otherwise identified as the contract goods.

A6 Division of cost

The seller must, subject to the provisions of B6, pay

- all costs relating to the goods until such time as they have been delivered in accordance with A4; and

- where applicable (Refer to Introduction paragraph 14), the costs of customs formalities as well as all duties, taxes, and other charges payable upon export

B6 Division of costs

The buyer must pay

- all costs relating to the goods from the time they have been delivered in accordance with A4; and

- any additional costs incurred, either because he fails to nominate the carrier or another person in accordance with A4 or because the party nominated by the buyer fails to take the goods into his charge at the agreed time, or because he has failed to give appropriate notice in accordance with B7, provided, however, that the goods have been duly appropriated to the contract, that is to say, clearly set aside or otherwise identified as the contract goods; and

- where applicable (Refer to Introduction paragraph 14), all duties, taxes and other charges as well as the costs of carrying out customs formalities payable upon import of the goods and for their transit through any country.

A7 Notice to the buyer

The seller must give the buyer sufficient notice that the goods have been delivered in accordance with A4. Should the carrier fail to take delivery in accordance with A4 at the time agreed, the seller must notify the buyer accordingly.

A8 Proof of delivery, transport document or equivalent electronic message

The seller must provide the buyer at the seller's expense with the usual proof of delivery of the goods in accordance with A4.

Unless the document referred to in the preceding paragraph is the transport document, the seller must render the buyer at the latter's request, risk and expense, every assistance in obtaining a transport document for the contract of carriage (for example a negotiable bill of lading, a non-negotiable sea waybill, an inland waterway document, an air waybill, a railway consignment note, a road consignment note, or a multimodal transport document). When the seller and the buyer have agreed to communicate electronically, the document referred to in the preceding paragraph may be replaced by an equivalent electronic data interchange (EDI) message.

A9 Checking - packaging - marking

B7 Notice to the seller

The buyer must give the seller sufficient notice of the name of the party designated in A4 and, where necessary, specify the mode of transport, as well as the date or period for delivering the goods to him and, as the case may be, the point within the place where the goods should be delivered to that party.

B8 Proof of delivery, transport document or equivalent electronic message

The buyer must accept the proof of delivery in accordance with A8.

B9 Inspection of goods

The seller must pay the costs of those checking operations (such as checking quality, measuring, weighing, counting) which are necessary for the purpose of delivering the goods in accordance with A4.

The seller must provide at his own expense packaging (unless it is usual for the particular trade to send the goods of the contract description unpacked) which is required for the transport of the goods, to the extent that the circumstances relating to the transport (for example modalities, destination) are made known to the seller before the contract of sale is concluded. Packaging is to be marked appropriately.

The buyer must pay the costs of any pre-shipment inspection except when such inspection is mandated by the authorities of the country of export.

A10 Other obligations

The seller must render the buyer at the latter's request, risk and expense, every assistance in obtaining any documents or equivalent electronic messages (other than those mentioned in A8) issued or transmitted in the country of delivery and/or of origin which the buyer may require for the import of the goods and, where necessary, for their transit through any country.

The seller must provide the buyer, upon request, with the necessary information for procuring insurance.

B10 Other obligations

The buyer must pay all costs and charges incurred in obtaining the documents or equivalent electronic messages mentioned in A10 and reimburse those incurred by the seller in rendering his assistance in accordance therewith and in contracting for carriage in accordance with A3 a).

The buyer must give the seller appropriate instructions whenever the seller's assistance in contracting for carriage is required in accordance with A3 a).

FOB - Free On Board (... named port of shipment)

«Free on Board» means that the seller delivers when the goods pass the ship's rail at the named port of shipment. This means that the buyer has to bear all costs and risks of loss of or damage to the goods from that point. The FOB term requires the seller to clear the goods for export. This term can be used only for sea or inland waterway transport. If the parties do not intend to deliver the goods across the ship's rail, the **FCA** term should be used.

THE SELLER'S OBLIGATIONS	THE BUYER'S OBLIGATIONS
A1 Provision of goods in conformity with the contract	**B1 Payment of the price**
The seller must provide the goods and the commercial invoice, or its equivalent electronic message, in conformity with the contract of sale and any other evidence of conformity which may be required by the contract.	The buyer must pay the price as provided in the contract of sale.
A2 Licenses, authorizations and formalities	**B2 Licenses, authorizations and formalities**
The seller must obtain at his own risk and expense any export license or other official authorization and carry out, where applicable (Refer to Introduction paragraph 14), all customs formalities necessary for the export of the goods.	The buyer must obtain at his own risk and expense any import license or other official authorization and carry out, where applicable (Refer to Introduction paragraph 14), all customs formalities for the import of the goods and, where necessary, for their transit through any country.
A3 Contracts of carriage and insurance	**B3 Contracts of carriage and insurance**
a) Contract of carriage	a) Contract of carriage
No obligation (Refer to Introduction paragraph 10)	The buyer must contract at his own expense for the carriage of the goods from the named port of shipment.
b) Contract of insurance	b) Contract of insurance
No obligation (Refer to Introduction paragraph 10)	No obligation (Refer to Introduction paragraph 10).
A4 Delivery	**B4 Taking delivery**
The seller must deliver the goods on the date or within the agreed period at the named port of shipment and in the manner customary at the port on board the vessel nominated by the buyer.	The buyer must take delivery of the goods when they have been delivered in accordance with A4.

A5 Transfer of risks

The seller must, subject to the provisions of B5, bear all risks of loss of or damage to the goods until such time as they have passed the ship's rail at the named port of shipment.

A6 Division of costs

The seller must, subject to the provisions of B6, pay

- all costs relating to the goods until such time as they have passed the ship's rail at the named port of shipment; and

- where applicable (Refer to Introduction paragraph 14), the costs of customs formalities necessary for export as well as all duties, taxes and other charges payable upon export.

A7 Notice to the buyer

The seller must give the buyer sufficient notice that the goods have been delivered in accordance with A4.

A8 Proof of delivery, transport document or equivalent electronic message

B5 Transfer of risks

The buyer must bear all risks of loss of or damage to the goods

- from the time they have passed the ship's rail at the named port of shipment; and

- from the agreed date or the expiry date of the agreed period for delivery which arise because he fails to give notice in accordance with B7, or because the vessel nominated by him fails to arrive on time, or is unable to take the goods, or closes for cargo earlier than the time notified in accordance with B7, provided, however, that the goods have been duly appropriated to the contract, that is to say, clearly set aside or otherwise identified as the contract goods.

B6 Division of costs

The buyer must pay

- all costs relating to the goods from the time they have passed the ship's rail at the named port of shipment; and

- any additional costs incurred, either because the vessel nominated by him fails to arrive on time, or is unable to take the goods, or closes for cargo earlier than the time notified in accordance with B7, or because the buyer has failed to give appropriate notice in accordance with B7, provided, however, that the goods have been duly appropriated to the contract, that is to say, clearly set aside or otherwise identified as the contract goods; and

- where applicable (Refer to Introduction paragraph 14), all duties, taxes and other charges as well as the costs of carrying out customs formalities payable upon import of the goods and for their transit through any country.

B7 Notice to the seller

The buyer must give the seller sufficient notice of the vessel name, loading point and required delivery time.

B8 Proof of delivery, transport document or equivalent electronic message

The seller must provide the buyer at the seller's expense with the usual proof of delivery in accordance with A4. Unless the document referred to in the preceding paragraph is the transport document, the seller must render the buyer, at the latter's request, risk and expense, every assistance in obtaining a transport document for the contract of carriage (for example, a negotiable bill of lading, a non-negotiable sea waybill, an inland waterway document, or a multimodal transport document). Where the seller and the buyer have agreed to communicate electronically, the document referred to in the preceding paragraph may be replaced by an equivalent electronic data interchange (EDI) message.

The buyer must accept the proof of delivery in accordance with A8.

A9 Checking - packaging - marking

The seller must pay the costs of those checking operations (such as checking quality, measuring, weighing, counting) which are necessary for the purpose of delivering the goods in accordance with A4.

The seller must provide at his own expense packaging (unless it is usual for the particular trade to ship the goods of the contract description unpacked) which is required for the transport of the goods, to the extent that the circumstances relating to the transport (for example modalities, destination) are made known to the seller before the contract of sale is concluded. Packaging is to be marked appropriately.

B9 Inspection of goods

The buyer must pay the costs of any pre-shipment inspection except when such inspection is mandated by the authorities of the country of export.

A10 Other obligations

The seller must render the buyer at the latter's request, risk and expense, every assistance in obtaining any documents or equivalent electronic messages (other than those mentioned in A8) issued or transmitted in the country of shipment and/or of origin which the buyer may require for the import of the goods and, where necessary, for their transit through any country.

The seller must provide the buyer, upon request, with the necessary information for procuring insurance.

DDU - Delivered Duty Unpaid (... named place of destination)

«Delivered duty unpaid» means that the seller delivers the goods to the buyer, not cleared for import, and not unloaded from any arriving means of transport at the named place of destination. The seller has to bear the costs and risks involved in bringing the goods thereto, other than, where applicable (Refer to Introduction paragraph 14), any «duty» (which term includes the responsibility for and the risks of the carrying out of customs formalities, and the payment of formalities, customs duties, taxes and other charges) for import in the country of destination. Such «duty» has to be borne by the buyer as well as any costs and risks caused by his failure to clear the goods for import in time.

However, if the parties wish the seller to carry out customs formalities and bear the costs and risks resulting therefrom as well as some of the costs payable upon import of the goods, this should be made clear by adding explicit wording to this effect in the contract of sale (Refer to Introduction paragraph 14).

This term may be used irrespective of the mode of transport but when delivery is to take place in the port of destination on board the vessel or on the quay (wharf), the **DES** or **DEQ** terms should be used.

THE SELLER'S OBLIGATIONS	THE BUYER'S OBLIGATIONS
A1 Provision of goods in conformity with the contract	**B1 Payment of the price**
The seller must provide the goods and the commercial invoice, or its equivalent electronic message, in conformity with the contract of sale and any other evidence of conformity which may be required by the contract.	The buyer must pay the price as provided in the contract of sale.
A2 Licenses, authorizations and formalities	**B2 Licenses, authorizations and formalities**
The seller must obtain at his own risk and expense any export license and other official authorization or other documents and carry out, where applicable (Refer to Introduction paragraph 14), all customs formalities necessary for the export of the goods and for their transit through any country.	The buyer must obtain at his own risk and expense any import license or other official authorization or other documents and carry out, where applicable (Refer to Introduction paragraph 1), all customs formalities necessary for the import of the goods.
A3 Contracts of carriage and insurance	**B3 Contracts of carriage and insurance**

a) Contract of carriage

The seller must contract at his own expense for the carriage of the goods to the named place of destination. If a specific point is not agreed or is not determined by practice, the seller may select the point at the named place of destination which best suits his purpose.

b) Contract of insurance

No obligation (Refer to Introduction paragraph 14)

a) Contract of carriage

No obligation (Refer to Introduction paragraph 10).

b) Contract of insurance

No obligation (Refer to Introduction paragraph 10).

A4 Delivery

The seller must place the goods at the disposal of the buyer, or at that of another person named by the buyer, on any arriving means of transport not unloaded, at the named place of destination on the date or within the period agreed for delivery.

B4 Taking delivery

The buyer must take delivery of the goods when they have been delivered in accordance with A4.

A5 Transfer of risks

The seller must, subject to the provisions of B5, bear all risks of loss of or damage to the goods until such time as they have been delivered in accordance with A4

B5 Transfer of risks

The buyer must bear all risks of loss of or damage to the goods from the time they have been delivered in accordance with A4.

The buyer must, should he fail to fulfill his obligations in accordance with B2, bear all additional risks of loss of or damage to the goods incurred thereby. The buyer must, should he fail to give notice in accordance with B7, bear all risks of loss of or damage to the goods from the agreed date or the expiry date of the agreed period for delivery provided, however, that the goods have been duly appropriated to the contract, that is to say, clearly set aside or otherwise identified as the contract goods.

A6 Division of costs

B6 Division of costs

The seller must, subject to the

- in addition to costs resulting from A3 a), all costs relating to the goods until

- such time as they have been delivered in accordance with A4; and

- where applicable (Refer to Introduction paragraph 14), the costs of customs formalities necessary for export as well as all duties, taxes and other charges payable upon export and for their transit through any country prior to delivery in accordance with A4.

The buyer must pay provisions of B6, pay

- all costs relating to the goods from the time they have been delivered in accordance with A4; and

- all additional costs incurred if he fails to fulfill his obligations in accordance with B2, or to give notice in accordance with B7, provided, however, that the goods have been duly appropriated to the contract, that is to say, clearly set aside or otherwise identified as the contract goods; and

- where applicable (Refer to Introduction paragraph 14), the costs of customs formalities as well as all duties, taxes and other charges payable upon import of the goods.

A7 Notice to the buyer

The seller must give the buyer sufficient notice of the dispatch of the goods as well as any other notice required in order to allow the buyer to take measures which are normally necessary to enable him to take delivery of the goods.

B7 Notice to the seller

The buyer must, whenever he is entitled to determine the time within an agreed period and/or the point of taking delivery at the named place, give the seller sufficient notice thereof.

A8 Proof of delivery, transport document or equivalent electronic message

The seller must provide the buyer at the seller's expense the delivery order and/or the usual transport document (for example a negotiable bill of lading, a non-negotiable sea waybill, an inland waterway document, an air waybill, a railway consignment note, a road consignment note, or a multimodal transport document) which the buyer may require to take delivery of the goods in accordance with A4/B4. Where the seller and the buyer have agreed to communicate electronically, the document referred to in the preceding paragraph may be replaced by an equivalent electronic data interchange (EDI) message.

B8 Proof of delivery, transport document or equivalent electronic message

The buyer must accept the appropriate delivery order or transport document in accordance with A8

A9 Checking - packaging - marking

B9 Inspection of goods

The seller must pay the costs of those checking operations (such as checking quality, measuring, weighing, counting) which are necessary for the purpose of delivering the goods in accordance with A4.

The seller must provide at his own expense packaging (unless it is usual for the particular trade to deliver the goods of the contract description unpacked) which is required for the delivery of the goods. Packaging is to be marked appropriately.

The buyer must pay the costs of any pre-shipment inspection except when such inspection is mandated by the authorities of the country of export.

A10 Other obligations

The seller must render the buyer at the latter's request, risk and expense, every assistance in obtaining any documents or equivalent electronic messages (other than those mentioned in A8) issued or transmitted in the country of dispatch and/or of origin which the buyer may require for the import of the goods.

The seller must provide the buyer, upon request, with the necessary information for procuring insurance.

B10 Other obligations

The buyer must pay all costs and charges incurred in obtaining the documents or equivalent electronic messages mentioned in A10 and reimburse those incurred by the seller in rendering his assistance in accordance therewith.

DES - Delivered Ex Ship (... named port of destination)

«Delivered Ex Ship» means that the seller delivers when the goods are placed at the disposal of the buyer on board the ship not cleared for import at the named port of destination. The seller has to bear all the costs and risks involved in bringing the goods to the named port of destination before discharging. If the parties wish the seller to bear the costs and risks of discharging the goods, then the **DEQ** term should be used.

This term can be used only when the goods are to be delivered by sea or inland waterway or multimodal transport on a vessel in the port of destination.

THE SELLER'S OBLIGATIONS	THE BUYER'S OBLIGATIONS
A1 Provision of goods in conformity with the contract	**B1 Payment of the price**
The seller must provide the goods and the commercial invoice, or its equivalent electronic message, in conformity with the contract of sale and any other evidence of conformity which may be required by the contract.	The buyer must pay the price as provided in the contract of sale.
A2 Licenses, authorizations and formalities	**B2 Licenses, authorizations and formalities**
The seller must obtain at his own risk and expense any export license or other official authorization or other documents and carry out, where applicable (Refer to Introduction paragraph 14), all customs formalities necessary for the export of the goods and for their transit through any country.	The buyer must obtain at his own risk and expense any import license or other official authorization and carry out, where applicable (Refer to Introduction paragraph 14), all customs formalities necessary for the import of the goods.
A3 Contracts of carriage and insurance	**B3 Contracts of carriage and insurance**
a) Contract of carriage	a) Contract of carriage
The seller must contract at his own expense for the carriage of the goods to the named point, if any, at the named port of destination. If a point is not agreed or is not determined by practice, the seller may select the point at the named port of destination which best suits his purpose.	No obligation (Refer to Introduction paragraph 10). b) Contract of insurance No obligation (Refer to Introduction paragraph 10).
b) Contract of insurance	
No obligation (Refer to Introduction paragraph 10).	

A4 Delivery

The seller must place the goods at the disposal of the buyer on board the vessel at the unloading point referred to in A3 a), in the named port of destination on the date or within the agreed period, in such a way as to enable them to be removed from the vessel by unloading equipment appropriate to the nature of the goods.

A5 Transfer of risks

The seller must, subject to the provisions of B5, bear all risks of loss of or damage to the goods until such time as they have been delivered in accordance with A4.

A6 Division of costs

The seller must, subject to the provisions of B6, pay

- in addition to costs resulting from A3 a), all costs relating to the goods until such time as they have been delivered in accordance with A4; and

- where applicable (Refer to Introduction paragraph 14), the costs of customs formalities necessary for export as well as all duties, taxes or other charges payable upon export of the goods and for their transit through any country prior to delivery in accordance with A4.

A7 Notice to the buyer

B4 Taking delivery

The buyer must take delivery of the goods when they have been delivered in accordance with A4.

B5 Transfer of risks

The buyer must bear all risks of loss of or damage to the goods from the time they have been delivered in accordance with A4.

The buyer must, should he fail to give notice in accordance with B7, bear all risks of loss of or damage to the goods from the agreed date or the expiry date of the agreed period for delivery provided, however, that the goods have been duly appropriated to the contract, that is to say, clearly set aside or otherwise identified as the contract goods.

B6 Division of costs

The buyer must pay

- all costs relating to the goods from the time they have been delivered in accordance with A4, including the expenses of discharge operations necessary to take delivery of the goods from the vessel; and

- all additional costs incurred if he fails to take delivery of the goods when they have been placed at his disposal in accordance with A4, or to give notice in accordance with B7, provided, however, that the goods have been appropriated to the contract, that is to say, clearly set aside or otherwise identified as the contract goods.

- where applicable (Refer to Introduction paragraph 14), the costs of customs formalities as well as all duties, taxes and other charges payable upon import of the goods.

B7 Notice to the seller

The seller must give the buyer sufficient notice of the estimated time of arrival of the nominated vessel in accordance with A4 as well as any other notice required in order to allow the buyer to take measures which are normally necessary to enable him to take delivery of the goods.

The buyer must, whenever he is entitled to determine the time within an agreed period and/or the point of taking delivery in the named port of destination, give the seller sufficient notice thereof.

A8 Proof of delivery, transport document or equivalent electronic message

The seller must provide the buyer at the seller's expense with the delivery order and/or the usual transport document (for example a negotiable bill of lading, a non-negotiable sea waybill, an inland waterway document, or a multimodal transport document) to enable the buyer to claim the goods from the carrier at the port of destination.

Where the seller and the buyer have agreed to communicate electronically, the document referred to in the preceding paragraph may be replaced by an equivalent electronic data interchange (EDI) message.

B8 Proof of delivery, transport document or equivalent electronic message

The buyer must accept the delivery order or the transport document in accordance with A8.

A9 Checking - packaging - marking

The seller must pay the costs of those checking operations (such as checking quality, measuring, weighing, counting) which are necessary for the purpose of delivering the goods in accordance with A4.

The seller must provide at his own expense packaging (unless it is agreed or usual for the particular trade to deliver the goods of the contract description unpacked) which is required for the delivery of the goods at the frontier and for the subsequent transport to the extent that the circumstances (for example modalities, destination) are made known to the seller before the contract of sale is concluded. Packaging is to be marked appropriately.

B9 Inspection of goods

The buyer must pay the costs of any pre-shipment inspection except when such inspection is mandated by the authorities of the country of export.

A10 Other obligations

B10 Other obligations

The seller must render the buyer at the latter's request, risk and expense, every assistance in obtaining any documents or equivalent electronic messages (other than those mentioned in A8) issued or transmitted in the country of dispatch and/or of origin which the buyer may require for the import of the goods.

The seller must provide the buyer, upon request, with the necessary information for procuring insurance.

The buyer must pay all costs and charges incurred in obtaining the documents or equivalent electronic messages mentioned in A10 and reimburse those incurred by the seller in rendering his assistance in accordance therewith.

DEQ - Delivered Ex Quay (... named port of destination)

«Delivered Ex Quay» means that the seller delivers when the goods are placed at the disposal of the buyer not cleared for import on the quay (wharf) at the named port of destination. The seller has to bear costs and risks involved in bringing the goods to the named port of destination and discharging the goods on the quay (wharf). The DEQ term requires the buyer to clear the goods for import and to pay for all formalities, duties, taxes and other charges upon import.

THIS IS A REVERSAL FROM PREVIOUS INCOTERMS VERSIONS WHICH REQUIRED THE SELLER TO ARRANGE FOR IMPORT CLEARANCE.

If the parties wish to include in the seller's obligations all or part of the costs payable upon import of the goods, this should be made clear by adding explicit wording to this effect in the contract of sale (Refer to Introduction paragraph 11).

This term can be used only when the goods are to be delivered by sea or inland waterway or multimodal transport on discharging from a vessel onto the quay (wharf) in the port of destination. However if the parties wish to include in the seller's obligations the risks and costs of the handling of the goods from the quay to another place (warehouse, terminal, transport station, etc.) in or outside the port, the **DDU** or **DDP** terms should be used.

THE SELLER'S OBLIGATIONS	THE BUYER'S OBLIGATIONS

A1 Provision of goods in conformity with the contract

B1 Payment of the price

The seller must provide the goods and the commercial invoice, or its equivalent electronic message, in conformity with the contract of sale and any other evidence of conformity which may be required by the contract.

The buyer must pay the price as provided in the contract of sale.

A2 Licenses, authorizations and formalities

The seller must obtain at his own risk and expense any export license or other official authorization or other documents and carry out, where applicable (Refer to Introduction paragraph 14), all customs formalities for the export of the goods, and for their transit through any country.

A3 Contracts of carriage and insurance

a) Contract of carriage

The seller must contract at his own expense for the carriage of the goods to the named quay (wharf) at the named port of destination. If a specific quay (wharf) is not agreed or is not determined by practice, the seller may select the quay (wharf) at the named port of destination which best suits his purpose.

b) Contract of insurance

No obligation (Refer to Introduction paragraph 10).

A4 Delivery

The seller must place the goods at the disposal of the buyer on the quay (wharf) referred to in A3 a), on the date or within the agreed period.

A5 Transfer of risks

The seller must, subject to the provisions of B5, bear all risks of loss of or damage to the goods until such time as they have been delivered in accordance with A4.

A6 Division of costs

B2 Licenses, authorizations and formalities

The buyer must obtain at his own risk and expense any import license or official authorization or other documents and carry out, where applicable (Refer to Introduction paragraph 14), all customs formalities necessary for the import of the goods.

B3 Contracts of carriage and insurance

a) Contract of carriage

No obligation (Refer to Introduction paragraph 10).

b) Contract of insurance

No obligation (Refer to Introduction paragraph 10).

B4 Taking delivery

The buyer must take delivery of the goods when they have been delivered in accordance with A4.

B5 Transfer of risks

The buyer must bear all risks of loss of or damage to the goods from the time they have been delivered in accordance with A4.

The buyer must, should he fail to give notice in accordance with B7, bear all risks of loss of or damage to the goods from the agreed date or the expiry date of the agreed period for delivery provided, however, that the goods have been duly appropriated to the contract, that is to say, clearly set aside or otherwise identified as the contract goods.

B6 Division of costs

The seller must, subject to the provisions of B6, pay

- in addition to costs resulting from A3 a), all costs relating to the goods until such time as they are delivered on the quay (wharf) in accordance with A4; and

- where applicable (Refer to Introduction paragraph 14), the costs of customs formalities necessary for export as well as all duties, taxes and other charges payable upon export of the goods and for their transit through any country prior to delivery.

The buyer must pay

- all costs relating to the goods from the time they have been delivered in accordance with A4, including any costs of handling the goods in the port for subsequent transport or storage in warehouse or terminal; and

- all additional costs incurred if he fails to take delivery of the goods when they have been placed at his disposal in accordance with A4, or to give notice in accordance with B7, provided, however, that the goods have been appropriated to the contract, that is to say, clearly set aside or otherwise identified as the contract goods; and

- where applicable (Refer to Introduction paragraph 14), the cost of customs formalities as well as all duties, taxes and other charges payable upon import of the goods and for their subsequent transport.

A7 Notice to the buyer

The seller must give the buyer sufficient notice of the estimated time of arrival of the nominated vessel in accordance with A4, as well as any other notice required in order to allow the buyer to take measures which are normally necessary to enable him to take delivery of the goods.

B7 Notice to the seller

The buyer must, whenever he is entitled to determine the time within an agreed period and/or the point of taking delivery in the named port of destination, give the seller sufficient notice thereof.

A8 Proof of delivery, transport document or equivalent electronic message

The seller must provide the buyer at the seller's expense with the delivery order and/or the usual transport document (for example a negotiable bill of lading, a non-negotiable sea waybill, an inland waterway document or a multimodal transport document) to enable him to take the goods and remove them from the quay (wharf). Where the seller and the buyer have agreed to communicate electronically, the document referred to in the preceding paragraph may be replaced by an equivalent electronic data interchange (EDI) message.

B8 Proof of delivery, transport document or equivalent electronic message

The buyer must accept the delivery order or transport document in accordance with A8.

A9 Checking - packaging - marking

B9 Inspection of goods

The seller must pay the costs of those checking operations (such as checking quality, measuring, weighing, counting) which are necessary for the purpose of delivering the goods in accordance withA4.

The seller must provide at his own expense packaging (unless it is usual for the particular trade to deliver the goods of the contract description unpacked) which is required for the delivery of the goods. Packaging is to be marked appropriately.

The buyer must pay the costs of any pre-shipment inspection except when such inspection is mandated by the authorities of the country of export.

A10 Other obligations

The seller must render the buyer at the latter's request, risk and expense, every assistance in obtaining any documents or equivalent electronic messages (other than those mentioned in A8) issued or transmitted in the country of dispatch and/or origin which the buyer may require for the import of the goods. The seller must provide the buyer, upon request, with the necessary information for procuring insurance.

B10 Other obligations

The buyer must pay all costs and charges incurred in obtaining the documents or equivalent electronic messages mentioned in A10 and reimburse those incurred by the seller in rendering his assistance in accordance therewith.

DAF - Delivered At Frontier (... named place)

«Delivered at Frontier» means that the seller delivers when the goods are placed at the disposal of the buyer on the arriving means of transport not unloaded, cleared for export, but not cleared for import at the named point and place at the frontier, but before the customs border of the adjoining country. The term «frontier» may be used for any frontier including that of the country of export. Therefore, it is of vital importance that the frontier in question be defined precisely by always naming the point and place in the term.

However, if the parties wish the seller to be responsible for the unloading of the goods from the arriving means of transport and to bear the risks and costs of unloading, this should be made clear by adding explicit wording to this effect in the contract of sale (Refer to Introduction paragraph 11).

This term may be used irrespective of the mode of transport when goods are to be delivered at a land frontier. When delivery is to take place in the port of destination, on board a vessel or on the quay (wharf), the DES or DEQ terms should be used.

THE SELLER'S OBLIGATIONS	THE BUYER'S OBLIGATIONS
A1 Provision of goods in conformity with the contract	**B1 Payment of the price**
The seller must provide the goods and the commercial invoice, or its equivalent electronic message, in conformity with the contract of sale and any other evidence of conformity which may be required by the contract.	The buyer must pay the price as provided in the contract of sale.
A2 Licenses, authorizations and formalities	**B2 Licenses, authorizations and formalities**

The seller must obtain at his own risk and expense any export license or other official authorization or other document necessary for placing the goods at the buyer's disposal.

The seller must carry out, where applicable (Refer to Introduction paragraph 14). , all customs formalities necessary for the export of the goods to the named place of delivery at the frontier and for their transit through any country.

The buyer must obtain at his own risk and expense any import license or other official authorization or other documents and carry out, where applicable (Refer to Introduction paragraph 14)., all customs formalities necessary for the import of the goods, and for their subsequent transport.

A3 Contracts of carriage and insurance

a) Contract of carriage

i) The seller must contract at his own expense for the carriage of the goods to the named point, if any, at the place of delivery at the frontier. If a point at the named place of delivery at the frontier is not agreed or is not determined by practice, the seller may select the point at the named place of delivery which best suits his purpose.

ii) However, if requested by the buyer, the seller may agree to contract on usual terms at the buyer's risk and expense for the on-going carriage of the goods beyond the named place at the frontier to the final destination in the country of import named by the buyer. The seller may decline to make the contract and, if he does, shall promptly notify the buyer accordingly.

b) Contract of insurance

No obligation (Refer to Introduction paragraph 10).

B3 Contracts of carriage and insurance

a) Contract of carriage

No obligation (Refer to Introduction paragraph 14).

b) Contract of insurance

No obligation (Refer to Introduction paragraph 14).

A4 Delivery

The seller must place the goods at the disposal of the buyer on the arriving means of transport not unloaded at the named place of delivery at the frontier on the date or within the agreed period.

B4 Taking delivery

The buyer must take delivery of the goods when they have been delivered in accordance with A4.

A5 Transfer of risks

B5 Transfer of risks

The seller must, subject to the provisions of B5, bear all risks of loss of or damage to the goods until such time as they have been delivered in accordance with A4.

The buyer must bear all risks of loss of or damage to the goods from the time they have been delivered in accordance with A4.

The buyer must, should he fail to give notice in accordance with B7, bear all risks of loss of or damage to the goods from the agreed date or the expiry date of the agreed period for delivery provided, however, that the goods have been duly appropriated to the contract, that is to say, clearly set aside or otherwise identified as the contract goods.

A6 Division of costs

The seller must, subject to the provisions of B6, pay

- in addition to the costs resulting from A3 a), all costs relating to the goods until such time as they have been delivered in accordance with A4; and

- where applicable (Refer to Introduction paragraph 14)., the costs of customs formalities necessary for export as well as all duties, taxes or other charges payable upon export of the goods and for their transit through any country prior to delivery in accordance with A4.

B6 Division of costs

The buyer must pay

- all costs relating to the goods from the time they have been delivered in accordance with A4 including the expenses of unloading necessary to take delivery of the goods from the arriving means of transport at the named place of delivery at the frontier; and

- all additional costs incurred if he fails to take delivery of the goods when they have been delivered in accordance with A4, or to give notice in accordance with B7, provided, however, that the goods have been appropriated to the contract, that is to say, clearly set aside or otherwise identified as the contract goods; and

- where applicable (Refer to Introduction paragraph 14), the cost of customs formalities as well as all duties, taxes and other charges payable upon import of the goods and for their subsequent transport.

A7 Notice to the buyer

The seller must give the buyer sufficient notice of the dispatch of the goods to the named place at the frontier as well as any other notice required in order to allow the buyer to take measures which are normally necessary to enable him to take delivery of the goods.

B7 Notice to the seller

The buyer must, whenever he is entitled to determine the time within an agreed period and/or the point of taking delivery at the named place, give the seller sufficient notice thereof.

A8 Proof of delivery, transport document or equivalent electronic message

B8 Proof of delivery, transport document or equivalent electronic message

i) The seller must provide the buyer at the seller's expense with the usual document or other evidence of the delivery of the goods at the named place at the frontier in accordance with A3 a) i).

ii), provide the buyer at the latter's request, risk and expense, with the through document of transport normally obtained in the country of dispatch covering on usual terms the transport of the goods from the point of dispatch in that country to the place of final destination in the country of import named by the buyer.

Where the seller and the buyer have agreed to communicate electronically, the document referred to in the preceding paragraph may be replaced by an equivalent electronic data interchange (EDI) message.

ii) The seller must, should the parties agree on on-going carriage beyond the frontier in accordance with A3 a)

The buyer must accept the transport document and/or other evidence of delivery in accordance with

A9 Checking - packaging - marking

The seller must pay the costs of those checking operations (such as checking quality, measuring, weighing, counting) which are necessary for the purpose of delivering the goods in accordance with A4.

The seller must provide at his own expense packaging (unless it is agreed or usual for the particular trade to deliver the goods of the contract description unpacked) which is required for the delivery of the goods at the frontier and for the subsequent transport to the extent that the circumstances (for example modalities, destination) are made known to the seller before the contract of sale is concluded. Packaging is to be marked appropriately.

B9 Inspection of goods

The buyer must pay the costs of any pre-shipment inspection except when such inspection is mandated by the authorities of the country of export.

A10 Other obligations

B10 Other obligations

The seller must render the buyer at the latter's request, risk and expense, every assistance in obtaining any documents or equivalent electronic messages (other than those mentioned in A8) issued or transmitted in the country of dispatch and/or origin which the buyer may require for the import of the goods and, where necessary, for their transit through any country.

The seller must provide the buyer, upon request, with the necessary information for procuring insurance.

The buyer must pay all costs and charges incurred in obtaining the documents or equivalent electronic messages mentioned in A10 and reimburse those incurred by the seller in rendering his assistance in accordance therewith.

If necessary, according to A3 a) ii), the buyer must provide the seller at his request and the buyer's risk and expense with the exchange control authorization, permits, other documents or certified copies thereof, or with the address of the final destination of the goods in the country of import for the purpose of obtaining the through document of transport or any other document contemplated in A8 ii).

Appendix E - Insurance

There is a new ACORD form changing the way insurance verification is processed. So what is the ACORD form? ACORD is a non-profit organization responsible for the publication and maintenance of standard insurance forms, such as applications, certificates and binders. These forms are widely used and supported in the insurance industry, and ACORD regularly monitors and revises these documents when necessary.

The ACORD form, known as the certificate of insurance, provides a summarized version of a policy and is commonly used to provide evidence of coverage in force. Logistics providers should be familiar with these forms when verifying the insurance coverage of carriers and subcontractors with whom they work. **ACORD updated its forms to replace certain text regarding policy cancellation, as noted below:**

Old Policy Cancellation Text	New Policy Cancellation Text
Should any of the above-described policies be canceled before the expiration date thereof, the issuing insurer will endeavor to mail__ days written notice to the certificate holder named to the left, but failure to do so shall impose no obligation or liability of any kind upon the insurer, its agents or its representatives.	Should any of the above-described policies be canceled before the expiration date thereof, notice will be delivered in accordance with the policy provisions.

The biggest change, as noted above, is that the insurance company now clearly has no obligation to inform certificate holders if a policy is canceled. With the new verbiage, most "policy provisions" only require that the first-named insured be notified that a policy is canceled. Typically, even an additional insured does not need to be notified. As a result, the new verbiage makes it more difficult for brokers, forwarders, shippers and other interested parties to monitor whether a carrier or subcontractor's coverage remains in force once any time has transpired since the certificate was issued.

It is important for logistics providers to verify the insurance of the carriers and subcontractors they work with to reduce their liability for negligent selection and reduce the overall risk of an uninsured loss. While a logistics provider or shipper could require a new certificate prior to each new shipment, this would be onerous and entail significant resource demands. One alternative could be a periodic requirement for evidence of insurance, such as monthly or quarterly, to provide statistical risk mitigation. The process would be less onerous, but would not guarantee the existence of coverage.

What is the Cargo Insurance Requirement/BMC-32?

The BMC-32 provided proof of a motor carrier's Cargo Insurance policy and was originally required by the Interstate Commerce Commission after many trucking companies experienced financial problems. The BMC-32 is an endorsement to a Cargo Liability policy that guaranteed a minimum level of coverage for loss or damage in transit at $5,000 per shipment.

Why is this important?

Claims submitted under the BMC-32 endorsement were not subject to deductibles or exclusions and were paid by the insurance company even if the carrier declared bankruptcy. This prompted many insurers to financially underwrite their clients based on this financial obligation. Now, because the FMCSA is no longer requiring Cargo Insurance coverage for motor carriers, insurance companies may not require a review of a Motor Carrier's financials as often since this is no longer a potential claim.

In the final rule, the FMCSA stated that elimination of the BMC-32 endorsement would make it "less convenient to confirm the existence of cargo insurance." Logistics providers know that verifying insurance is an important part of the carrier qualification process. With the implementation of this rule, however, logistics providers must find a new method for verification, such as obtaining certificates of insurance from the carrier. If the logistics provider obtains certificates of insurance from the carrier, they must remember to verify coverage limits and effective dates. This process has become more cumbersome, however, with the issuance of the new ACORD insurance form, as the certificate holder may not be informed if a policy is expired.

With the elimination of the Cargo Insurance requirement, it's more important than ever for transportation brokers to investigate a carrier's safety record, claims history and insurance status. If a claim occurs, shippers or injured third parties could allege that the broker engaged in negligent selection. Unlike other types of insurance, cargo policies are unique and include exclusions that vary from insurer to insurer. If a carrier declares bankruptcy or if their limits are insufficient or if coverage is excluded, the logistics provider can be held liable.

Appendix E - Insurance

How can logistics providers protect themselves?

Several types of liability insurance policies are available to protect logistics providers when they are held liable for claims arising from cargo loss or damage and third-party liability.

Non-following form Contingent Cargo Insurance provides coverage when the motor carrier's insurance does not pay a claim and the motor carrier is unable to pay. Coverage is typically triggered only in situations where the motor carrier is negligent.

Errors & Omissions Insurance protects the transportation broker if an error or oversight in the course of business causes a customer to suffer a financial loss. A transportation broker should ideally obtain a combined policy form with Errors & Omissions Insurance and non-following form Contingent Cargo coverage. A combined form is not the same as purchasing separate policies. Separate policies can create both gaps as well as overlaps in coverage.

Contingent Automobile Liability Insurance is also available to protect transportation brokers when they are held liable for death, bodily injury or third-party property damage claims as a result of the motor carrier's negligence.

Policies widely vary and coverage is subject to numerous conditions or exclusions. On a Contingent Cargo policy for example, some policies could limit coverage in a variety of instances. Typical limitations include a locked vehicle endorsement, which only provides coverage if the vehicle is locked. Another frequent requirement is for the broker to obtain evidence of insurance prior to the transit of a brokered load. The timeframe may vary, and the condition could state that a certificate of insurance needs to be on file annually, quarterly or perhaps monthly, but with the increasingly cumbersome requirement of verifying certificates of insurance, this could place significant resource demands on your business if a new certificate of insurance is required prior to every shipment.

It's important to work with an insurance provider who understands your business and regularly reviews your policy with you. Limitations may not be realized until after a claim has occurred and these conditions apply.

Appendix F - Mexican Logistics

Importing and Exporting

The handling of Mexican traffic is quite different from shipping domestically. Many factors influence the flow of goods between the U.S. and Mexico. Some of these factors are the buyers' and sellers' needs, U.S. and Mexican Government regulations, market conditions, and currency exchanges. Importing and exporting may seem difficult but it is not impossible since thousands of trucks cross the border each day.

Customs Brokers and Forwarding Agents

Regardless of whether the shipment is to or from Mexico, there are always U.S. and Mexican customs brokers involved. Typically, the consignee will select the customs brokers.

It takes an average of two days to prepare documents, pay applicable duties, and obtain customs clearance. Therefore, it is important to provide complete and correct documentation two days prior to the freight arriving at the border so it can progress rapidly through customs. Generally, trailer detention charges at the border average $75 per day.

Import and Export Documents

Shippers are responsible for providing the proper and complete documents to the customs broker or forwarding agent. The standard export documents are:

• Commercial Invoice

A complete commercial invoice should include the following: seller's federal tax ID number, descriptions, quantities, unit costs, total cost, weights, number of packages, serial numbers, and the buyer's and seller's names and addresses. Catalog numbers or style numbers alone without a complete description of the merchandise are not allowed.

• Packing List

The packing list provides additional description required by the customs broker for classification.

When preparing packing lists, include each product's function and composition. Itemize the contents of each box or crate. Number the packing lists and packages unless the contents of all packages are identical.

• Import and Export Licenses

Some products require import or export licenses. Check with your customs broker to see if they are required. Most licenses take several weeks to many months to obtain.

• Bill of Lading

A copy of the bill of lading will help expedite a shipment at the border. Bills of lading should indicate the names, addresses, and telephone numbers of the consignee and customs broker or forwarding agent.

• U.S. Customs Documentation

For most U.S. exports, a Shippers Export Declaration (SED) is required. The shipper or their customs broker can prepare this document.

U.S. Customs requires a Formal Entry for most U.S. imports. In-bond documents are used when shipments are not cleared at the point where they enter the U.S. This merchandise might clear Customs at an inland port or possibly not even enter the commerce inside the U.S. at all. The T&E, IE, and IT are the most common in-bond documents.

• Mexican Customs Documentation

The "Pedimento" is the document used in Mexico for imports and exports.

• NAFTA Certificate of Origin

Regardless of whether a shipment is going into or coming out of Mexico, there will always be U.S. and Mexican customhouse brokers involved. Typically, the importer of record will select the customhouse broker and is responsible for any customs duties, freight forwarders and customhouse broker related fees. The shipper (or seller) is usually responsible for the preparation of all export documentation including but not limited to: the commercial invoice, packing list, bills of lading and the "Certificate of Origin."

Since the North American Free Trade Agreement (NAFTA) was approved, there have been some changes to the paperwork that must accompany freight moving between the U.S., Canada, and Mexico. The new NAFTA Certificate of Origin must be used if the goods shipped were manufactured in the U.S. or Canada.

What Is It?

The NAFTA Certificate of Origin (also referred to as CBP form 434) is a uniform document created to make sure that goods imported into the member countries (U.S., Canada and Mexico) qualify for preferential tariff treatment under NAFTA. There are copies of this document printed in English, French, and Spanish. The exporter determines which version to use, but the importer must provide a translation to their customs officials if requested.

A NAFTA Certificate of Origin can cover a single shipment or multiple shipments over a 12-month period (called a blanket certificate).

Claims for preferential treatment under NAFTA can be made up to four years from the date the document was signed. This would come into play for shipments that are imported in-bond and held at a warehouse until they are ready for use.

Appendix F - Mexican Logistics

When Is It Used?

A NAFTA Certificate of Origin is required for all shipments of U.S., Mexican, or Canadian origin that are valued at US $1,200.00 or more. However, it is recommended that a NAFTA Certificate of Origin accompany each shipment to expedite the clearance process.

Why Is It Important?

This form must be used to get the preferential tariff treatment provided for in NAFTA. Without a valid NAFTA Certificate of Origin, there is no break on tariffs.

What Must the Exporter Do?

The exporter has the responsibility for completing and signing the NAFTA Certificate of Origin. If the exporter has not actually produced the goods, the exporter can still complete the Certificate relying on:

- His/her knowledge of the origin of the goods

- The producer's written statement of the origin of the goods

- A Certificate of Origin for the goods provided by the producer

Exporters are also required to keep records of export for at least five years (maybe longer depending on their own country's requirements).

Any changes to the shipment that could affect the accuracy of the certificate must be communicated to anyone the Certificate was given to.

What Must the Importer Do?

The importer is responsible for providing a NAFTA Certificate of Origin to his/her country's customs officials upon request. The importer must also provide a corrected import declaration and pay the accompanying duties if there is reason to believe the original Certificate was not accurate. Like exporters, importers must keep records of imports for at least five years (maybe longer depending on their own country's requirements).

Where Can I Get the Forms?

The easiest way to get the NAFTA Certificate of Origin is to download it directly from the U.S. Customs and Border Protection (CBP) website at http://www.cbp.gov. After you log onto the site, go to the forms section and look for form CBP 434.

Appendix F - Mexican Logistics

When Is It Used?

A NAFTA Certificate of Origin is required for all shipments of U.S., Mexican, or Canadian origin that are valued at US $1,200.00 or more. However, it is recommended that a NAFTA Certificate of Origin accompany each shipment to expedite the clearance process.

Why Is It Important?

This form must be used to get the preferential tariff treatment provided for in NAFTA. Without a valid NAFTA Certificate of Origin, there is no break on tariffs.

What Must the Exporter Do?

The exporter has the responsibility for completing and signing the NAFTA Certificate of Origin. If the exporter has not actually produced the goods, the exporter can still complete the Certificate relying on:

- His/her knowledge of the origin of the goods

- The producer's written statement of the origin of the goods

- A Certificate of Origin for the goods provided by the producer

Exporters are also required to keep records of export for at least five years (maybe longer depending on their own country's requirements).

Any changes to the shipment that could affect the accuracy of the certificate must be communicated to anyone the Certificate was given to.

What Must the Importer Do?

The importer is responsible for providing a NAFTA Certificate of Origin to his/her country's customs officials upon request. The importer must also provide a corrected import declaration and pay the accompanying duties if there is reason to believe the original Certificate was not accurate. Like exporters, importers must keep records of imports for at least five years (maybe longer depending on their own country's requirements).

Where Can I Get the Forms?

The easiest way to get the NAFTA Certificate of Origin is to download it directly from the U.S. Customs and Border Protection (CBP) website at http://www.cbp.gov. After you log onto the site, go to the forms section and look for form CBP 434.

Appendix F - Mexican Logistics

Where Can I Get More Information About NAFTA?

You can get more information on NAFTA and Certificates of Origin at the CBP website mentioned above and also from the NAFTA Secretariat at https://www.trade.gov/north-american-free-trade-agreement-nafta.

The following are guidelines about how a NAFTA Certificate of Origin should be completed. The back of the form (not shown here) contains detailed instructions on how to complete it and provides references.

Completing a Certificate of Origin

1. The full legal name, address (including country) and legal tax identification number of exporter: Canada—use the employer number or importer/exporter number assigned by Revenue Canada. Mexico—use the federal taxpayer's registry number (RFC). U.S.—use the employer's identification number or social security number.

2. Complete these fields if the Certificate covers multiple shipments of identical goods that are imported for a period of up to one year. "FROM" is the date the Certificate goes into effect; "TO" is the date the certificate expires.

3. The full legal name, address (including country) and legal tax identification number of the producer. If goods from more than one producer are included on the Certificate, attach a list of additional products (including addresses and tax identification numbers). Reference them to the applicable goods described in field #5.

4. The full legal name, address and tax identification number of the importer. If not known, state "UNKNOWN." If there are multiple importers, state "VARIOUS."

5. A complete description of each commodity, relating it to the invoice description and the Harmonized System (HS) description. If this is a single shipment, include the commercial invoice number, and use another unique number as a reference number (e.g., shipping order number).

6. For each commodity, identify the HS tariff classification to six digits (or eight digits if the commodity is subject to a rule of origin included in Annex 401), using the HS tariff classification of the importing country.

7. State which criterion applies to each commodity (one must apply in order for the shipment to receive preferential treatment). Review the criteria (A-F) included on the back of the form to determine which one applies.

Appendix F - Employee vs. Independent Contractor

In 2005, the Bureau of Labor Statistics reported approximately 10.3 million workers, or 7.4% of the U.S workforce, were classified as independent contractors. Today, that number is likely dramatically larger. According to government studies, many workers classified as independent contractors are actually employees. Consequently, worker classification has become a hot topic for the IRS, state departments of revenue, and other federal, state and local government agencies. In addition, the plaintiff's bar has taken note of this issue and the opportunities for individual and class action lawsuits against businesses. This article highlights some of the worker classification rules, the risks of misclassification, and general guidelines for businesses and advisors.

New Scrutiny on Worker Classification

Although worker classification has been an area of focus for many years, current economic and political pressures have pushed it to the forefront of governmental attention. Congress' Joint Committee on Taxation has concluded there is a significant loss of tax revenue associated with worker misclassification. Consequently, the IRS is dramatically increasing audit activity, targeting worker misclassification as a means of reducing budget deficits. State and local governments have followed suit and are aggressively scrutinizing businesses and industries which commonly utilize independent contractors. The states and local governments have the same motivation to prevent worker misclassification as the federal government—to generate revenue, increase compliance, and ensure workers are properly treated under their employment laws. States and local governments are particularly concerned about payment of income taxes and ensuring their unemployment insurance and workers' compensation systems remain healthy. Federal and state legislatures, and local administrative agencies are reviewing a wide range of proposals and recommendations related to reducing worker misclassification.

Misclassification

Many businesses have legitimate business reasons for classifying workers as independent contractors, such as when the workers perform temporary, specialized services for the business and perform the same services for others through independently established businesses. In some industries, the use of independent contractors is a common practice (e.g., construction and transportation). Workers in these industries often prefer to be independent contractors because they like the freedom to be their own boss and to own and operate their own businesses. It is not uncommon for businesses to pay independent contractors more than the wages they pay employees because the contractors are responsible for their own costs of doing business, including payroll taxes, benefits, tools, equipment and liability insurance. So, classification of workers as independent contractors does not automatically result in cost savings. Nevertheless, some government regulators perceive businesses are solely motivated to classify workers as independent contractors to avoid payroll and other "employee-related expenses," circumvent minimum wage, overtime, anti-discrimination and other employment laws, or avoid union organization. As a result of this widespread perception, along with the significant need for governments to cure budget deficits, the focus on worker classification has recently intensified throughout the United States. Businesses and their legal advisors need to pay careful attention to this important issue.

Risks of Misclassification

The risks of misclassifying workers, whether or not intentional, are significant. If the IRS determines an independent contractor is really an employee, it may assess amounts which should have been withheld from payroll for federal payroll taxes (i.e., Social Security and Medicare) and income taxes, as well as penalties and interest. Other federal agencies, such as the Department of Labor or the National Labor Relations Board, may also assess penalties, fines and interest, in addition to disqualifying retirement plans. State and local agencies are also quick to assess taxes which are based in whole or part on employee payroll, including unemployment taxes, withholding taxes, workers' compensation insurance taxes and public transit taxes, as well as assessing penalties, fines and interest.

Federal, state and local taxes are not the only areas of concern. The workers themselves may initiate private lawsuits seeking damages for breach of contract and compensation for failure to pay for tools and equipment, workers' compensation insurance, pension contributions and benefits, sick pay, vacation pay, business expenses, and other employee benefits. When many workers are involved, class action lawsuits may evolve. The costs of defending worker lawsuits or battling government audits can be staggering. Likewise, the publicity from worker lawsuits can hurt business goodwill. Moreover, the distraction to management resulting from worker lawsuits or government audits usually has a negative impact on business operations.

General Classification Rules

Worker classification is not an exact science. While some types of workers should clearly be classified as employees, there is a significant gray area with respect to other types of workers. Moreover, although workers are often classified in groups based upon occupation, classification should technically be done on an individual-by-individual basis. Additionally, state and local rules may differ from federal rules, such that a worker may potentially be classified as an employee under state law and an independent contractor under federal law. Making matters more complex, state and local rules may differ within a single jurisdiction, depending upon the application within the jurisdiction. For example, it is not uncommon for some of the classification rules applicable to workers within a state to differ for purposes of unemployment taxes, workers' compensation insurance taxes and withholding taxes. These differences are often less than obvious and make compliance difficult for most businesses.

Federal Law

Under federal law, certain workers are classified by statute as employees (i.e., corporate officers and commission drivers, home workers and salespersons), but most others are classified under common law rules. Under the federal common law rules, an employment relationship exists when the person for whom the services are performed has the right to control and direct the individual performing the services, not only as to the result to be accomplished, but also as to the details and means by which that result is accomplished. It is not necessary that the employer actually direct or control the manner of performance; it is sufficient if the employer has the right to do so. If an employment relationship exists, any other designation of the relationship by the parties (including designation of independent contractor status) is immaterial.

The IRS and other agencies look to a variety of factors in determining whether a right to control a worker's performance exists. Twenty common law factors are discussed in Revenue Ruling 87-41, which for years was the standard by which worker classification determinations were made. Nearly all tax practitioners and employers have some familiarity with the "20-factor test."

In the two decades since issuing Revenue Ruling 87-41, the IRS has modified and updated its approach to worker classification. In an attempt to ensure the focus is on the "right to control," the IRS now encourages its auditors to look beyond the twenty factors contained in Revenue Ruling 87-41 and to focus on three categories of factors: (1) Behavioral Control Factors; (2) Economic Control Factors; and (3) Factors Evidencing How the Parties Perceive their Relationship. This evolutionary approach essentially groups many of the factors from Revenue Ruling 87-41 into these three general categories and gives some factors more weight than others. Regardless, application of the test remains quite subjective.

State Law

Federal law does not control worker classification for state and local law purposes. States use a variety of different tests to classify workers. The majority of states use some variation of a three-prong common law test often called the "ABC Test" which analyzes whether:

- The worker is free from direction and control over the performance of services;

- The services are either outside the employer's usual course of business or performed outside of the employer's business premises; and

- The worker is engaged in an independently established trade occupation, profession or business.

If the ABC Test is met, the worker is an independent contractor. If one of the three prongs is not met, the worker is an employee. Although the ABC Test is based in common law, many states have codified variations of it. One common variation uses only the first and last prongs, and is often called the "AC Test." Some states allow workers to be classified under alternative tests. For example, Washington's unemployment tax statutes utilize two similar, but alternative, tests to determine whether a worker is an employee.

The variety of state law tests and differences from federal law creates significant confusion and hazards. A worker may be classified differently for federal and state purposes, differently from state to state, and even differently within the same state! For example, Oregon has codified a variation of the AC Test for purposes of its workers' compensation, unemployment, and withholding tax laws. Oregon's test differs from the federal test, so workers in certain industries are frequently found to be independent contractors by the IRS, but employees for Oregon tax purposes. This statutory test does not apply to other employment-related determinations in Oregon, such as when an independent contractor sues for employment-related benefits or for determining an employer's liability for acts of its employees. A different common law test is used in such cases. These differences can be hazardous to unsuspecting businesses!

Businesses and their advisors must be prepared for increased federal, state and local government scrutiny of worker classification. Businesses and their advisors should regularly discuss the risks of misclassification and review worker classification decisions as this area of law is in a state of flux. Business owners should not assume a worker who is an independent contractor for one purpose is automatically an independent contractor for all purposes. They are well-advised to enlist their attorneys to periodically review their worker classification decisions and determine if possible problem areas exist. Assistance of qualified legal counsel should also be obtained when appropriate, including when:

- Drafting and reviewing independent contractor agreements;

- Analyzing differences between relevant state, local and federal laws, and the application of those laws to a group of workers; and

- Undergoing state, local or federal worker classification audits or exams.

Proper worker classification has always been a concern for federal state and local agencies. Due to recent economic and political pressures, however, worker classification is currently and will likely continue to be at the forefront of government regulation. The risks associated with worker lawsuits or government audits are significant. Businesses need to be well advised in this area. Consequently, periodic reviews and adjustments, if necessary, prior to worker classification decisions are warranted.

Appendix G - Regulations added in 2016

#1. The Unified Registration System Will be Implemented

The two phases of the URS were rolled out. It affects all motor carriers, freight brokers and other entities currently registered with the Federal Motor Carrier Safety Administration.

The URS does away with all registration numbers currently in use, such as the MC, MX and the FF, and replaces them with the USDOT numbering system in one comprehensive database. This is predicted to save time and money for the industry, thanks to reduced paperwork and processing times. It also makes it easier for FMCSA to track down high-risk small and mid-sized carriers trying to evade enforcement action.

#2. New Safety Fitness Rule Proposed by the FMCSA

In January 2016, FMCSA proposed a new rulemaking that aims to make it easier to evaluate safety fitness of motor carriers and identify non-compliance.

The proposed Safety Fitness Determination rule introduces a new safety ranking "by integrating on-road safety data from inspections, along with the results of carrier investigations and crash reports, to determine a motor carrier's overall safety fitness on a monthly basis." The previously used model had three levels: satisfactory, conditional, unsatisfactory. The new rule will replace it in favor of an "unfit" score, meaning that a motor carrier would have to take immediate action and improve its rating or discontinue operation.

#3. Driver Coercion Mandate Has Just Begun

FMCSA has been working on a coercion mandate. It aims to prevent fleet owners from harassing their drivers, but the rule also applies to freight brokers and shippers. FMCSA defines driver coercion as an action occurring when motor carriers, shippers or freight brokers "take employment action against, or punish a driver for refusing to operate in violation of certain provisions" of regulatory authorities. Drivers are now able to file complaints with FMCSA within a 90-day period of when the coercion occurred.

#4. More Training Required for New Drivers

At the end of 2015, a proposal to update training requirements for entry-level drivers was moved into the Office of Management and Budget for approval, which is the last step before it gets published in the Federal Register.

Many trucking groups, however, disagree with the minimum hours rule on the basis that there is no statistical evidence to back it up. In addition to that, the Entry Level Driver Training Advisory Committee has compiled a 10-page curriculum of performance-based requirements every new driver must fulfill.

#5. Speed Limiters Installed on Heavy Trucks

This is an issue FMCSA has been trying to tackle for several years, and progress has been slow. In the middle of 2015, the administration postponed setting a deadline for implementation once again, but 2016 may be the year it finally happens. The rule is simple: FMCSA wants carriers to install speed limiters on heavy trucks (defined as vehicles with a GVWR of 26,000 pounds or more) in an effort to reduce the number of fatal crashes. According to the administration, the measure will not prove to be costly, as most of these trucks already have speed limiters installed but have not set limiting parameters.

#6. A CDL Testing Database to be Established

In the first half of 2016, we saw the publication of the final rule of the drug and alcohol testing clearinghouse, a requirement of the Moving Ahead for Progress in the 21st Century highway funding act. The rule has established a database of drivers who have refused to submit to or have failed a drug and alcohol test. Carriers need to query the database before hiring a new driver. They would also have to report all incidents in which one of their drivers was cited for driving under the influence.

Appendix H - New Regulations for 2018

#1 Nationwide Speed Limit

65mph may be the new limit on Freight Trucks since the FMCSA is working on speed limiters on vehicles over 26,000 lbs., but they have not said yet what that limit would be.

#2 Suspension of HOS

A study was done by Virginia Tech University along with the FMCSA that will decide whether or not the suspension will be permanent or not.

#3 Overtime Rules Lawsuit

An update to overtime rules was stopped from taking effect this year because of a lawsuit from 21 states. The new law was going to increase overtime pay exemption up from $23,660 to $47,476. They would also be able to include 10% of commission or bonus pay to someone total compensation if it is paid quarterly. This would primarily affect dispatchers, salespeople and other salaried personnel since drivers are usually paid by the mile.

#4 Updating of FMCSA's Registration System

Instead of having an MC, FF and MX number for operating an authority, there is now a Unified Registration System (URS). For registration details, visit: https://portal.fmcsa.dot.gov/UrsRegistrationWizard/

#5 ELD Mandate

As of December 16, 2018, all truck drivers who are required to track Hours of Service will have to use an Electronic Logging Device (ELD) to do so. One of the few exemptions is drivers of vehicles manufactured before 2000.

Appendix I - New Regulations for 2020

#1 ELD Mandate

The ELD mandate went into full effect on December 17, 2017. However, some commercial vehicles that were still using the Automatic On-Board Recording Devices (AOBRDs) were excluded from this new ELD rule. However, those fleets still using AOBRDs are expected to switch to the new ELDs by December 17, 2020.

#2 Hours of Service Reform

All of the controversies around the ELD mandate shed some light on something the trucking industry has known for a long time: the current hours of service regulations are outdated and don't give drivers the flexibility they need to do their jobs well. New guidance was expected early this year around four specific hours of service areas:

- Expanding the on-duty time for drivers who use the 100 air-mile exemption
- Extending the on-duty limitation for the adverse conditions exemption
- Revising the current 30-minute break requirement
- Providing more flexibility around sleeper berth time

More than 5,100 comments were received this fall when the agency asked for public feedback on the suggested changes—confirmation of the industry's passion for hours of service reform. To give them more time to focus on this issue (and review all of the comments more quickly), the agency recently canceled the split-sleeper berth study that was supposed to kick off this year. The goal of the study was to evaluate whether giving drivers more flexibility in managing their sleeper berth time impacted their overall safety on the road. The agency felt that continuing this study was "moot," as sleeper berth time is one of the hours of service areas being considered for reform.

#3 DOT Drug & Alcohol Clearinghouse

The clearinghouse rule was approved but is in a holding pattern, since the Department of Health and Human Services must develop guidelines for hair testing before DOT can change the rule.

Federal Bill HR 6 was signed into law on October 24, 2018, which reaffirms that the FMCSA Commercial Driver's License Drug and Alcohol Clearinghouse will go into effect January 6, 2020, and that within 60 days, the FMCSA administrator must submit a status report to Congress on the Clearinghouse status.

The Act mandates HHS to update Congress on implementing the process of publishing hair testing guidelines for DOT-mandated testing within 60 days of enactment of the Act, and every 180 days until guidelines are published. Until guidelines are published, hair testing is not allowed for DOT-tests.

#4 Minimum Wage

With the new minimum wage raise, the Truckload Carriers Association (TCA) is telling truckers to be mindful of the new requirements that have taken place in many states in 2020. The legal counsel from TCA states, "Employers with operations in different states must take care to monitor these various state law requirements, and when they change. This is significant for the trucking industry because carriers are often targeted with wage and hour lawsuits brought by drivers and other employees."

#5 DOT Hair Testing

A recent legislative package that was signed into law is holding the Department of Health and Human Services responsible for finishing the hair testing guidelines that were due by December 2016. These guidelines are the first step in making hair follicle drug testing a DOT-approved drug testing method. Although many trucking companies already use hair testing as part of their pre-hire process, urine must still be collected for all DOT-regulated tests.

#6 Sleep Apnea Update

With 28% of commercial truck drivers likely suffering from mild to severe sleep apnea, these drivers are five times more likely to be involved in a crash, and the total cost of collisions related to apnea is estimated at $15.9 billion a year, according to research from the National Safety Council.

In March 2016, FMCSA and FRA published their proposed rule for sleep apnea. NTSB recommended a higher degree of sleep apnea testing. However, there was lots of industry push-back.

#7 Speed Limiter Rule

National Highway Traffic Safety Administration (NHTSA) and FMCSA in August 2016 issued a rule regarding speed limiters for commercial trucks. The rule was to require that all commercial trucks have a speed limiter device. Even though the rule has been outlined, the top speed has not been decided on. The following speeds have, however, been discussed – 60, 65, and 68mph.

#8 CME Registry Hack

Back in December 2017, the CME Registry was hacked. Since then, they have been trying to fix the website. The ability to search for examiners was restored first. Then the ability to add new examiners was created in a new process. The examiner portal is partially restored, and examiners and MEAA can upload determinations, though glitches still exist in the system. Expect more updates as they push to fully restore the CME Registration website.

Appendix J - New Regulations for 2020

#1 Drug and Alcohol Clearinghouse.

All parties involved in the drug and alcohol testing process for CDL holders will be required to register, including motor carriers (employers), consortiums/TPAs, service agents, medical review officers/substance abuse professionals, and drivers – at least most of them over time. Not every driver will have to register. (Those who are long-time employees and who have never failed a drug/alcohol test probably won't be required to register.)

Beginning Jan. 6, carriers will be required to query the system when hiring and annually for all current CDL holders in their employ. Carriers will conduct a limited query first, which only tells them if there is a record in the database on that driver. If the query comes back "yes, there's info, "then a full query is required.

Driver consent is required to query the database. That can be a consent form included in the application packet for limited queries, but for full queries, drivers must give their consent through the clearinghouse. Queries are $1.25 each – there are bundles offered, but there is no price break. Carriers have to have money in their account before they can query. There is a no-limit annual fee of $24,500, but only a few carriers in the country would need the unlimited plan.

Carriers have three business days to report violations, including refusals to be tested.

A record of each query and information obtained from the clearinghouse must be kept for three years. For the first three years, employers must both query the clearinghouse and conduct manual queries for an applicant's former employee, since it will take some time for the database to be populated with data. After Jan. 6, 2023, employers must only use the clearinghouse.

#2 Entry-Level Driver Training
Entry-level driver training rule is slated to take effect in February 2020 and requires new training rules applicable to those applying for a CDL, CDL upgrades (from Class B to Class A, or instance) or for S/P/H endorsements.

Those seeking a CDL are required to obtain training from a certified provider in order to take a CDL skills test.

This rule also requires CDL training providers to register with the FMCSA's training provider registry (TPR). Training providers registered must deliver FMCSA's required curriculum. It is believed that this rule was created to raise the "entry bar" for new drivers, which could affect the supply of drivers. The training is likely to be more expensive as well.

#3 Hours of Service Rule Changes
Among the changes are adjustments to the 30-minute rest break rule, changes to the sleeper berth rule, a change to the 14-hour running clock rule that would allow it to pause, or stop, between 30 minutes and 3 hours for break time, a change in the short haul-driver exception to 150 air miles and 14 consecutive hours versus the current 100 air miles and 12 consecutive house. There is a belief that this change could

allow more drivers to be exempt from the EDL rule. Also among the changes is a proposal to extend the 14-hour on-duty window by two hours due to adverse driving conditions.

Many of these changes could end up being part of the HOS rule, but a few may not make the cut.

#4 CSA Changes
The CSA has been around for some time and has been plagued by problems from the beginning. An independent study in 2017 recommended wholesale changes with a new scoring model needed.

A revised model may have fewer BASICS and predicted that the industry probably would see a new CSA that focuses on violations that matter in terms of safety as opposed to those that don't, such as paperwork violations. While such violations could still result in a citation, they would be included in the CSA score.

#5 Under-21 Driver Initiatives
There is a pilot program that allows 18- to 20-year-old drivers with military driving experience to obtain CDLs.

A better solution would be a graduated CDL that has limitations and restrictions, as those imposed in some states on auto drivers between 16 and 18 years old, with the limits gradually increased as the drivers gain experience.

Made in the USA
Las Vegas, NV
09 November 2023

80525182R00116